Love and Lollipops

Charles Hackeling

Contents

CONTENTS

Preface

OUT OF STEP

This December your mother and I will have been married fifty-five years. Sounds like a long time doesn't it? ...To me it was like yesterday.

It seems I was courting your mother and dreaming about every moment I could be alone with her. I couldn't get enough of her. To hold her in my arms was like being in paradise. It still is.

I tell you this because it's part of a history that, unless I tell you now you may never know how happy I was in your mother's arms. And unless I tell you what I know of the people who make up this family, the Hackelings and Corrys - what their lives were like- you may never know what they or their times were like. You would lose their history forever. Wouldn't that be a shame?

I thought a long time about what my last words to each of you should be. Should I start with Mom, go down the list of children, Stephen, Michael, Susan, etc. leaving each of you a small note, like the stocking stuffers? The problem with that is when you tell someone you love them, and how much they have meant to you over the years, and you repeat this again and again, it gets repetitive and starts to sound insincere. I don't want that to happen. I love each and every one of you equally . . . yet differently. Now that you are parents yourselves you know there is no such thing as loving one child more than another. So I decided to write two notes, one to all my children, and the other to my loving wife and lifetime friend. You will find these notes in separate envelopes. They are not part of this history.

The balance of this story will be about YOUR family - the ones that have come before you, the one that is here now, the good and the bad. Being one of the oldest in the family I can tell you I have loved every minute I've spent getting to know you. You have made my life worth living. I can't imagine going through this life without you. Believe me when I say I love you with all my heart....because I do. Take care of each other. Your time together is precious and short, and I will see you soon on the other side in the hands of God.

Enjoy!

Love and Lollipops

CHAPTER I

EARLY BEGINNINGS

In an effort to leave you a meaningful legacy, let me tell you about your heritage. I may jump around a bit but it will come together as we go along.

Every family network starts with two people. In this case that would be me, Charles Hackeling (hereafter referred to as Charlie) and Mary Anne Corry Hackeling (hereafter referred to as Mae). It then expands forward and backwards in time. Some of these relatives went before us and it is they who make up our DNA. We cannot dismiss them since it is their lives that make up the platform for our existence.

Now, those people who were here some time ago, those who are here now, and those who are yet to come make up the family. They include our parents, grandparents, our brothers and sisters, cousins, aunts and uncles, and finally, dear friends.

Therefore, when we examine our family we find it had its beginning with Charles Creighton Christopher Hackeling and Mary Anne Corry. We've selected photographs to add to the story, in hope that you will get to know us even better.

So the Hackeling Family Tree starts with Charlie and Mae. It goes back to my Grandfathers, Johannas Christianis Van Hackeling and James Keeling, Sr. My Grandmothers were Theresa Dietrich Hackeling and Anna Maultz Keeling.

Theresa

Anna

Mae's grandparents were Andrew Curry (1867-1947) and Mary Gorman (?-1950). Sorry, no photographs available.

But, before we get into our parents and grandparents, who am I? Who is Charles Creighton Christopher Hackeling? And then, who is Mary Anne Corry?

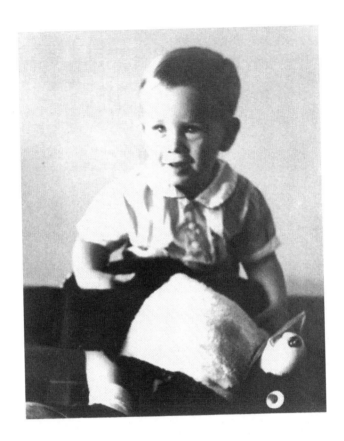

Charlie 1932 Age 2

CHARLES CREIGHTON
CHRISTOPHER HACKELING

I was born September 10, 1930 in the Bronx, New York City, and raised in the same house as my mother, 1160 Taylor Avenue. My mother's name was Edna Francis Keeling and my father's name was Carl Herman Armound Hackeling. I was the oldest of three boys; Ronald followed, and last was Walter. There were two years between each of us.

I was not only the oldest but also the biggest. Ronald, trailing behind me, was the thinnest. But don't be fooled by Ron's size, he was the most talented in the family. Walter was the last of us, also very talented. He was always at the top of his class.

As a young boy I went to Blessed Sacrament Grammar School, directly across the street from my home. The Sisters of Mercy taught there. I still remember my first grade teacher, Sister Jane. She was very young and pretty. Like every young boy, I was in love with her. It didn't make any difference that she was a nun. Little boys of six overlook small details like that. What I remember most about her was that she would take us up on the roof of the school and play punch ball with us. Imagine, punch ball on the roof of your school. I was good! I could punch the ball clear over the roof wall. Of course, then I had to go down four flights of stairs, into the street and look for the ball while my classmates yelled directions to me from the rooftop. They didn't always send me in the right direction. And watch out for the cars. Some fun!

One of the nice things about living across the street from my school was I could always go home for lunch. My mother would have hot soup and a sandwich waiting. It tasted especially good on winter days when the snow was two feet high and the wind was blowing icicles and snowballs.

While I was in grade school I was in love with Mary Jane Whan, Mary Cashel, Patsy O'Conner, Rita Holston, and several others whose names I can no longer remember. Sometimes I loved them all at once. Other times I would rotate them depending on how I felt that day. Unfortunately, none of them even knew I was alive. As a matter of fact, if any one of them had even talked to me, I would have fainted on the spot. I was a true Charlie Brown.

The truth is - I was scared to death of girls. My mother was a very private person, and I didn't have a sister so there was very little female influence in my home. I was interested in girls and wanted to spoon with them, because the guys I hung out with always said how much fun it was, but darn it, I wasn't even sure what spooning was. And kiss a girl? I'd have rather kissed a pig. No, that's not true. I really did want to kiss them. I just didn't have the courage to confront them.....a true coward.

Oh! I was also in love with baseball. I played the outfield and was a good hitter - a home run hitter. Most of our teams were what they called pick-up teams. We would get nine or ten players if we were lucky, guys who promised to be available every Saturday and Sunday for a baseball game. The hardest position was pitcher. Tommy Naughton and Eddie Herald always pitched. Ernie Herald was the catcher. I was always in right or left field. I loved the game so much that I would often dream about playing for the New York Yankees. But if the truth be known, I didn't have the passion to pursue the dream.

Another fond memory from my childhood that will help give you an idea what life was like back in the 1930's, is the tale of Christmas Stockings. It is one of my favorite memories.

1930's CHRISTMAS STOCKINGS

When I was a child, my brothers and I hung our stockings on the kitchen windowsill adjacent to our bedrooms in the back of the house. Christmas was always a special time of year for the Hackeling family. On Christmas Eve my brothers and I went to bed early, afraid Santa might make an early visit and find us awake, and bypass us.

I remember how we would awake long before dawn, sneak out of our beds, steal into the kitchen, and check on the status of the Christmas stockings. Were they empty? Were they full? Had Santa been here yet? We had to be quiet or our parents would yell for us to go back to bed. Santa hadn't arrived yet. If we were lucky enough to reach the stockings without waking our parents, we would know firsthand if that was true, simply by touch!

In those days, stockings were knee length and came up to the bottom of our knickers. All boys wore stockings with knickers. Knickers were long pants cut off at the bottom of the knee, with elastic bands attached to the bottoms to keep them tight about the leg. Long pants were for grown-ups. Christmas was the only day in the endless year when we were grateful for the long stockings. They looked so fine stuffed from top to toe. There was always a horn sticking out of the top and the toe always looked like it held an apple or an orange. So round! So fully packed!

Oh! Those stockings! I can still feel my fingers groping up and down the outside, squeezing ever so gently, with my ears attuned to the sound of cellophane wrapped lollipops, paper wrapped candy bars, all the while trying to guess what was inside. There was always a piece of fruit in the toe. It had to be round so it filled out the stocking and gave it a base, and heavy enough to pull the cotton fibers of the stocking down, making the stocking longer. There would be at least half dozen walnuts next, most of the times. Little trinkets came next - candy, a harmonica or a small toy. It's amazing how a new harmonica takes on a life all its own. Maybe a Mickey Mouse watch if you were lucky. A yo-yo and a top were always welcome. A jack-knife, when you were old enough. And on top...... a horn, a banana, or a candy cane and sometimes a chocolate Santa. Oh! Those were delicious moments. Sharing each other's joy with the unexpected gifts; all the while tasting the sweet fragrance of Christmas morning.

Today, stockings are different. Knickers and their associated knee length stockings have disappeared. Today's store-bought stockings are large and red with names in gold on fluffy white tops. And they vary in size; the bigger they are, the cheaper they look. But kids don't seem to get the same pleasure from the store bought stockings. They quickly turn the stockings upside down and spew the contents all over the floor. Yes, they hold more than my knee-length knicker-stocking, but where is the joy that? Gone with the need to use one's imagination to visualize Aladdin's gift as your fingers groped the outside of your treasured stocking. Where has the mystery of what is contained gone? Oh, to return to those days of yesteryear, when stockings were vehicles of wonder and delight.

STOCKING STUFFERS

There were times that were especially exciting and warm to the heart. Times you remember the rest of your life. Christmas was always one of those times. It was truly the time when Jesus visited us; how we hoped the feeling of Christmas would last forever. Here is how I remember those joyful days.

Excitement fills the house as the children stretch to reach the mantle above the old stone fireplace, to hammer in the nail that will hold their stocking. The heat from the fire casts a warm, rosy glow over their faces. They giggle and chatter; it's Christmas Eve. Dad and Mom help the youngest reach the top of the mantle, lifting her so she can pound in her nail. With the stockings hung: all step back and admire the work with round, bright happy faces, smiling from ear to ear. Tonight they will dream about these bare, limp stockings, and how they will look on Christmas morning. Like 'horns-of-plenty,' with Santa's gifts stuffed from the bright red toes to the sparkling white tops.

Thirty years later, how could I have forgotten? It was Christmas Eve again. Only now, I'm the father and Mae is the mother. Between us were eight busy children hanging up stockings and adding last minute trimmings to the Christmas decorations.

I remembered to buy the gifts for under the tree. But I completely forgot the stocking stuffers. Other concerns occupied me this season. Not that that was any excuse. Mae's father and mother were ill this past year. Business had suffered, and money was scarce. Still! How could I have forgotten the stocking stuffers?

As the children ran around full of Christmas spirit, I felt a sinking feeling in my stomach. As happy as they were then to see the empty stockings hanging over the fireplace, what would it be like on Christmas morning, when the stockings are still limp and empty? Perhaps, I told myself, the presents under the tree will make up for the empty stockings. But I knew this was a false hope. I was contemplating the disappointment the children would experience on Christmas morning when suddenly Mae announced dinner was ready. The children huddled around the table, talking in hushed tones, all being very good.... even to each other. Tracy, the youngest said, to everyone and to no one in particular, "I can't wait to see my stocking, bulging with stuff!"

My heart sank. My mind raced for a solution to this awful dilemma. At this hour stores are closed! Nothing extra in the basement or attic! What could I say to the little ones on Christmas morning? Santa forgot! Not likely! No! I had to find a way to fill the stockings.

As I looked at each child seated round the table, I thought of how much I loved them. Then it dawned on me. We're a family of ten. If ten people write one small note to each other, there would be nine notes in every stocking. The notes could say how much we love and appreciate each other. The notes wouldn't fill the stockings completely, but they would be a good start. Besides, I told myself, we commercialize Christmas too much. We make too much of gifts and rarely think about the real purpose of the holiday. Maybe it's time we took a few minutes to think about how blessed we are just to have each other. I resolved to write my notes immediately after supper. Now I just had to figure out how to get everyone else involved. I needed a clever way to introduce the idea to the children. Dinnertime, even when the children are being good, is hectic. I asked everyone to be quiet for a moment as I had something to suggest. Of course I couldn't tell them I had forgotten the stocking stuffers, so I said, "Children, as I look at each of you I'm so grateful for the blessing of having you. Wouldn't it be a great idea, if each of us wrote a short note to the others, saying what we really like about them, or what we really appreciated them doing for us this past year?"

I finished with a broad smile upon my face and the happiest expression I could muster. But, I was the only one smiling. The silence took my breath away. Everything stopped. The children were staring at me in disbelief . . . finally, they replied, "Are you kidding? On Christmas Eve? Say I love you? Are you nuts? God forbid. Forget it" . . . and then silence!

I was shocked. "Wait a minute," I said. "Aren't we losing sight of what Christmas is all about? Are you only interested in what Santa brings?"

A resounding, "Yes!" . . .

Even from the little ones . . . more than shocked, I sat stunned. Mae broke the silence saying she thought it was a good idea. "As for the rest of the family," she continued, "if you want to do it, fine. If you don't, you do not have to."

It was settled. Supper continued . . . in silence. When dinner ended, the children ran off to finish wrapping presents and then went about their Christmas Eve activities.

After cleaning the table, I set about to write my notes. It wasn't easy to write nine different notes. Each child, although part of the same family, is so very different. Each has their own unique personality. I tried to concentrate on what I loved most about each. When I finished, it had reached the magic hour. Christmas morning was approaching. I was suddenly very tired. The younger children were asleep awaiting Santa's visit. The older children were returning from Midnight Mass. I put the gifts under the tree, went to the mantle and placed my notes in each of the stockings along with the few trinkets I had scrounged up from the basement. It was time to retire to bed. My notes were the only notes in the stockings on the fireplace mantle.

On Christmas morning, after a fitful night, tormented by the disappointment I knew awaited the children, I wearily descended from my bedroom to the living room below. As I entered pandemonium erupted. The children rushed to greet me with cries and shouts of joy.

"Merry Christmas Dad!"

Not what I expected.... I glanced at the fireplace. To my surprise, the stockings were full. They bulged from top to toe. I didn't know the full story about how those stockings became gorged with gifts until many years later.

Mae and I were retiring, selling our house, and moving. As I cleaned out the basement, I had the chore of throwing out all the old high school and college memorabilia stored by the children. Each child had his own box and footlocker. Each had its collection of coins, rings, pictures, cups declaring "The best of 1967", old stockings, hats, scarves, mittens, notebooks, text books, comic books, class papers, diaries, golf balls, and a million other things they didn't have space for when they left home. Inside Susan's box was a copy of a composition she wrote her first year in college. What caught my eye was a note on the front page from her teacher. It said, "You get an A, but Dad gets an A+." Well, you know I had to read it. Here's what Susan had submitted:

SUSAN'S STORY

I remember the day my mother told me there was no real Santa Clause. It was two days before Christmas and she was dragging me by the hand as she shopped in the mall. After three hours of having me yank on her arm and continually ask if there was a REAL Santa Clause, she finally conceded and let me in on the secret.

I remember how she tried to ease my disappointment by telling me how there was a real Saint Nicholas. Since then, I have never had a truly happy Christmas. I tried everything. Singing the loudest during Christmas Mass to reading the sections of the Bible about the birth of the Baby Jesus, over and over again, hoping I would miraculously recapture the lost holiday spirit. I usually ended up lying awake on Christmas Eve thinking about how I'd have to wait another 365 days for my next chance to feel "Christmassy."

This past Christmas was different, however. Finally I learned at the advanced age of eighteen that Christmas does not have to lose its magic with the loss of Santa Claus. The excitement, anticipation, happiness, and love that I had known during the Christmas' of my childhood were back again, but experienced in a different way. After attending all of the usual Christmas Eve festivities, I returned home utterly exhausted. My only intention was to wash up and hit the sack. En route to the bathroom, I passed the kitchen where my father was leaning over a mass of papers on the dinner table. It seemed a little odd to me that my father, the man who religiously goes to sleep after the 11 o'clock news, was still up at 2 a.m.

Over the past few years I had seen my father age tremendously because of the stress of his new job. My friends, who used to comment how young my father looked for a man of fifty, were now commenting on his balding head, his graying hair, and his sagging eyes. By the time I returned to the kitchen my father had disappeared. 'Good', I thought, 'he deserves some sleep.'

I continued on to what was now my bedroom-the living room with two fold-out couches, one for me and the other for my sister, Maureen. When we left for college, our four younger sisters took over our rooms. I found my sister sitting up in bed with her lap covered in sheets of paper and loose envelopes.

"May I inquire as to why everyone in this house has the sudden urge to write letters at 2 a.m., on Christmas?" I asked.

Maureen proceeded to tell me that she was writing 'stocking notes' and that she thought Dad was upset because no one else had done likewise. My father had tried to start a new tradition in our household this year; instead of stuffing the stockings with junk, he suggested that we stuff each person's stocking with notes, stating what we thought was good about that person. With ten people in the family, each person would receive nine little heartfelt notes.

I had completely forgotten about his suggestion. Now I understood what he had been doing at the dinner table. I tried to imagine how he must have felt when this Christmas Eve had passed and not one person had taken him up on his suggestion. I wondered if he had been hurt by our thoughtlessness.

"Got any extra paper, Mau?"

"Yeah," she sighed, "sit down."

I hadn't realized how long it would take to write nine notes. After finishing three of them I bargained with Maureen, "You don't have to write me one, if I don't have to write you one. Okay?"

After finishing my fifth note, I started to run dry. It was very difficult to find something nice to say in a note when the hands of the clock are creeping up on 4 a.m. Although I was tempted to use the same note, and just change a few of the words, I did not, but continued to write a brief personal statement. With eight letters finished I stretched out on my bed and stared at the pitifully limp stockings hanging over the fireplace. Obviously Maureen had been thinking the same thing because when I glanced at her she just shook her head and moaned. The two of us decided that we had to do something to aid those sickly looking stockings before the younger children awoke. So we began to scavenge the house for trinkets and other fillers.

Maureen took the last of what was remaining in the fruit bowl and added it to the stockings to give them some 'body'. I, in the meantime, found a box of Raisin Bran with a recipe for bran muffins on the side panel and began baking. After the muffins entered the oven, I attacked the Christmas tree; stole all the candy canes off of it, and added them to the fattening stockings. My muffins, wrapped in tin foil and tied off with stray ribbons were the last item to garnish the stockings-an excellent topping, I thought.

As we crawled back into our beds, Maureen suggested we read our letters from Dad.

"Na!" I said, "I'm too tired and I'll start bawlin' if I read any sentimental stuff."

So, as a last noble deed before retiring, Maureen crept around the house leaving messages on everyone's door to write their 'stocking notes' before Dad woke up. I continued to write my last letter. Of course it was to my father. I've always had a bad habit of leaving the hardest until last. What the heck am I going to write to this stubborn, sensitive man who's too good to everyone but himself, I thought. I found that by writing just what I was thinking, it was not that hard after all.

As I placed my note inside his stocking I became curious to know what he had to say to me, so I returned to my bed with his letter in my hand. From the opening of "To my dearest Susan:" I cried. I could tell he had really opened himself up and was letting me in on his buried feelings about me, and they were beautiful.

I reluctantly put my letter back into its place, and though I knew I shouldn't have, I drew out all of the other notes he had written, from the other stockings, and read them too. He sure did know how to make everyone feel loved and special.

That night I found the joy I used to know at Christmas. The feelings of warmth and security, serenity and love filled me again. They had come, not with presents under the tree, but by observing how my father had openly given of himself. By expressing his deepest feelings with each member of our family he had left himself vulnerable to the criticism of being 'corny,' he had also offered the people he loved a rare chance to understand him better and to love him all the more.

Although my 'stocking notes' were not nearly as revealing as my father's, they were the beginning of what I will carry out as a life-long tradition with the hope of stirring others as my father had stirred me.

~

The Christmas evening that started out as a disaster became a family tradition. I can't begin to tell you the joy and pleasure I received from the children's short notes...even the youngest ones. I'd take them to my bedroom to read in privacy. I didn't want them to see a grown man cry.

CHAPTER 2

MY BROTHERS & ME

As mentioned earlier, I was the oldest boy in my family. My brother Ronald, two years behind me, was the thinnest. My father always said the first time he saw Ronald he thought he was a frog, all arms and legs. Ron was the most talented in the family. He could draw and paint anything…whatever he put his mind to, he accomplished. But he inherited the Hackeling stubbornness. I remember when he was about six, he had an argument with Dad about his use of the basement. He told Dad if it couldn't be his way he would run away from home.

"Good," Dad said, "and I'll help you pack your bag. Where are you going?"

"West!" was Ron's answer.

After Ron got a bag, he put in his pajamas and two boxes of breakfast Cheerio's cereal. That was enough. He didn't want his suitcase to get too heavy. After all, he had his paints and brushes in the basement to consider. As he stepped out of the front door of our Taylor Avenue home, all of our family was at the upstairs windows and all of the Keelings, our cousins, were at the downstairs windows. Likewise, the

McMullens, the neighbors next-door, were at their windows. In those days, neighbors were part of your extended family. Ron looked up the street and down the street before he turned to face us at our window and asked, "Which way is west?"

Dad pointed up the street.

Since it was summer, storm clouds were growing and thunder was starting. Rain was about to start. Ron took several tentative steps up the street when a loud thunder clap let loose with a bolt of lightning to follow. Ron turned on his heels and started to run for the house. Dad had followed Ron down the stairs as far as the door between the outside of the house and the foyer. Then he locked the door. Ron couldn't get in the house. Rain started to come down in torrents. He struggled with the door but couldn't get it open. He was panicking when Dad, hidden up until now, unlocked the door. In flew Ron through a veil of tears. We never heard another word about going west.

Walter, the youngest of us, was also very talented. Walter was always the lead character in every school play. He could sing and dance and was as handsome as any twelve year old boy could be. All the girls loved him. Academically he did well up until the eighth grade. But something happened to Walter during the summer preceding the seventh grade. He caught diphtheria. He spent several weeks in bed, isolated from the rest of us and was never the same after he recovered. Prior to his getting the disease, he was always at the top of his class. He was smart and his teachers loved him. He participated in everything at school; the plays, academic contest, spelling bees, things the teachers asked him to do. He did them, and did them well. But once he got diphtheria, he seemed to lose all interest in school. His grades started to slip until he was failing everything. His teachers were alarmed and were often found with my mother huddled over an approach to Walter's problem. As it turned out, Walter's solution was for my father to sign him into the Navy as soon as he turned seventeen. Walter no longer participated in any school activities. No sports, no plays.....nothing. Walter lost interest in everything except smoking, drinking and playing pool at the local pool hall.

At seventeen, my father signed Walter into the Navy. He became a Sonar man and rose to the rank of Second Class Petty Officer. But that was just the beginning. He was headed for the rank of Chief Petty Officer when his drinking reversed his climb. He wound up in bar fights that caused him to lose a rank. He missed ship, which is a capital offence in the Navy. Again, break in rank. By the time his nonsense was over he was reduced to the rank of Seaman, and lucky he wasn't sent to the brig. What a shame!

Ronald on the other hand, spent his time isolated in the basement of our house on Taylor Avenue. He spent every spare moment painting or going on exploratory trips to the abandoned docks at Whitestone Park. It was a rundown section of the Bronx where old boats were abandoned. They lay piled one on top of the other. But Ron saw beauty in them and captured it on canvas. This he brought home and reworked into pieces of beauty. No sports for Ron. No female interest, but no male interest except for Mr. Orish, an immigrant artist who lived around the corner from us and saw the talent in Ron's eye and hands. Mr. Orish was well up in his sixties or even seventies when he met Ron. He liked Ron immediately and took to tutoring Ron in the finer points of art and Ron blossomed under his tutelages. Ron graduated from the School of Industrial Arts in Manhattan and took first place in thirteen of the fourteen art fields. Not only was he accomplished in drawing and painting, but also in sculpture. His works were pieces of beauty. Just prior to the end of his senior term, the school was broken into one night and Ron's work was the only work stolen. The art teacher said this was his final humiliation. They didn't steal a single piece of his art, but all of Ron's.

Ronald worked for a firm illustrating medical magazines in New York City, but the daughter of the president of the firm was getting too possessive of Ron, so he decided to flee to the School of Art at Mexico City College. While there he visited the Aztec Ruins deep in the jungles of Mexico. He contracted a form of fever and lay in a lean-to waiting for a train to take him back to civilization and a doctor. He lay there for a week. Finally a train came and Ron was able to get back to Mexico City and treatment.

Ron's next adventure was to Germany where he attended the University of Fine Arts in Munich. He spent three years in Europe, met Siv, married and returned to the United States to complain about all the things that are wrong here. One day he'll realize all the good that comes out of this country and its citizens. One day...

Ron was a joy to my mother. I learned years later that all the time he was in Europe and in Mexico, he communicated with Mom via mail. We regret that we didn't save Ron's and her letters. They would add immensely to the history of this family.

Let me give you an example of the sort of story from my younger years that may help you understand what life was like for me and my brothers as children. This story relates to Ron, and is about his love of peanut butter and jelly sandwiches.

RONALD AND A PEANUT-BUTTER SANDWICH

My brother Ron was always different. He was thin. Not heavy like the rest of the family. Thin. He had classical Greek features pronounced by his thinness. He had thin blond hair, always neatly combed. His eyes were a clear blue, deeply set, and seemed to smolder. He was quite handsome. He didn't roughhouse like the other kids in the neighborhood. He preferred to draw and paint. He was the artist in the family, and possessed a great talent.

When he was six years old, he was painting beautiful large oils, and turning out a new painting every week. Because of his talent, he had special privileges. The basement of our house became his studio. He could stay up late at night whenever he was in a painting frenzy. Even when money was short, my parents found enough to buy him paints and canvas. But what I remember most about him was his love for peanut-butter and jelly. No matter what my mother served at mealtime, Ron always asked for, and received, a peanut-butter and jelly sandwich.

I remember one holiday when my parents took us to a fancy restaurant for dinner. I was ten years old, Ron was eight, and Walter was six. Seated around the restaurant table among the crushing Easter crowd, my mother, regal in her finest new dress, read the menu, then ask, "What would you like Charles?"

Being the oldest, I was always asked first. "Turkey! Roast turkey!" That was my favorite.

The waiter scribbled on his pad and smiled, turning to my mother for the balance of the order.

Walter followed with a "Me too! Turkey!" Walter was not the shy type. He liked turkey and insisted on getting his order in early, lest they run out. That made two orders placed. The waiter smiled a pained smile again, hesitated, pencil poised, awaiting the balance of the order.

My mother then turned her attention to Ron. She smiled and quietly asked, "And what would you like Ronald?"

"Peanut-butter and jelly," was Ronald's reply.

My mother stiffened, looking like she was about to go into shock. She quickly recovered, straightened her back, and, unobtrusively leaned over in Ron's direction to whisper, "Ronald, order something big!"

Ron, leaning in my mother's direction said, "Peanut-butter and jelly."

Flustered and embarrassed, my mother tried again to change Ron's order. She smiled at Ron and said, "Wouldn't you like turkey, like Charles and Walter?"

"Peanut-butter and jelly!" Ron insisted.

Starting to panic, my mother added, half pleading, "Maybe you would like roast beef? I like roast beef!"

"Peanut-butter and jelly."

My father, aware of the waiter's growing impatience, interrupted to relieve the tension. He gave the waiter his order and then said to my mother, "Edna, have you made up your mine what you want?"

A wave of my mother's hand and my father knew, don't bother me. With that my father would turn to the waiter and say, "She'll have the same as me."

Four orders placed-one to go. The waiter smiled a forced smile, sighed and raised both his pencil and eyebrows. My mother was becoming desperate. Her strategy changed.

"If you eat something big Ronald, I'll make you a peanut-butter sandwich when we get home. Now what would you like, the roast beef or the turkey?"

"Peanut-butter and jelly."

My father started shifting in his seat, obviously embarrassed by the whole affair. The waiter was anxiously waiting to complete the order and move on to another table. Annoyed with both my mother and brother, Dad said to mother, "Oh, for God's sake! If he wants peanut-butter and jelly, let him have it!"

"He can't order peanut-butter and jelly," my mother growled, "They'll think he's adopted. He should order something big!"

What adoption had to do with ordering something big I will never know, but it was important to my mother that Ron order something big.

My father, getting close to the end of his rope, finally said to the waiter, "Give him a peanut-butter and jelly sandwich."

"Sorry!" came the waiter's reply, "We're all out of peanut-butter and jelly."

To this day, Ron still likes peanut-butter and jelly. However, he doesn't order it in restaurants. It's not big enough.

CHAPTER 3

HIGH SCHOOL

I attended high school at La Salle Academy, located in the Bowery of New York, on 2nd Avenue and 2nd Street. I had to take the subway (that's a train that runs on tracks elevated above the street), from St Lawrence Avenue in the Bronx, to Bleaker Street, in Manhattan. About a one-hour train ride. The Christian Brothers were our teachers. They taught us our subjects and you either learned the material or got hammered for not being prepared. You see, they never thought for a minute that we couldn't learn. If we were not getting good grades it was because we weren't applying ourselves. I still remember Brother Cagedin, the Librarian, Brother Ambrose, The Principal and Brother Luke, my homeroom teacher. Mr. Canavatchel was my freshman year Latin teacher. He also holds the distinction for giving me my first bloody nose. I learned never again to give my homework to anyone to copy. If you didn't do it, you were going to get the bloody nose, not me. He had me come to the front of the class, and then proceeded to pummel me with both hands until my nose started to bleed. Then he told me I could go back to my seat. He knew I wouldn't tell my father because my father believed if I got hit by my teacher, I probably deserved it. And

I didn't dare cry. If the guys saw me crying they would never let me live it down. You just had to suck it up.

I played baseball on the La Salle Baseball team, but gave it up to take a home news route. Delivering papers was one of the few ways a young boy could earn money in my neighborhood. Somehow, I felt the money was more important than baseball. As I look back I realize we never had a guidance counselor or anyone else to help guide us in after class activities…..no one to tell us which subjects to take or what athletic activities to pursue. If you found something you liked you were lucky to make the team and luckier to know where and when to catch the bus to take you to the field.

In our first game, I was the only one to get a hit. Two hits as a matter of fact, a single and a double. No one else even came close to the ball. When the results of the game were posted the following day in the cafeteria, several classmates came up to congratulate me. No one from the school's administration even mentioned it to me. Not even the coaches. I felt they just didn't care and therefore I quit the team. I delivered papers instead. Sure was a big mistake for a young boy.

After High School, I worked for a firm in New York City in the credit department. Requests came to us first before any order was put into action. We checked the applicant's credit rating before extending the credit. The job was boring and I found it hard to concentrate after an hour or two of looking up credit reports. The department consisted mostly of middle aged women, the boss and me. Besides being boring, it was lonely.

I had to get up at six o'clock in the morning, five days a week in order to catch a train so I got to the office by eight-thirty. Then I'd leave the office at five-thirty and get home by seven-thirty, except for the days I had to stay downtown to take my college course. I had registered for classes at Pase College. I attended classes three nights a week. After six months of this grueling agenda I was starting to feel like there had to be something better for me. I was bored and tired and looked forward to Saturdays so I could get together with my old friends. The trouble was they were going to college full time and their schedules were very different from mine.

Never mind that I had more money than they, it didn't do me any good when they weren't anywhere to be found. Finally, I realized my life was going nowhere and I looked to make a change.

UNITED STATES NAVY

Charles Hackeling

I was 18 when I enlisted in the United States Navy for one year with a nine year reserve commitment. I had never been away from home for more than a week at a time, so the one year away concerned me. I thought... how bad could it be? No matter how bad it was I would be out in a year. I gave very little thought to the nine years of reserve time.

I did my basic training at The Great Lakes Training Facility just outside Chicago. It was here that I leaned to wrestle and how to take care of myself. I was given the task of carrying the General Orders from New York City to the base in Chicago. I wondered why I was selected out of a group of thirty. Maybe it was because of my size (6'1").

After Basic Training I was assigned to Radio School in Norfolk, Virginia. I was at the top of my class, graduating number one. This was the first time I was number one in anything. It shocked me but gave me a different slant on Charlie Hackeling. After Radio School I was assigned to the USS Beltrami, a cargo ship out of Norfolk. It was during a voyage to the Mediterranean that something very mysterious happened.

THE MYSTERIOUS AZORES

As I mentioned, my first assignment in the Navy, after Boot Camp and Radio School, was to serve aboard the USS Beltrami and take supplies from Norfolk, Virginia to Casablanca, Morocco, then on to Tangiers, and finally Athens, Greece before turning for home. It was my first real sea adventure. We left Norfolk and steamed east across the mighty Atlantic Ocean.

After several days at sea, very early one morning, as the mist was rising off the ocean's face, we passed through the Azores Islands. It was like a dream. All around me hung a diaphanous cloud. It was everywhere. What was here one moment, was gone the next. I wasn't sure if the islands were there or not. As I leaned over the side of the ship I could see fires burning dimly on the mountain side and on the shore. It was quiet, except for the sound of the water passing under the side of the ship. So quiet! Only the sound of the ship cutting through the water. *Swissssh*. It had a mysterious quality to it.

As the ship slid through the water the ocean responded... *swissssh*. The water passed along the ship's bottom and reappeared again at the stern of the ship... *swissssh*. Where were the sirens? It appeared to me that, like Ulysses, I was being called by the Sirens of the ocean depths. I expected to see mermaids at any moment. My heart beat wildly. All around me everything seemed to disappear except me, the ship and the sea. As the sun came up I cried to see the dream disappear. But disappear it did, and gradually the sun replaced the cool mist and ocean spray. Only the ship and sea continued their harmony- swissssh, swissssh..... swissssh.

Our first port of call was Casablanca. We made port about six-thirty in the morning and the sun had not yet broken the horizon so a heavy mist hung over the entire port. We made fast to a dock where there was one long storage building after another, as far as you could see. I was on the flying bridge watching the docking procedure. How smoothly the deck hands slid the lines through the halters to the stanchions on the dock. The ship had settled into its berth and deck hands were preparing to off-load our cargo as soon as the civilian crew was available. The storehouses were starting to open their doors to receive their cargo. I half-heartedly expected to see Humphrey Bogart appear from behind one of the buildings. Next to him would be Lauren Bacall. There is a mysterious quality about the ships and the sea, especially when they dock amid fog, rain, and early morning mist. This incident was so vivid and seemed so real that it left me wanting more when it gradually fell apart as the sun rose above the horizon.

For me it was quite an adventure. Not only did I get to go to foreign lands like Casablanca in Morocco, Tangiers in Tunisia, Athens in Greece, and Barcelona in Spain but I got to experience a hurricane on the way back from the

Mediterranean Sea. We had to run ropes from the bow of the ship to the stern so we could hold onto something and avoid being washed overboard as we tried to move forward and aft on the ship. The radio shack was located in the aft quarter of the ship and the flying bridge forward in front of the Captain's Quarters. It was quite a walk. Not a trip I would like to take again. Every time a weather report came into the radio shack, we had to take it immediately to the Captain who was always on the flying bridge. It was the worst storm I had ever experienced and it lasted two full days. We were sure it was following us and we were cursed for our thoughts when we were touring the harems in Casablanca.

While in Casablanca, we sailors were invited to tour a home with a harem attended by some very large eunuch. A look-but-don't-touch attitude prevailed. The girls were clothed in veils and flimsy shorts and tops. They lived in separate quarters close to the owner's living space. All I could think about was how nice it would be to spend a couple of weeks living the life of the harem's owner. At the age of eighteen young boys fantasize and dream but do little else. With the eunuchs around that was all anyone could do. What is a eunuch you ask? A large man, usually of African descent and about seven feet tall and 250 pounds, who, with a large sword was capable of cutting off your head in a single swing. You would be surprised at how they take your desire away.

Charles Hackeling

In Barcelona we attended a bull fight. Unfortunately for me, I wasn't careful enough the morning of the bullfight and ordered a ham omelet at one of the restaurants in town. In a matter of minutes, I knew the best place for me was back aboard the ship. My stomach was starting to grumble and my temperature was rising. I could feel it. I bid my shipmates goodbye and headed for the ship. Fortunately for me I got back just in time to catch the heaves…from both ends. I retired to my bunk and started to run a fever. I asked the person who was on guard duty to look in on me every time he made his rounds and to replace my small towel for a fresh cool one. I spent the rest of that day and the next heaving and pooping. When there was nothing left in me, I turned myself into sickbay and spent the next three days in and out of fever. Once the fever subsided I was able to report for duty. Just in time for another wicked storm.

We completed our cruise, emptied our hole, supplied our troops and now, before we headed for home we took aboard three hundred troops, all anxious to get home.....back to the USA.

As my one year enlistment was coming to an end, I was discharged from the Navy Base in Rhode Island and assigned to a reserve unit at Fort Schyler in the Bronx. I was there about one year when the Korean War broke out. The Navy immediately called our reserve unit back into active duty. My new assignment was aboard an aircraft carrier, the Antietam. The ship was being retrofitted with a new canted deck in the Philadelphia Navy Yard. This meant that we would be at least another few months in Philadelphia. Good for me, that meant I could go home almost every weekend. This worked out fine because I was just beginning to know this new girl in my life. Her name was Mary Anne Corry.

EASTER

Up until this time I was a very shy young man. As I mentioned earlier, I was scared to death of girls. I liked to be with them, but I was always afraid they would embarrass me or make fun of me. If they did, I didn't know how to respond; I had no sisters, so girls were foreign to me. I was always on my guard.

For Easter of that year I decided I'd send my mother a picture of her son in uniform. The picture turned out so good that the photographer used it as the centerpiece for his spring window display. There I was the star of the show, right in the center of the main window display. As I passed by each day on my way to a liberty, I had to agree, that was one handsome sailor. My mother was thrilled and for the first time in my life I saw myself as a hunk. I was starting to build some muscle mass because I had taken up wrestling aboard ship and we worked out five times a week. Girls would be crazy to pass me up now.

Yep! I was hot! From that day forward I saw myself in a different light. It changed me completely. I knew girls would like me if I only gave them the chance. And for some reason, I wasn't afraid of them anymore. I guess part of that could be attributed to the fact that while aboard the Beltrami, I volunteered to be the ship's librarian. That meant I was responsible for all the books in our library, and I decided what new books we could order, what the library hours would be, and who could borrow the books. It also meant I got first crack at every book that came aboard. It was like I hit the jackpot. I started to read everything I could get my hands on. Was it ever fun. I also read from cover to cover and over and over again a book titled, "30 Days to a More Powerful Vocabulary." I felt it was the power I needed to feel comfortable with the girls. It made me feel good about myself. I could hold my own in any conversation.

One day however, I realized there was still something lacking in my approach to young women. When I went out on Sunday evenings to the local church dances it always turned out that the girls were on one side of the church ballroom and the boys on the other. Once the disc jockey started the music the girls would dance together while the boys looked over the field. I noticed that only one of my friends ever got out and danced; Bill Flack. Wild Bill, as he was called, was less than six feet tall, skinny with slightly bucked teeth and far from good looking. Our mutual friends all thought of Bill as the low man on the totem pole when it came to desirability by the girls. But he could dance. And he had a girl for every dance and usually a different girl each time. We, the cool crowd, use to laugh at him, but it was more envy than anything else.

We were jealous because he was out on the dance floor swinging his arms in every direction and quite often holding the girls... tightly. He was enjoying himself and so were the girls. I figured if the girls would dance with Wild Bill just because he was a good dancer, they'd like to dance with me so much more if I were a good dancer.

LEARN TO DANCE

I was determined to learn to dance. I was home on liberty so bright and early the day after a dance, I showered, put on my best fu-fu juice, took my entire ward of seventy-five dollars and headed into New York City. Arthur Murray's beckoned and I was happy to be on my way to becoming the next Fred Astaire. I imagined it would take at least three or four lessons before I became accomplished but I was prepared for that; I had seventy five dollars. As I stepped out of the subway and into Arthur Murray's studio, I noticed how nice and thick the carpet was beneath my feet. No wonder they were good dancers, you could bounce on the carpets. I sauntered up to the counter and quietly asked the young lady behind it if I could see someone about dance lessons. Gosh! She was pretty.

"Why sure," was her coy reply, "Who shall I say is calling?"

"Eh! Charles Hackeling," I whispered, "I want to learn to dance."

As I looked around, I started to realize that maybe I was in over my head. This was some swanky place. No wonder the carpets were so thick; I was starting to sweat. Water was running off my palms, and I could feel sweat sliding down the sides of my chest. I started looking for an exit, but just as I was ready to make my break the girl behind the counter came out, came up to me, smiled, took my hand in hers and said, "I'll bet you're nervous. Come over here and let me show you some of our graduates who felt just like you are feeling now."

We walked, hand in hand, over to the wall that contained one picture after another of young men dancing with beautiful girls. The girl who was holding my hand was beautiful herself. I'd let her hold my hand forever. She started to tell me about the men in the pictures and I had to feign interest, when all I could feel was her hand in mine. It felt good.

I was looking at the pictures on the wall, Fred Astaire, Gene Kelly, Donald O'Connor and a bevy of other dances.

"Of course these guys could dance, but there was a time when these men couldn't dance, and they felt just like you do now," she said.

She smiled at me, squeezed my hand and sashayed over to another wall with even more pictures. It started to relax me. I could see myself in their shoes. Boy! The girls would surely go for me if I could dance like these people. From behind me I heard a delightfully soft voice whisper, "Can I help you?"

I spun around and stared into the eyes of a beautiful blond young lady, about my age, but much older. The receptionist immediately dropped my hand and retreated to the back of her desk. I was now in the hands of an angel.

"Err!" I stammered. "Hi! I want to learn to dance."

Boy, wasn't that a cool opening. Talk about being a boob! I was looking into two beautiful eyes, my mouth had gone to cotton and all I could say was, "Err! Hi!"

But all I could think of was, "Wow! Am I a lucky guy? I drew a beautiful dancer....and what a figure!"

She smiled and continued, "Is there any particular dance you want to learn or are you open for suggestions?"

She took both my hands in hers, leaned back, smiled and started to lead me to God knows where. She could have led me right into hell and I wouldn't have minded.

"My name is Sandy. What's yours?" she continued.

"Charles! Eh! Charlie" I said. Again, another smooth line.

She took me and we went behind the wall which separated the receptionist from the rest of the staff and clients, and then into a large room walled with mirrors. In one corner were a small table, two small chairs, and a sound box tucked into the upper corner. Sandy reached up and turned on one knob on the music box. Immediately the room was flooded with music. Sandy came very close, took my right hand and placed it in the small of her back while taking my left hand in hers. She had a small delicate hand and she smelled like a field of flowers on a spring day. She looked up into my eyes and started to move ever so gently.

After I stepped on her toes about six times, she exhaled and said, "Your left foot first, then the right."

I was as stationary as the George Washington monument in Sheridan Square. She tried three times to move me. I was at a standstill, afraid to move for fear this beautiful creature would disappear. It was a miracle but she finally got me moving and in the right direction. But it was hard work and she finally said, "OK! Let's try a Fox Trot and then a Waltz."

Was she kidding, I thought. I was lucky to be able to spell the words, no less do the dance. She walked over to the music box, turned the dial to Fox Trot and returned. All the time, I had my eyes glued to this vision of loveliness as she glided across the floor. Boy! She had some shape. I was envisioning her stark naked and I'm sure the grin on my face must have given me away because as she took me in her arms again she looked up at me, smiled and said, "What? Why are you smiling?"

I couldn't tell her the truth so I muttered, "Oh! I was just admiring how gracefully you walk."

We made several attempts at the Fox Trot, then the Waltz, but they all ended with me stepping all over her feet. I must have said "*I'm sorry!*" fifty times. When she couldn't take it anymore, she sighed, stepped back, took my hand in hers and walked me over to the table and chairs. She invited me to sit. As she took a pad out of the desk and opened it, she looked at me with smiling eyes and said, "Now that I have some idea of your dancing skills, I suppose the best place to start would be with the Fox Trot. It's the most basic. Do you agree?"

I nodded my head while admiring her beauty, and the fool that I was; I probably would have agreed to start on the moon if she suggested it.

She continued, "After the Fox Trot, the next dance would be the Rumba. It gives you a different beat but the two together will make all the other dances easier to learn."

It made sense to me so I just kept grinning and shaking my head 'yes' at every suggestion. Sandy went through a litany of dances. I kept shaking my head yes. What an idiot I was. When Sandy finished going through all the dances I said I wanted to learn, she started to calculate the cost. Of course all I could look at was Sandy. What a great time I'm going to have learning to dance with this gorgeous creature. I couldn't wait to get my hands around her again.

"There!" Sandy said. "I think, based on what we just went over, that you will have a terrific plan and it isn't that expensive. Would you like to put down a deposit now?"

"Sure!" I said feeling very sure of myself and imagining how desirable I'd be when I dance like Fred and Gene. I started to withdraw my wallet when she asked, "Will five be too much?"

"Oh! Hell no! I've brought seventy-five with me."

I was starting to open my wallet when Sandy interrupted with a little giggle, "No! Not five dollars Charles, I mean five hundred dollars?"

Wow! The wind went out of my sails as I gulped, almost fell over the back of the chair and asked, "Five hundred dollars?"

"Yes!" Sandy said again, "Five hundred dollars."

"How much is this program?" I asked as it was beginning to dawn on me that I was not going to be a Fred or Gene, I might just wind up Charlie two left feet. I was in over my head. Goodbye Fred and Gene.

"The total program is fifty-five hundred dollars," Sandy said apologetically.

Fifty-five hundred? I thought, it will take me the rest of my life to earn that much. From here on out I had only one objective. Get out of here and go home. Put your five dollars back in your wallet and run as fast as you can for the next subway. Sandy must have expected something like this was going to happen. She realized I was starting to hyperventilate, so she stood up, smiled, took both my hands in hers and said, "Don't worry about the money now. You're entitled to a free half hour lesson. Let's just dance and relax. We'll talk about the money later."

Again, sweat had started to form on my forehead. But I began to dry out when Sandy took me in her arms, turned on some low, quiet music and put her head on my shoulder. She glided me over the floor and I was amazed at how much I had learned while sitting at that little table. After a few moments, time for my heart to stop beating like an African war drum in a Tarzan movie, we drifted over to the music box.

"You're doing fine," she said as she changed the music from slow and mellow to a Rumba.

"Let's try the Rumba," Sandy said.

Sandy took both my hands in hers, turned around so her back was facing me, placed my hands upon her hips, palms down and a little lower than hip high, and started to gyrate to the music. She turned her head over her shoulder, smiled at me and said, "Are you starting to get the feel of the music?"

Oh yeah! I was starting to get the rhythm all right. Her ass was moving like a cat on a hot tin roof and my hands were holding on for dear life. The sweat returned. Only not just on my forehead. I was sweating from head to toe. Sweat was running down the sides of my body, wetting my pants and filling up my shoes. Oh! I was feeling the music all right, in every part of my body, and I was hoping she wouldn't turn around just then. My pants were doing the Rumba better than the rest of me. A quick turn on her part would reveal a very embarrassing condition.

After we danced for another few minutes Sandy again maneuvered me over to the table and chairs.

"Let's sit for a few minutes" she said. Taking my hands in hers she looked into my eyes, smiled and said, "Is fifty-five hundred too much for you, right now?"

"Err! Well, err! Yeah! I was thinking more like five-hundred, not five- thousand," I had to admit, feeling very embarrassed.

"Well, don't worry about the money right now. Suppose I could arrange for you to take private lessons with me, would that be agreeable?"

"Sure. How much?" was all I could manage to say.

"Let's start at fifty dollars a session and we can go from there." We can meet at my apartment and work from there.

She smiled. She was always smiling. Fifty dollars was still a lot of money to me, but as I looked into Sandy's eyes it seemed to get much smaller. Hell, right now I could afford one and a half lessons and after my next payday, I could afford a few more. Needless to say, I spent over seven hundred and fifty dollars with Sandy. But now I was a good dancer…and it was worth it, especially the Rumba.

CHAPTER 4

A NEW CAREER

After my one year commitment was over and I was home in the Bronx, I had to get a job and start a new life. I had not yet met Mae and the Korean War was still in the future.

I went to work for my father in his delicatessen on Underhill Avenue, in the Bronx. All my friends were working for thirty-five dollars a week. My father was paying me one hundred dollars a week. It was a dream job! I took orders, delivered them and usually got a nice tip for the delivery. Little did I know about the big changes ahead.

Shortly thereafter, Dad suggested we ought to support the neighborhood where we earned our living. One Saturday evening, I attended a minstrel show at the Catholic Church, a block away from the store with a friend of mine named Tommy Naughton. While there I was seated at a table with five girls from Saint Catherine's School of Nursing. One in particular caught my attention. Her name was Mary Anne Corry. She went by the nickname of Mae.

After the feature presentation the dancing began. It was now time for me to meet Miss Mary Anne Corry.

MEET MARY ANNE CORRY

She was attending Nurses Training and with three of her friends, took the night off and decided to come to the minstrel show. We were sitting at the same table and got to talking. Before you knew it the minstrel was over and we were on the dance floor. I was dancing with Mary Anne. She smelled good and felt even better in my arms. I didn't want the music to stop because it gave her an excuse to move away from me. She was awfully nice. I didn't want the dance to end; Mae felt so good in my arms. Again my trousers were way ahead of me when it came to the dance and I was trying to hide my discomfort if she moved away from me too quickly. But all good things do come to an end, and the dance ended. After the dance we withdrew to the local pub, the Ratscheller, just a short drive from the church. I had borrowed my father's car, so getting around was no problem. After a beer, I asked Mae if I could take her home. I was really nervous about her answer because if she said 'no' it would mean that I really was striking out. To my relief she agreed. Off we went to Underhill Avenue and since it was cold and dark that night Mae asked if I would like a cup of hot coffee before venturing home.

"Sure!" I said, while I thought, 'what a fast chick I have here. Pretending to offer me coffee when all she wants to do is get me alone in her apartment. Upon reaching her apartment, a fifth floor walk-up, she asked me in and directed me to the couch in the living room.

"Wait here," she said, "I'll go put on the coffee."

The front door of her parent's apartment led into a small hallway that divided the apartment, the kitchen on the left, the living room on the right. The hall extended past the kitchen and living room to the bedrooms and bathroom directly behind the front two rooms. I took off my coat and put it over a chair then got settled on the couch. I don't know exactly what I expected, but was hoping for something. I sat on the living room couch, allowing plenty of room for Mae to join me when she returned. Time passed, and I wondered what was keeping her. Suddenly, from the direction of the kitchen, I smelled something burning. I rose from my seat and slowly started in that direction when I heard a roar from one of the rear bedrooms.

"Glory be to God, child! What have you done?"

It was Mae's mother, running down the hallway with her hair up in curlers, in her nightshirt and bathrobe. She and I arrived at the kitchen about the same time. She gave me a shove and I flew into a chair at the kitchen table. On the stove was a coffee pot as red hot as the burner under it. With one quick motion Mae's mother knocked the pot from the stove to the sink, which was right next to the stove, and turned on the faucet. Clouds of water vapor filled the air. I was trying to say excuse me to Mae's mom, for bumping into her, when Mae appeared out of nowhere. Turning to Mae, her mother said, "Child, you have to add water to the pot to make coffee."

Then she looked at me, now sitting on the edge of the kitchen table and continued, "And who might you be?"

Mae gave a brief introduction and quickly ushered me out of the house.

"Coffee will have to wait!" is all she said as she started to close the door.

I wanted to kiss her goodnight, but with her mother behind the half open door, and the kitchen and coffee still in doubt, I thought it wise to say goodnight and forgo the kiss. Before I left, however, I asked Mae for her telephone number. She looked me in the eye and said, "If you want it bad enough-you'll find it," and smiling closed the door.

'What a smart ass she is,' I thought. 'I ought to just forget her.' But I didn't.

I found her number and we dated on and off for about three months. As the Korean War started to heat up I was recalled back to active duty and assigned to the USS Antietam, an aircraft carrier assigned to the Atlantic Fleet. It was in the

Philadelphia Naval Yard undergoing retrofit for a canted deck. The first of its kind in the Navy.

For those of you who don't know what a canted deck is, it's a flight deck that is shaped so it can receive planes coming in for a landing while still launching planes from another part of the deck.

When the retrofit was complete, about three months after I arrived on board, we set sail for the Caribbean for a shakedown cruise. This cruise was designed to shake out the little defects in the ship that were missed in the yard. The cruise lasted about six weeks and we then sailed to Guantanamo and the Virgin Islands before heading for our home port. It was during this time I lost track of Mae. I know I had promised to write, but never got around to it....a big, big, big mistake!

Upon arriving home, I assumed Mae would be delighted to see me. My assumption was another big mistake. Goes to show how little I knew about girls. I had no idea Mae would be so mad. She was spitting mad and I couldn't understand why. Now normally when a girl was as mad at you as Mae was at me, you would just write her off and look for another girlfriend. But Mae's influence over me had a stronger hold than I ever imagined. I thought a lot about home and Mae during all the time I was away, but it was sporadic. However, on our way home, one night I had the most unusual dream.

THE DREAM

It was late when I turned in. Maybe one o'clock. I don't always dream. In fact, I seldom dream. But this night was different, and it changed my life. I dreamed that I was home on leave, talking to my mother in our home on Taylor Avenue.

"I think I'll call Mae Corry," I said to my mother.

"Oh! Haven't you heard," my mother replied, "She's married and has twins."

Shocked, startled, upset, I began to shout in a loud voice, "Oh! No! No! No! That can't be! No!"

My mother was looking at me in the strangest way, as if to say, "Well what did you expect? You waited too long!"

I was pained beyond consolation and woke myself up screaming and shouting, "No! No! No!"

That never happened to me before. **Never**. The Duty Officer on watch came running over to me and asked if I was O.K. I told him I was and that it was just a bad dream. But why was I so disturbed by this dream? I never felt so bad in all my life. It was like I had just lost my best friend. Worse! I awoke and was wet from the top of my head to my shoulders, sweating, but I had no fever. I dragged myself out of my bunk, dressed and went up on deck, heartsick. Maybe the fresh air will clear my thoughts. The more I thought about Mary Anne Corry, married with twins, the more upset I became. I started to wonder, 'What can I do?' I didn't want Mae to marry. I wanted her to wait for me. But wait for what? I wasn't ready for marriage! Or was I?

Why am I so upset? I kept thinking. We only dated for a few months. We were not lovers beyond holding hands and necking.

What could this dream mean, and why could I not shake this terrible feeling? When the ship returned to its home port, I grabbed a ride to New York with one of my fellow shipmates, and soon arrived at my parent's home. It was with much trepidation that I asked my mother what she had heard about Mae Corry.

"Why nothing," she responded.

A tremendous sense of doom lifted from my shoulders. I was anxious to talk to Mae and confirm she was not married, so I reached for the phone and dialed her number. The phone rang three times before a woman answered. It was Mae's mother. The woman I met in her nightgown at two in the morning.

"Oh! Hello Mrs. Corry" I said. "This is Charlie Hackeling ... is Mae home?"

"Ah! Sure and she is, how nice to hear from you. Wait, I'll call her."

That was a surprise. She sounded pleased to hear from me. Through the phone I could hear her calling, "Mae.... Oh! Mae, it's for you."

I heard Mae's voice but I couldn't decipher what she said. I guessed she must have asked, "Who is it?"

Her mother replied, "It's that nice boy Charlie ..."

She didn't finish and I plainly heard Mary Anne Corry's reply, "Oh! Him! Tell him to go jump in the lake."

Now that was not good. Her mother, God bless her, responded, "I will not! Tell him yourself."

I knew then that my future mother-in-law liked me, but her daughter was questionable. 'That a way mom' I thought,' don't let her off the hook. Make her talk to me.' I knew now that not writing was a big mistake. Mae must have come to the phone because now I could hear them real well. They were arguing about who should take the call. My concern was if she hangs up and didn't give me a chance to explain why I hadn't written I would be sunk.

From the tone of her voice I realized she was steaming mad. I felt certain that if I could get her to talk to me I could convince her to see me, and if I could get her to see me I could use the old Hackeling charm to win her over. The phone made a terrible noise, like it had fallen to the floor: I held my breath, hoping she would not hang up. After all, if she hung up, my pride would be so wounded I didn't think I could call again. Finally, Mae picked up the phone and said, in a sarcastic tone of voice, "Hello! What do you want?"

Hi! Mae," I said, "It's good to talk to you."

"Oh! I'll bet. Where have you been the last four months?"

"Gosh! Has it been four months? I thought it was only three."

I was trying to be funny, but I still wasn't sure if she was married. She had no idea how much I wanted to be with her. How much I really cared for her.

"Four, three, what's the difference?" she said.

"Well you see," I began, "I was recalled ... to active duty ... because of the war in Korea."

I thought I could play on her emotions. Perhaps she would have some feeling for those serving their country.

"I'd like to come over and see you if you're free this evening?"

"Forget it!" she replied. "You still haven't answered my question. Where have you been?"

I could sense she was steaming over the time lapse. I was in a bind. I knew I could not smooth away four months of neglect over the telephone. My only chance was to get eye-ball to eye-ball and try to calm her down and reassure her of my sincerity.

"I'm really sorry I didn't write," I explained, "But if you give me a chance to see you, I'll try to make it up to you."

"Oh! That ought to be a good one... Well," she hesitated, then continued, "Make it in an hour. I've got a busy evening. And your explanation had better be good." She was not a very happy puppy.

I recruited my cousin Jimmy to go with me. Guess I needed his moral support. It was a cold evening and promising to be an even colder night. I borrowed my father's car, stopped for some gas and flew over to Mae's apartment. Arriving in front of her apartment, with my heart pounding and wondering what I was going to say, I reasoned that if I left the keys in the ignition while I was talking to Mae, Jimmy would run the radiator and run down the battery. I couldn't have that, so as I parked, I turned off the ignition and palmed the keys, jumped out of the car and ran for the vestibule of the building. I heard

Jimmy yelling something, but it was too cold to turn around and debate. I climbed the five flights of stairs in record time and rang the bell. Mae answered, not smiling. She opened the door, but not far enough to let me enter.

"OK! Now what do you want to say?" she asked, no preface.

My body went limp and I could feel all my blood draining down into my feet. I felt like an icicle. My mouth wouldn't work, and my brain was empty. I stumbled, which was unlike me, "Gee! It's good to see you, Mae!"

And it was. Just looking at her brought life back into my limp torso.

"Any chance I could come inside?"

Reluctantly, she admitted me to the living room.

"I want to explain why I didn't write," I began. As I sat on the living room couch Mae chose a chair ten feet away with room for one only. I didn't want the whole world to hear my confession, so I tried to whisper, but she couldn't hear me. I finally blurted out, "You aren't married, are you?"

Mae looked shocked, "Are you crazy? Of course not! Why?"

"Whew!" I said, and with my heart beating double-time. I continued, "You see Mae ..."

Whatever I said after that I do not recall. I only know that I put all I had into convincing her to see me again. I was piling it on using two shovels and a fork, working as fast as I could. She cancelled her plans for the rest of the evening and we went out for a hot chocolate. I vowed to take up writing and never let this young girl out of my sight, until she married me. It wasn't until years later that I told Mae about my dream. I still get goose bumps when I think of what I would have missed, had she been married with twins.

That was my dream. I will never forget it because it was the first real clue that this girl, Mary Anne Corry, meant something more to me than I could fathom at the time. When we came down to the car I realized I had been gone for over two hours. Jimmy looked frozen and I was afraid hot chocolates wouldn't revive him. But they did, and after four hot chocolates he was alive and forgave me.

"You took the keys on purpose didn't you?" he said. I looked at Jim and smiled, "Yea! I knew you would run down the battery and we would never get to the diner for the hot chocolates. I just never expected it to take so long. I was fighting for my life. She didn't give in easily."

THE NAVAL ACADEMY

Remember I was still in the Navy and with the Korean War still engaged I had no idea when I might be discharged. I could be in the Navy for the balance of nine years.

My assignment aboard the Antietam grew weary after awhile and so I wised off to my chief. In exchange for my caustic remark he gave me the pleasure of assisting the cooks. Starting at 3 o'clock in the morning and lasting until after dinner about seven each evening. Seven days a week. When we weren't cooking, we were scrubbing pots and pans. The temperature ranged about 100 degrees. Sweat was a constant companion. One evening as I was headed for my bunk I ran into our Radio Operations Officer, Lt. Jarvis. He stopped me and said, "Hackeling, I've been reviewing your personnel records and it appears to me that you might be a good candidate for the United States Naval Academy. Any interest?"

"You bet, Sir!" I responded, "What do I have to do to qualify?"

"Meet me in my wardroom this evening and I'll go over it with you."

"Yes Sir!"

The Naval Academy! What an opportunity. I raced down to my quarters, showered, changed uniforms and waited patiently for my hour of reclamation to arrive. When Lt. Jarvis returned to his stateroom I was there with my anxiety hanging all over me. Is there any chance I could qualify for the Naval Academy? He invited me into his quarters, explained to me what was involved and suggested we get started immediately if this was something I was interested in. It was already pass the time for the fleet exam, but he suggested I send a letter to my Congressman and Senator requesting any appointment they might have available. With his help I sent off both letters and Lt. Jarvis and I started my preparation for the entrance exam by going over some old exams he had stashed away in his safe. To my surprise, I scored extremely high. There was only one problem, he said. Since I was already twenty-one, and the requirements for entrance into the Academy are you had to be under twenty-two when you entered. I would have to make it on my first try. There would be no second chance. Since the fleet exam for the class of fifty-six had already been given, I had little chance of getting a fleet appointment. That took the wind out of my sails, but I wasn't going to give up. My appointment had to come from a Congressman or a Senator. In the meantime I spent the next several weeks cramming, not just because I wanted to improve my skills, but because I felt so different when I was in his cabin, in officer's territory. I felt I belonged there. It felt good.

We completed the shakedown cruise and were returning to our home port, but before we got there the Captain thought it would be good for crew moral to put into Miami for ten days of leave and liberty. As we were docking at the Miami port, we received early mail call. I had several letters in my hands, one from my Mom, with the usual five dollars, and two official looking envelopes. I was just coming off kitchen duty and found a large coil of line to relax on while I opened my mail.

First, Mom's letter with the God-saving five dollars. The next letter was from my Senator. Senator B---- said he admired my enthusiasm for a career in the Navy, but unfortunately, he had already used up his allotment of appointments. Keep up the good work. Little did he know that at that moment I was scrubbing pots and pans in the galley, and going through the most humiliating inspection known to man every morning. Please dear God, help me out of this awful situation. As usual, He did.

The next letter was from my Congressman. As I was about to open this letter, knowing it was probably my last chance to get into the Academy, there was a call over the ships loud-speakers, "Would Radioman Hackeling please report to the Captain's Quarters?"

The Captain's Quarters? My God, what did I do now?

I was scared half to death. Nobody went before the Captain unless you were ready for the firing squad. I raced down to my bunk and changed uniforms. I had to look presentable for the Captain; after all, this was the first time I would meet him face to face. Believe me I was scared. I kept thinking, what have I done that the Captain wanted to see me. Oh! Well! There goes any chance I would have at the Academy. As I was ascending the ladder up to the Captain's Quarters I noticed the gangway crowed with officers. They were talking and laughing and patting Lt. Jarvis on the back. As I entered the Captain's Wardroom, he got up from his seat, asked if I was Radioman Hackeling, extended his hand, smiling all the time, and started to pat me on the back.

"Congratulations young man!" the Captain said, "We are all proud of you and hope you will do great things at the Academy."

All the time he was shaking my hand and patting me on the back. Soon all the ships officers were crowded around me shaking my hand and singing my praises. It appeared I couldn't do anything wrong. I wasn't being called up for a reprimand; instead, I was being congratulated by every officer aboard ship. But for what?

They had all just heard that I had been appointed by my Congressman to the Academy. It seemed every officer on board wanted to congratulate me, shake my hand and give me advice. It wasn't until later that evening I realized the letter I hadn't opened yet was still on my bunk where I dropped it while getting ready to see the Captain. This letter was from Christopher McGrath, my congressman, confirming my appointment as his second alternate to the Naval Academy. What a thrill!

Before I left the Captain's Quarters, he sat down at his desk, called me over and said, "I can cut orders for you to go directly to the Prep School in Bainbridge, Maryland now, or I can wait until we're over the ten days of liberty here in Miami. What would you like me to do?"

"Well Sir," I said, "I've never been to Miami."

"Enough said," The Captain responded, "We'll cut the orders in ten days. Until then, you're on official liberty."

What a break. No more pots and pans.

Ten days after my indoctrination in the Captain's Quarters I was standing on the pier at nine in the morning with my sea bag on my shoulder and orders in my hands, waving good-bye as the Antietam made its way out of the harbor. From here I hitched a ride over to the military airport and caught a flight to New York and home. Mom and Dad were about to hear the good news and so was Mary Anne Corry. I wondered whether Mae was going to like it.

I knew Mae would be happy for me, but I also knew she would realize it meant four more years of schooling before we could think of marriage. And four years was a long time. I was concerned she wouldn't wait for me. Or perhaps she would fall in love with a young doctor. After all, they saw the same beautiful girl I was dating. How was I going to assure that this Irish beauty would wait for this thick headed Dutchman, if he decided to go for it? I was heart sick. I was in love and only wanted to be by her side. For the first time in my life I didn't know what to do.

I entered the Naval Academy in June of 1952 and graduated in May of 1956. The Academy had a profound effect upon my life. As tough as it was, it was the one single most important part of my development and future life. I felt like the gentleman they told me I was when I put that uniform on - I was transformed into a Naval Officer, and proud of it.

MIDSHIPMAN'S BALL

During the Christmas leave each year, the Naval Academy Alumni Association throws a Ball in honor of the first year midshipmen. This is usually given in New York City. During my freshman year it was given in the Waldorf Astoria on 5Th Avenue. There was a picture taken, and I am not sure how, but Mae and I wound up right in the middle of the class. It was a night to remember.

It was a cold bitter night as I drove Mae home from the Midshipman's Ball. We had taken the train from the City to the Bronx, but we had to get to Hillside, where Mae lived. I parked the car on Taylor Avenue a convenient place to catch the train into the City. But from here on, most of the trip would be under the elevated train tracks. More than once the car slid on the icy patches that formed under the elevated tracks. Each time I brought the car under control before we hit the El stanchions. Good thing too - it was my father's car. We reached the complex of apartments off Gun Hill Road just a little after one o'clock in the morning. After finally finding a parking place, and on our way to Mae's apartment, we passed through a series of semi-covered passage-ways. The wind howled and blew around our feet in little circles, as though it meant to pick us up and carry us away. Dead leaves rustled in the courtyard and scurried from corner to corner. Before we entered Mae's building, I stopped. I took Mae in my arms and kissed her. Midnight darkness encircled us as we stood pressed together like one, just outside the front door. Silently, I pleaded for the night not to end. Good thing her mother couldn't see us now, I thought, as I pressed even closer. I wanted to stay like this forever, but I knew Mae's mother, strict Catholic that she was, could turn my knees to water and my heart to ice with just one penetrating look. Mae broke the silence and said, "It's too dangerous for you to drive home this evening! You'll have to spend the night."

She turned, put the key in the lock, opened the door and, taking my arm, led me into the darkened apartment.

Mae lived with her mother and father in a two bedroom apartment. A comfortable but small apartment. I liked the idea of staying overnight; awakening to breakfast with Mae would be a real treat! But the thought of Mae's mom gave me a chill far colder than the winter night.

"What about your mother?" I asked timidly.

"Don't worry about Mom," Mae replied.

'Easy for you to say!' I thought. Once inside the apartment, Mae suggested I take the bed in her room. She quickly added,

"I'll sleep with my mother. My father is working tonight."

Always a gentleman, I wouldn't think of putting Mae out of her bed. I would, however, consider spending the night on the living room couch, anything to be close to Mae. But what would her mother think if she found me in Mae's bed and her daughter on the couch? The very thought made me cringe. But Mae insisted I take her room.

"I'll be perfectly comfortable with my mother. I sleep with her whenever my father works nights or we have guests."

After much discussion, I finally agreed, but added, "If you promise me you won't spend the night on the couch!"

I liked the idea of us sharing the couch together, but there was her mother, only a wall away. Besides, Mae would never agree to it. Too bad. And so it was I went to sleep that cold winter's night, in Mae's bed, in Mae's room. The following morning as dawn lifted the darkness from the city, I awoke. I was delighted with the thought of breakfast with Mae. After all, I was in love and the more time I spent with Mae the better I liked it. Although still very early, I arose quietly, dressed, and walked bare-footed through the hall toward the kitchen. I would start the coffee and go to the local Deli for rolls and bagels. That would be a good idea. It might even impress Mae's mother. Couldn't hurt to get on the good side of Mom! As I passed the living room I glanced in the direction of the couch. To my astonishment, there was Mae, still asleep on the couch. A light blanket covered her from head to toe. But there she was. She had deceived me! I no longer felt the noble gentleman. What would Mae's mother think of me, depriving her daughter of her bed? In a moment of rash judgment, I decided to make the most of the situation and teach Mae a lesson. Slowly, ever so slowly, I slipped into the living room and knelt by the couch next to her head. In my mind, Prince Charming couldn't have handled the situation better. I would teach her a lesson she would not soon forget. I would awaken the Princess with a kiss. She would feel it from her lips to her toes. I leaned over her head, my lips just inches from her covered face, and gently, with both hands lifted the blanket. Slowly, ever so slowly I raised it while my lips lowered to embrace hers. Oh! What a kiss this would be! As the blanket disclosed Mae's head, I looked into the wide open eyes, not of my love, but of her mother. We were eyeball to eyeball.

My lips froze. My eyes previously half closed in a lovers trance became as wide as saucers. Mom just stared at me. Naturally, I panicked. Jumping up, I let out a scream and dropped the blanket back over Mom's face. My heart, which a moment ago floated in the ecstasy of love, was trying to jump out of my chest, run away and hide. "This must be a night-mare" I thought. Mae's mother, on the other hand, having the blanket irreligiously dropped back over her head, reached up with a hand and removed the blanket looking directly into my eyes and said, in her fine Irish brogue, "Well? Damn it! Aren't you going to kiss me?"

Shaking, and too unsettled to kiss anyone, I stammered, "I'm sorry! ... I'm sorry ... I thought it was Mae!"

"I'll bet you did!" Mom replied as she started to rise, "And what were your intentions?"

She was too much of an old fox to let an opportunity like this get away. I, on the other hand, was at that point in a young man's life where I didn't know whether to shit or go blind. So I just stood there shaking and waiting for the axe to fall. Mae having heard my screams jumped out of bed and ran to the living room. Mom looked at Mae and started laughing hysteri-cally. She said, "You better hurry up and marry him; he's a real Don Juan."

Still stuttering, I was trying to explain. First to Mom, then to Mae, but nothing seemed to come out right. I broke out in a cold sweat. Perspiration covered my forehead while my mouth went cotton dry. Finally, Mae smiled and answered, "Do you really think so?"

DECISION TO GO TO THE ACADEMY

Before I had to make any decision about the Academy, I had to go to the Navy Prep School to prepare for the entrance examination to get into the Academy. The Navy Prep School was in Bainbridge, Maryland. I received my appointment letter in late September and arrived in Bainbridge in October. I was a little too late for regular classes; they began in May of the same year, so I was given the books to study on my own. I realized if I didn't qualify for the Academy I would be sent back to the fleet, as a reject. Back to the pots and pans, and then some. I studied hard to complete one year in 3 months since the exam was going to be given in January.

The decision to go or not to go to the Academy was left right in my lap. I qualified both academically and physically both under the Prep Schools quota and also under my Congressman's second alternate appointment since both the principal and first alternate failed one or the other exams. I knew Mae was anxious about marriage, but she also wanted what was best for me. I, on the other hand, knew how proud my parents would be if I decided to go to the Academy. I had no idea what a degree from the Academy would mean in my future work career. In a sense I really did feel different when I thought about a career in the military. If I stayed in the military the only way to go was as an officer. That meant the Academy. Several of my fellow classmates were in similar situations and we discussed it into the wee hours of the night. To go or not to go? One of my closest friends, William Doherty, suggested we give it a go and if we didn't like it we could quit halfway through our first year, be free of our military commitment, and finish college on our own. That sounded good to me because it put the real decision about the Academy off for at least six months. After talking to Mae we decided this was the best course of action and so I entered into my first year as a midshipman.

We were sent from Bainbridge to Annapolis and arrived there about six o'clock one evening during the month of June, 1952. I recall it very well because I was anticipating what life as a midshipman would be like. We were divided into companies and assigned as the incoming class of Plebes. There were about fifteen hundred of us and at the 'Swearing in Ceremony' I recall the Superintendant saying two things; one, we were the cream of the crop as far as our country was concerned - that made me feel really special- and second, to look at the Plebe next to us because there was a good chance one of us would not make it through the next four years. This was going to be a tough grind.

I was assigned to the Ninth Company 3RD Battalion. My room was directly across from the Company Office and although this was thought to be bad because we were under the eyes of the Company Commander, it turned out pretty good. It held down some of the harassment the upperclassmen gave to the Plebe Class.

BIG FOOT BROWN

In our little group of misfits who came out of the service, there was one Marine by the name of Bigfoot Brown. His father was a General in the Marines, having been one of the very few Officers who came up through the ranks from Private to General. What an achievement! But this put great pressure on Bigfoot to perform. We were all trying to think of a way to get out of the military without owing the government any more time. Bigfoot tried to resign from the Academy outright. One afternoon, as we were all wondering what would happen to Bigfoot now that he submitted his resignation, his father showed up in a Marine Corp Car with flags flying. Bigfoot had an ass chewing from Pop about what a stupid thing he had attempted…then his father took him back to Camp Lejeune and put him back in the Marines for 4 more years, as a private. His father was to be his director of duty stations. We all took notice of this because it meant we could not just resign and not owe the government any time back. It was a real blow to our plans. Unless we wanted to go back into the Navy as a white hat again, we would have to wait until graduation before we could even dream of leaving the service. Of course, once we reached our senior year we still had the option of going into the Navy, the Marines, or Air Force.

At the Naval Academy, during the fifty's and prior to that, the Air Force was entitled to get twenty-five percent of the graduates since they were required to pay twenty-five percent of the bill for putting the class through four years of training. Now the way they decided who was to get the slots allocated to the Air Force was by lottery….a blind lottery. Fortunately for me I drew number 26. That meant I was the

26th person to declare which branch of service I would select. There was no doubt but that I would pick the Air Force. I wanted so much to marry Mae and start a family. There was no way I was going to pick the Navy. Picking the Navy was a guarantee that you would spend the next three years at sea. Not the best way to start a marriage. So when my time to declare came, I picked the Air Force.

The rest of the senior year was pure heaven. Every chance we got, Mae either came down to see me or I traveled up to see her. Graduation came around and we all were given our assignments. I was going to be commissioned as a Second Lieutenant in the United States Air Force and go to flight school in Tucson, Arizona for pilot training. A new adventure was about to happen for Mae and I. My orders called for me to take flight training at the Mariana Air Force Base in Tucson. This was June of 1956.

It wasn't all that bad. After graduation Mae and I attended Bill Peters' wedding to Betty Ann in Maryland before starting out for New York and our folks. I had thirty days of leave before I had to report back to an air base in Tucson, Arizona for flight training.

My Uncle Jim got me a job running an elevator in one of the buildings he managed in New York City. It was a chance for us to earn a thousand dollars before we ventured to the far west and the advent of our first child.

CHAPTER 5

MAE'S EARLY YEARS

Grandma or Mary Anne Corry (Mae) was also born in the Bronx on May 8, 1930. Her father's name was Michael Curry and he was born in Liscannor, Ireland, on September 24, 1905. Mae's mother was Catherine Ahern and she too was born in Liscannor, Ireland, on July 28, 1906. They came to the United States separately but found each other, married in 1927, and raised a beautiful family. Mae was the second of three children.

First her sister Catherine, then Mae, and Jackie last. They lived in an apartment by St. Anslum's Church along with other family members and friends from Ireland.

Although they were only two years apart in age, Mae and her sister were worlds apart. Catherine was the glamour princess of the family and Mae was responsible for taking care of Jackie. Since Jackie was short for his age, he always had to prove himself by fighting the biggest and toughest kids around. When they got the better of him, Mae would step in and deliver the beatings. Boy could she fight!

Mae's father, Michael Curry was one happy man, and loved by all. Mae remembers her father this way:

A GLEAM IN MY FATHER'S EYE
(Told by Mae)

One day, at the age of four, I came upon a family portrait. Frustrated at not finding myself, I shouted to my mom, "Where am I?"

My mother smiled and replied that when the picture was taken, I was still a gleam in my father's eye. Now this answer did not satisfy my childish curiosity. But it did make me happy to know that I was a part of my father. And because I loved him so, I accepted it until I could understand. Looking back, I realize I arrived in 1930 with the depression. Both Charlie and I were needed like a hole in the head! As luck would have it, UPS could not return "bundles of joy." And so I got to stay. I marvel at how insulated I was from the anxiety and deprivation my family experienced during the depression. When I was hungry, I cried and my mother nursed me. When I was wet, I howled, and again my needs were met. Changed, cuddled and cooed, I couldn't understand the hullabaloo about the depression.

My dad's concerns never seemed to cloud his joy. He would twirl me around, dance and play with me and leave me feeling secure in my little world. Looking into his eyes, I could see the magnificent beams of love. And now I understand what my mother meant. Despite the problems of the depression, I remained a gleam in my father's eye.

I remember Charlie saying that he wished he had known me as a child. I often thought that if he did, he probably would have gotten a bloody nose from me. Some of my favorite memories of my childhood years were of the times I spent playing with my older sister Catherine and younger brother Jackie. I can recall telling Charlie about how when I was a little kid I was the toughest kid on the block. I had to be because my mother put me in charge of my younger brother, Jackie. He was always getting into fights and I was the one to bail him out. I got real good at fighting. When they would pick on Jackie, I would make them pay. Fists would fly and I always gave more than I had to take to even up the score.

Charlie once said, "You sure were a tough kid! Maybe it is a good thing I didn't know you back then."

Despite the depression and the hard times back then, our parents insulated us so we never knew they were experiencing hard times. That was real love.

Looking back I remember St. Anslem's Grammar School as always being within walking distance to my home. We moved a lot but always remained in the same neighborhood. A wonderful Catholic foundation was given to me by the sisters of St. Dominic. They imbued me with the ability to discern how to make a right moral decision. For that especially, I'm forever grateful.

The eighth grade was a particularly happy time. Having made many classmates good friends- we had a lot of fun together. Next was Cathedral High School. Because I had to commute by train into Manhattan and knew no one, I had very little time to socialize and felt left out. There were no extra-curricular activities after school so I began to work at the age of fourteen in Woolworths Five and Dime store.

Graduation from high school led to me going to St. Catherine's Nursing School. Three years of around the clock working, studying, and making solid friends was an eye-opening experience to life. I would not have exchanged this part of my life for anything.

Then I met Charlie. He must have stepped out of the sun because he radiated lots of love. For that gift of love, I have been truly blessed!

MAE & THE 40's

The 40's were a wonderful time to be alive! During these years, I was entering my teens and experiencing tremendous changes. I remember the eighth grade well. As fate would have it, because the school was overcrowded, I was the cut-off student sent to another class. I was prepared to be miserable, separated from my old friends. Surprisingly, my new classmates mirrored to me that I was O.K. Hormones surfaced at this time, and changed the way we all saw each other. It suddenly became important to socialize.

Weekend church dances provided the opportunity to further the art of socialization. They provided us with a way to meet new people. Some of these people became future dates, prom escorts and lasting friends. Dancing provided a healthy outlet for our youthful energies.

The problem of carrying two pairs of shoes arose, as the girls grew taller than boys in the teen years. Heels were worn for the same size or taller escort, and flat shoes for the shorter partner. Comparing that problem with problems that youths face today, I am ever grateful the 40's were my time to grow up.

Looking back, I realize that the stage was set by our Catholic teachers to prepare us for an honorable way to conduct ourselves. They inspired us, taught us to excel and to value ourselves. They did this by leading exemplary lives. They served as wonderful role models, demonstrating how to appreciate life and love ourselves and each other.

MAE'S BAPTISMAL CERTIFICATE

Charlie commiserated:

On one of those rare occasions when we could get Pops and Nana to sit for us for a week, Mae and I went on a vacation that led to a discovery about some very interesting data concerning our family. You see, to this date I'm not sure to whom I am married.

Your mother and I were applying for a passport for a trip to Bermuda. We couldn't find Mae's birth or baptism certificate which was required for entry into the country of Bermuda. Since we were going into the Bronx to see Mae's mother the following day we decided it would be an ideal time to revisit Mae's old stomping grounds and visit St. Anslum's Church to get a copy of her original birth certificate. Mae insisted the church would be easy to find since it towered over all the other buildings in the neighborhood. Well, Mae remembered her neighborhood as it was in the 1930's. Here we were in the year 2001, seventy-one years later. The gigantic church she remembered was now dwarfed now by apartment houses on both sides, up and down the entire block. The only remnant of the neighborhood Mae grew up in was the church, which now hid like a little church mouse between two giant build-ings. We must have spent the better part of an hour driv-ing around the neighborhood looking for this gigantic church Mae spoke of. Just as we were in the process of giving up I spotted a church down a lonely side street.

"Is that it?" I asked Mae as I pointed to this little church huddled between the behemoths of today.

"Yes," she said haltingly, "I - - -I think so."

We drove slowly down the street as Mae tried to bring back the memories of seventy years ago. It was slow going as I realized she was adjusting to the fact that time had passed and with it, the memories of long ago. I'm sure to a little girl of four or five, no matter the condition of the neighborhood; it was fine and full of happy thoughts. Now it was gone and age had taken its place.

We stopped in front of the church, and since there was no parking on the street I told Mae I would wait in the car while she went in and got a copy of her baptismal certificate. It wasn't long before Mae came out of the front door of the church with a copy of her certificate in hand. As she entered the car I asked to see the certificate since I wouldn't relish having to make this trip again. When I opened the envelope and extracted the sheet of paper I quickly noticed there were some mistakes.

"I think you got the wrong birth certificate!" I said.

"What do you mean?" she answered, now a bit annoyed as she tore the paper from my hand.

"Look," I said, "This certificate is for an Anna Marie Curry, nor Mary Anne Corry!"

We both jumped out of the car and this time I said, "I'll go with you."

We both headed up the steps of the church toward the rectory from which Mae had just come. We entered the church, walked briskly up to the woman behind the desk and Mae said, "I think there must have been some mistake. I asked for Mary Anne Corry!"

Mae handed back the document which the woman quietly took. She withdrew from a drawer in the desk, a large, hard covered book which had obvious been in use for many and many a year. She opened the book to the page where the 1930's were registered. After a brief review she handed the book to us and said, "Oh! There's no mistake. Look for yourself. The only baptism that day was for Anna Marie Curry."

We were floored.

"What does that mean?" I asked Mae. "Who am I married to? And what about the children? Are they legitimate?"

Of course I was kidding (with) Mae at this point and she quickly saw the gleam in my eye. She played along with it quite well.

"Well," she said, "At last I'm free. Free as a bird. No kids and no husband. What a life!"

"Wait a minute," I quickly corrected her, "You're not going to get away with this just because you weren't baptized correctly. You know what happened?" I asked knowing full well she knew exactly what happened. Before Mae had a chance to respond, I continued, "Your Godfather, Uncle John talked your Godmother, Aunt Mae into having a drink before the christening then they became confused about the names. Mystery solved."

With the new information in hand we left the church with the baptism certificate for Anna Marie Curry.

"We won't say a word to anyone in the family, especially the children!" I said, as we descended the church steps towards the car.

The ride home was fun. We laughed as we thought about the different scenarios that could come about because of the small error made by two very tipsy people awarded the honor of baptism. Oh well, it could be worse. I don't know how but I'm sure it could be worse. But I'm still not sure to whom I am married?

CHAPTER 6

PARENTS, OURS: GRANDPARENTS, YOURS

You have just been given a brief introduction to your mother's and my early childhood. Now for some tales about your grandparents and their parents as far back as we are able. We'll explore the people who gave us the DNA that makes us who we are. It's a voyage into the past. There are two branches that we will follow; one is the Corry and Ahern branch, the other is the Van Hackeling and Keeling branch. We are going to try to give you some of the flavor that made up their lives thereby giving you some idea of who they were and how they lived.

POP'S WISDOM

How often I think back on the times I use to have with Pops (Mae's father) and wish I could relive them. Pops was full of wisdom. We don't appreciate it until it's gone forever.

Mae and I lived in a small house on Long Island with our eight children. It was a short distance from New York City and my in-laws. Our house was small and always in need of repair. If it wasn't already broken, the children could fix that. Every weekend I faced the challenge of repairing the house. It was always the children's alterations that needed immediate attention. Not that our children were unnecessarily destructive, they just did what children normally do. In our case, because we had so many of them, it was hard to keep up. Windows were especially vulnerable. Cracked panes and torn screens were everywhere. No window escaped the wrath of the children. Doors, of course, came off hinges nicely. Furniture fell apart from the not-so-gentle way the children scaled the rugs and coffee tables, to land, in a tummy tuck, safely on the couch cushions. New furniture turned into antiques in a matter of weeks. Floors, even after a waxing, looked like a herd of buffalo just passed through. In minutes, a paint job that took hours could be made to look like it had been on the walls for years.

Toilets were also a favorite. For children under two, splashing in the toilet bowl was great fun. Over two, soap, small boats, plastic soldiers, combs and curlers wound their way to the cesspool accompanied by a flush. Every so often, they got stuck. When the snake didn't work, the only solution- replace the object in question. Mae would call Pops.

"Pops! Please! Can you come out and help Charlie this weekend?"

Pops always came. It was during these 'crisis visits' that I got to know him. After breakfast we would start the repairs and work until supper. Two people always work better than one alone. And Pops was a pleasure to work with. Never rushed and never flustered. He would examine the job and find the simplest solution. But it was the times between jobs that were most revealing. Every couple of hours or so, Pops would say, "Charlie! Let's take a 'blow'!" Pops' term for a break.

He would ease his six-three, one-hundred-sixty pound frame into an old lawn chair, pass his fingers through the thin graying hair on his head, look at me over his Ben Franklin glasses, and ask, "Charlie! What would you like to talk about?"

Pops could talk about anything. He had the unique ability to break complex problems into small, manageable pieces. His depth of understanding amazed me. 'How,' I thought, 'could this man, who has very little formal education, have such insights into the people, places and things that make up our world today?' As a boy, Pops left Ireland before he finished grade school. He came to the States or 'Colonies' as he liked to refer to them, and went to work for Con Edison. He married and raised three children. Now, in the twilight of his life, he could talk about people, events, and world conditions with unbelievable insight and clarity. He had reasonable solutions. And they made sense. Yet he never sought to impress or impose his views on me or anyone else. He expressed his thoughts and feelings with a sincere and humble, "It just seems to me ..."

I envied his ability to see things so clearly. I had the advantage of college and graduate school, but with all my education and degrees, I was no match for him. Of course, that didn't stop me from giving him my thoughts on a subject. I wondered how he developed his unique insight. One day, while attending a seminar at a local college, I discovered the answer.

"Wisdom," said the professor "is a ball of knowledge, massaged by life's experiences." He raised his arms, clenched his hands together, and massaged an imaginary ball.

'That's the difference,' I thought, 'between Pops, and me.' I often wondered why some people see things so clearly, while the rest of us have to struggle to understand. My father-in-law was one of those people.

"Wisdom is knowledge, massaged by life's experiences."

I had more formal education than Pops, true. I had more knowledge, true. And I was thirty years younger. 'Ah! That's the rub!' I was thirty years younger. Time enough to get lots of information, but little time for massaging. Pops had a lifetime of experience; a lifetime of massaging. He had massaged his knowledge well. Life had taught him that wisdom was for those who were ready to receive it.

Pops died shortly after I learned the difference between knowledge and wisdom. I think about him often and wonder why I didn't spend more time listening to him and less time telling him what I thought. I miss him.

THE CORRY - AHERN BRANCH
A GRAND LOVE AFFAIR

For our thirty-fifth wedding anniversary the children gave Mae and I a trip to Ireland, the birthplace of Mae's mother and father. Neither Mae nor I had ever been to Ireland. Our only exposure to this emerald island was what we heard when her parents would talk about 'the old sod'. But they were both dead now. Wouldn't it have been nice, we thought, to have made this trip with them? To have brought them home. But that was not to be, so we did the next best thing. We went ourselves.

Upon arrival in Shannon, we decided we would like to visit the county in which Mae's parents lived, possibly find someone who would remember them. We went to the Irish Cultural Center and asked where we might start to look for their birthplace. We knew they lived in County Clare, but where in Clare? The Center needed some help before starting the search. Mae's father was one of eleven boys and two girls, a total of thirteen. Even for Catholics this is a large family. They isolated our search to a parish in the south of Clare, in the town of Liscannor. We went there to visit the local church and ask about the family birth records. We arrived about five o'clock in the evening. Too late to visit the church, the doors were locked. We decided to stay at a local Bed-and-Breakfast. We arrived in time for tea with the lady of the house. She asked about our visit and was told of our mission, and Mae's maiden name, Curry. Mrs. Reynolds asked if Mae might be a cousin of Andrew Curry. He and his family live on a small farm only a short, walking distance away. Mae wasn't sure, but her father had a brother by the name of Andrew.

He had never left Ireland. This might be his son. Since the sun was still some hours from setting, Mrs. Reynolds suggested we visit them.

"They'll be delighted to meet you!" she exclaimed.

We walked down the lane and the dusty dirt road that led to the farm. The house was a typical farm house reminiscent of Early American farm houses. There was no bell to ring or buttons to push, so I knocked on the front door. A young woman, with a small child upon her hip and an assortment of young boys and girls swirling around her feet, answered. She took one look at Mae, startled, as if seeing a ghost and said, "My God! You must be a Curry!"

"Yes," Mae quickly interjected, "How did you know?"

"Ah!" She sighed, "They all look alike."

We introduced ourselves, and in turn were introduced to the children; all eight of the bright, well behaved, beautiful, happy children. Andrew, Mae's cousin, was not home from work, but was expected shortly. We apologized for coming at the dinner hour, and tried to retreat explaining that we would return at a more convenient hour. Hanna, for that was her name, wouldn't hear of our leaving, and the children, having discovered an aunt from America, laughed and jumped with joy.

"Please let them stay," they pleaded, "Please?"

And, as is the way of the Irish, they meant it. Saint Patrick himself could not have received a more warmhearted welcome.

Andrew arrived shortly thereafter, and after giving his wife and children a hug and kiss, was introduced to Mae and myself. He was delighted to meet us, especially Mae, a blood relative. We spent the next hour or so talking around the dinner table while the young children climbed upon our laps and buried their heads in our bosoms. The older children wanted to hear all about America and our families. The younger ones just wanted to be held. After a while Andrew asked if we would like to visit the farmhouse in which Mae's father had been born and raised. Of course we jumped at the chance. The sun was starting to creep under the horizon, but it was still remarkably light as we walked across the road to the original homestead. It was just as we imagined it. There was one big house that looked like a converted barn and the road walked up to the front door. They had, this year, installed electricity. A bright bulb hung down from the ceiling and cast a gloomy glow over the entire inside of the house. Behind the house was an old barn, a field and twenty or so cows. After a brief review of the house we walked across the road to an old dilapidated, broken down church and graveyard. Here were buried most of the Curry clan and their offshoots. From there we wandered over to the other side of the road. Sitting on the remains of a broken down wagon was an old man, smoking a pipe and mussing with a younger lad. Andrew walked up to the elderly gentleman, still robust in the ninetieth year of life, and introduced us.

"Shawn," he said, "do you remember my Uncle Michael Curry?"

"Mick Curry?" the old man replied with a jump in his stature. "Yes, a fine lad! He went to America! Ah! Sure and I do! Many a night we sang our hearts out on the road home from the pub."

"I'd like you to meet his daughter, and my cousin," Andrew said.

Mae walked up and took the old gentleman's hand in both of hers. "Hello! I'm Mae. I understand you knew my father?"

"Ah! Sure and I did!" he replied as he eyed Mae in amazement. "I always knew Mick would have beautiful children." He continued, and he showered Mae with the warmest smile this side of Shannon.

Mae smiled and returned, "Did you know my father well?"

"Yes indeed," he replied, "I can still remember the night before he left for the Colonies. We partied all evening and said our 'Good-byes' on the dock the following morning. We were the best of friends."

He threw his head back, smiled and continued as if reliving that time so long ago.

"As I remember, Mick was going with a pretty young girl from the south of Clare. A fiddler.….. Catherine by name."

"Yes!" Mae interrupted with an exciting lilt in her voice, "That was my mother. She played the violin."

"Ah! The old man continued, "But she didn't leave with him. Mick left alone."

"Yes," Mae repeated, "She came over after my father. They met again in Boston and married."

"Ah!" cried Shawn, as he leaned back with a smile of contentment upon his face, "Twas a grand love affair . . . And you my dear," he continued, "are living proof of its beauty."

Mae seemed to glow with the thought of her parents as young lovers. I thought the old man possessed a silver tongue. Is this blarney? If so, he had mastered the craft. A look into the old man's eyes told me, no, it was the love of one old friend for another. That evening, Mae and I cuddled under our comforter to keep out the damp, cold Irish air. She whispered, "I'm glad my father had such a wonderful friend."

After our visit with the old gentleman, Mae and I were escorted to an old grave yard sitting on the back of a run down and abandoned church.

"It's old, but you'll find a host of Curries and Aherns here in this graveyard," said Andrew. "You can take as long as you like looking for your Grandparents."

Mae appreciated the opportunity to walk quietly among the headstones. The grass had overgrown most of the head-stones, so we had to pull the grass back to identify the occu-pant. It was fun, especially since Mae had heard just about all the names of the people here from her mother and father.

Mae's family tree goes back as far as Great-Great-Great-Grandfather, Andrew Curry and Great-Great-Great-Grand-mother, Mary Gorman.

Now let me clear up the confusion over the Curry-Corry name. Actually both are correct. When Pops was a young man immigrating to the United States from Ireland he landed at Ellis Island in New York City. The clerk who pre-pared his paperwork inadvertently listed Pops as Michael Corry, rather than Curry which was the name Pops used in Ireland. Being the kind of man he was, Pops didn't want to embarrass the clerk by making him redo the form, so Pops just decided to go through life as a Corry rather than a Curry.

"After all, what difference does it make?"

That was Pops' attitude about everything in life. What difference does it make as long as you are enjoying your life and doing no harm to another? A beautiful philosophy, for a beautiful man.

CATHERINE AHERN (Nana): EARLY BEGINNINGS

Catherine, Mae's mother (hereafter referred to as Nana), was raised on a farm in Ireland, along with her brothers and sisters. They lived in a small house that sat atop a hill with green grass running clear down to the coast where it dropped off into the Atlantic Ocean. Their house was considered one of the better homes in the community because it had an indoor privy. For those of you who do not know what a privy is, it's a bathroom that contains a toilet. Most homes had outhouses. As a little girl, Catherine carved her initials on the inside bottom of the privy door. Many years later, her granddaughter Maureen, was able to identify the house by those initials on the privy door.

Now Catherine was a scamp. A hard worker, but at things she liked to do. Catherine was a determined and willful child. It was almost impossible to get her to do things she didn't like. Especially the gardening.

WEED THE GARDEN

Her mother was especially fond of Catherine and tried to find simple jobs for her to do around the house. One of those jobs was weeding the garden. Little did her mother know Catherine hated weeding. To grumble and grouse about the job might get her out of weeding for today, but tomorrow she knew she would have to fight the battle all over again. How to end this drudgery once and for all? It dawned on her that occasionally when she wasn't paying attention to the task at hand she would pull up the vegetables instead of the weeds. What a terrible mistake. With a sly smile upon her face Catherine began to pull up all the flowers and veggies instead of the weeds. By the time her mother caught her, Catherine had weeded about half of the garden. Her mother's scream was enough to assure Catherine she would not be called on to weed the garden any more.

CATHERINE AND THE DOCTORS

Catherine was one tough lady. I remember one day Nana wasn't feeling well so we took her to her regular family doctor. After examining Nana he told her that what she needed was an operation on her stomach to relieve the congestion she was experiencing. But, he added, he couldn't perform the operation because he had already operated on her stomach so much that there was nothing left but scar tissue and if he operated there was no guarantee that the wound would heal. He did say however that there was a new doctor on Long Island who might try it. We got his name and we were off to Queens Long Island.

When we met Doctor Gerhart we were surprised to find he was young and from South Africa. After examining Nana he said he would be happy to help her. What he proposed was to cut Nana from the top of her breastbone to her belly button, and then move the skin and flesh back on both sides. He could then arrange Nana's insides so that she had a clear flow of food and gasses through her system. By using two major muscles from her thighs, he could fold them under her hips, bring them up to her chest, and attach them to her sides. He could open them and attach them to new muscles, vest like. Of course he said with a twinkle in his eye, "I would never do this operation if you were a young girl and planning to run in a marathon, or do any other strenuous exercises."

"Oh! Yes!" Nana responded, "I'm thinking of entering the next Olympics."

She always had a great sense of humor and was quick with a response when it was needed. The operation was performed and Nana recovered completely. When we asked the doctor why more surgery like this wasn't being performed here in this country he replied, "Litigation!"

When Catherine first came to this country she stayed with her sister Minnie who lived just outside Boston. Although Catherine was an accomplished musician, and was offered a position with a concert band, her sister, who was older than Catherine, would not allow her to take the position since it would require she be out after dark. It wasn't considered good manners for single girls to be out after dark. You can see the blending of cultures did not always go smoothly. It took a considerable amount of time for the two to integrate.

NANA AND THE LAMB CHOPS

As Nana got older her health began to fail, so she came to live with us in Centerport. Perhaps, we thought, the country air would help her. Oh! How foolish could we be? Neither weather, climate, change of venue or housing was going to change Nana. As I said, Nana was getting on in age.

It was Nana's 83rd birthday. But Nana was not a happy person. She didn't seem to care about anything since Mick, her husband, passed away several years ago. During the last year, Mae noticed her mother getting more and more melancholy. Mae, wanting to make this a happy day for her mother so she asked, "Mom, today is special! What would you like for supper?"

Nana, in her Irish brogue replied, "I think baby lamb chops would be nice."

'Lamb chops,' Mae thought. 'We haven't had lamb chops in years. And baby lamb chops at that. They're expensive.' With a household of ten to feed, lamb chops weren't served very often. But Mae was determined to make this a memorable day for Nana. She set out to buy her mother the best baby lamb chops she could find. She toured the neighborhood, butchers to supermarkets, until at last she found the right baby lamb chops. Boy were they expensive! $9.99 a pound. We couldn't possibly afford enough for the entire family. But today was Nana's day so Mae was determined to spend what was required to make Nana's day a pleasant one.

Mae returned home happy with her find and called to her mother, "Mom, I found the baby lamb chops! Look here! Aren't they beautiful?"

"They sure are," returned Nana, with neither a glance at the chops nor with any enthusiasm.

It was mid afternoon and Nana was too engrossed in General Hospital to care what the lamb chops looked like.

"Shall I put them on for you?" Mae asked, thinking her mother might be hungry.

"No!" came Nana's reply. "I'm not hungry...maybe later!"

Mae felt hurt. Nothing she did seemed to brighten her mother's spirit. No day seemed to have the joy that Mae remembered her mother exhibiting when Mick was alive. Well, life had to go on.

"All right Mom," Mae said sadly. "If you're not hungry now, I'll put the chops in the refrigerator until later. Maybe you'll be hungry then."

Mae, having spent a good deal of the day trying to locate the chops, decided to take a shower and freshen up while her mother watched TV. Tracy, the youngest of the clan, returning from school, climbed the stairs and retreated to her bedroom. She didn't want to be stuck with the chore of watching Nana, who was becoming forgetful.

Mae, unhappy over her mother's melancholy and concerned about her health, followed Tracy upstairs. She needed a few moments to herself. She felt exhausted. The shower proved a delight. The cool water danced over her head and shoulders and ran down her back. She imagined herself under a waterfall in Hawaii. So delightful was the shower that she resented having to leave it. As she emerged and started to dry herself, she caught a whiff of smoke. She panicked and quickly threw on a towel, sarong like. Opening the bathroom door she saw smoke coming from the direction of the kitchen. Mae raced hysterically down the stairs, shouting to Tracy as she passed her bedroom to get out of the house. She passed the living room where her mother was still seated watching TV. She yelled at her mother to flee the house for safety to the front lawn. She reached the kitchen in time to see dense black smoke emerging from the oven. She knew she hadn't put anything in the oven, but she guessed, rightly, her mother had started the chops.

Across the street, Pat Fallon, a volunteer fireman, was returning from work. Hearing Mae's screams, he ran across the lawn, in through the front door, and headed for the kitchen.

"Get out of the house," he said to Mae. "I'll take care of the fire."

Mae, still clutching her towel, raced into the living room. "Mom, get out. The house is on fire."

"I will not." replied Nana. "I'll catch me death of cold."

"Get out," Mae repeated as she unceremoniously hustled her mother into the center-hall. She grabbed Nana's coat from the coat-rack, tossed it in her direction and started up the stairs for Tracy. Meanwhile, Tracy, hearing all the commotion came out of her room and demanded to know what was happening. Mae raced upstairs taking the steps three at a time, yelling, "The house is on fire. Get out."

"I will not," Tracy screamed. "I'm not dressed. Suppose people see me. I'll be embarrassed. What would my friends think?" she asked, not really expecting an answer.

"Who cares!" Mae shot back as she raced into the master bedroom, dropping the towel and jumping into the house-dress she had put on the bed before taking her shower. Underwear would have to wait.

Out like a flash Mae came running and grabbed Tracy who was standing at the head of the staircase. Tracy knew better than to mess with Mae. At the bottom of the staircase, Nana was standing, pout on her face and yelling at Pat who headed towards the kitchen, "Save the chops... Save the chops!"

Mae pushed Tracy out the front door and then, just as unceremoniously, took her mother's arm and escorted them both to the middle of the lawn. As she started back toward the house, the fire truck was pulling into the driveway. Firemen jumped off the engine and rushed toward the house. But, thanks to Pat Fallon, the kitchen fire was already out. Pat emerged from the house, blackened by the smoke and said to Mae, "Everything's OK Mae! It was the oven."

Mae replied without blinking an eyelash, "Yes Pat! Thank you! But let me ask you....did you save the chops?"

MAE'S FAMILY

Mae's family tree goes back as far as Great-Great-Great-Grandfather, Andrew Curry and Great-Great-Great-Grandmother, Mary Gorman. Michael (Pops) came to the States and when he found Catherine, they got married. They wasted no time before Catherine, their first daughter, was born. Next came Mary Anne (Mae) and last, but not least, John (Jackie).

They lived as an extended family in the vicinity of Tinton and Union Avenues in the Bronx. Aunts and uncles were everywhere, as were friends. Nana and Pops were quick to help the family. They helped their siblings get settled and find jobs and introduced them to other friends.

One relative was Thomas Flanagan who came over to the States when he was about twenty years old. Tom was as good as gold and was equally generous when it came to helping the family. Some stories about Tom are worth repeating. One was the time Nana found a mouse in the house just as Tom was returning from work. Tom, excited by Nana's screaming and yelling, grabbed the first thing he could lay his hands on. It was a ball peen hammer. Tom chased the poor mouse into the bathroom and cornered it in the bathtub. Bamb ... bamb ... bamb. Tom was swinging the hammer from side to side, determined to get that poor scared mouse. Well, he finally got it. And with it the entire porcelain tub, which was now pot marked from front to back with ball peen hammer marks. The porcelain could be swept up but the tub was doomed. Nana took one look at her tub, where she loved to soak and rest at the end of a long day and began to beat poor Tom over the head with her purse. Tom ran out of the house not sure why he was being pillaged by Nana but happy to escape her rage.

On another occasion, Nana had a habit of secretly hiding her purse in the oven, especially on pay days. On one such day Nana came home exhausted, hid her purse and went into her bedroom to take a much needed nap. Tom, in the meantime, also arrived home shortly after Nana retired and brought with him half of a pizza pie. Without looking, he put the pizza in the over and turned it on to heat up his dinner. The first clue Nana got that all was not well was when she smelled something strange burning in the kitchen. Like a flash she was up on her feet and flying towards the kitchen. Tom was also moving towards the kitchen but at a much slower pace. He knew what was cooking. Nana bowled him over. She arrived at the stove; flung open the oven door, whipped out the pizza, and then retrieved her purse. It was smoldering. Nana tossed the purse back and forth between her hands until she could get it to the sink where she put it under the cold water. When she withdrew the purse it was wet but major damage was not done. Her pay was cooked to a nice roomy temperature. She extracted her funds and started after poor Tom with her purse. Before Tom knew what was happening, he was the target of Nana's rage. She chased him around the apartment, out the door to the fifth floor landing and down all five landings to the street, calling him every Irish curse word she could think of, all the time swinging her purse at Tom's head.

But all things considered, Tom was a good and loyal soul who was a blessing to the family. When times were tough and money short, Tom could be called upon to help until times improved. He did so graciously. Enough about Tom.

Grandma Mae was the middle child of three. Her older sister is named Catherine and her younger brother is named

Jackie. Grandma Mae went to grammar school and high school and then onto to nurses training at Saint Catherine's School of Nursing. After graduation she worked at the Veterans Administration Hospital in the Bronx. We met and dated while I was working with my father. Soon after, I was recalled to active duty in the Navy.

CHAPTER 7

THE VAN HACKELING AND KEELING FAMILY LINE

Now what do we know about the Hackeling and Keeling lines? Not as much as I would like to know but we have some stories that cast a general feeling about their lives. For example, my father, Carl Hackeling, never talked very much about his childhood. Although I tried several times to get him to open up about his past, I realized it was probably because he didn't have a very happy childhood. His father died when he was one year old. His mother, being relatively new to this country didn't realize she was entitled to veterans' benefits when her husband died, so she did what she knew how to do. She took in laundry from the rich folk, did the laundry and whatever sewing she could get. They lived in an inexpensive apartment in the Hell's Kitchen area of Manhattan. It was a cold water flat with a pot belly stove in the center of the apartment. My Uncle John and my father attended the local public school. They were poor. I don't think my father ever had a visit from Saint Nick. His stockings probably had holes in every toe. Not like ours.

My father rarely talked about his father. A good reason for that would that he never knew him. My Grandmother Theresa, my Dad's mom, grew up under the tutelage of Tonda

Fritz. She lived in lower New York City, went to school there, and began to work as Tonda's assistant after graduating from grammar school.

Some years later, Theresa met and married a young man named Johannes Van Hackeling. He migrated to the United States in 1897. His homeland was Groningen, Holland, where he was a physician. But here in the United States, he had to operate as a pharmacist.

The story was told that as a young doctor in Amsterdam he was invited to the royal palace for the evening. During dinner one of the royal families started to choke, but luckily there was a doctor in attendance, Dr. Van Hackeling, and a life was saved. The royal family was so grateful they rewarded him with a position at court. Dr. Johannes Van Hackeling was present at the birth of a royal daughter, who later became Queen Wilhelmina. While at court Johannes dallied with one of the Queens ladies in waiting. This caused a royal embarrassment and the young doctor was advised to leave the country. He sailed for America in the 1890's.

Upon entering this country, it was suggested that he Americanize his name by dropping the Van. He reluctantly complied. Although he had been educated in Holland, he couldn't be accredited as a doctor in this country, so he became a pharmacist. He met and married Theresa and soon had a son who they named John. A little while later Theresa was again with child, Carl. Shortly after the birth of Carl, Johannes was inducted into the military. What happened to Johannes during his time in the service is not known, but during his tour of duty, he died. Theresa, being unfamiliar with the customs in this new country did what she had to do to survive - she took in laundry.

BLACK GOLD

Needless to say, money was always scarce in the Hackeling household and many a day went by when there was no food or heat in the house. My father used to tell me how, at the age of five, during the winter months, he and his brother would climb the fence that surrounded the railroad yard which was only a few blocks from where they lived to search for lumps of coal. Once inside the yard, they would pick up the lumps of coal that fell off the trains as they pulled out of the yard. The coal lay on both sides of the train tracks. Yes, it was dangerous to cross the tracks again and again, but to my father and his brother it might mean the difference between sleeping in a warm kitchen or a cold one. In those days many of the tenements were heated by coal stoves only, usually located in the kitchen in the center of the house. The year was 1906, and trains burned coal. So did the railroad flats. Coal was expensive and money was always short.

A danger they faced when they scaled the railroad fences was the railroad policemen who patrolled the yard. To them, these boys were stealing the railroad's property. To the boys these men were big strong bullies who took pleasure out of beating the young hooligans. They would chase them and if they caught them they would beat them across the back of their legs with their Johnny sticks. When they were done you could hardly stand no less pull yourself back over the fence and crawl home. He recalled how he felt the stick of the railroad guard across the back of his legs as he scrambled back over the fence, his pockets full of coal. My father called the coal, 'Black Gold.'

"Without it," he would say, "the long, cold winter nights never seemed to end." But to go home with the prize of several pieces of coal was worth the smile it brought to their mother's face.

They lived in poverty until, years later when John, her oldest son became an accountant and realized his mother should have been eligible for some veteran benefits. He applied for them and Theresa became a rich widow. She would always say she came into money when it really didn't matter.

WATCH MY BACK

A practice the two brothers always adhered to was helping defend one another. Being in a fight was commonplace in their school yard. There was always an ample supply of bullies, anxious to show off their tactics. Grandpa was an easy target because he was small. Bullies always pick on the small kids because they know they can push them around.

My father was small for his age. He never grew taller than five-foot six-inches. But that five-foot-six-inch was all badger. When provoked, my father would out-fight any kid in school, regardless of their size. He was a hungry tiger let loose in the midst of all those kids. No one wanted to fight my father once he beat to a pulp the biggest kid in school. It took more than one kid to beat Dad. One day a gang of thugs decided they would teach my dad a lesson and ganged up on him. He held his own for a while, but the numbers finally beat him down. He went home a wreck, told his brother what happened, and they set about avenging the beating. From that day forward, they always defended each other and watched one another's back. They decided that if they could get each boy alone, and let him face my father single handedly, that would be a fair fight. One by one each of that gang was found, isolated from his friends, and allowed to fight my father, one-on-one. Carl was small for his age, but was dynamite in a small package. One-on-one they were no match for my father and he thrashed each and every one of them. The word was out and no one bothered the Hackeling boys again.

MY DAD'S EDUCATION ENDS

My father says of his education, that it ended after the sixth grade. It seems that on the first day of class when the roll was being taken, his new sixth grade teacher, a huge bulk of a man, called my father by name. When my father answered, the man looked up from his paper, growled at my father and said, "By Jesus, if I can get my hands on you I'll break every bone in your body."

That was all my father had to hear. He didn't need an invitation. He would make sure the man never got within one row of seats before my father picked up his books and got out of the classroom. Why the man would say such a thing, or why the man disliked my father, my dad never knew. Perhaps it had something to do with my father's older brother, or perhaps there was some other explanation. He just knew it was wise to always be one step ahead of him. And that was what he did. He had a small mirror which he set up on his desk so he could see anyone coming up the aisle from behind him. From there my father would go into the school yard and play handball. My father's education ended there. Too bad, he had a great head for numbers. Grandpa loved mathematics.

CARL HERMAN ARMOND HACKELING

When my father died he left a good many friends behind. One was Bob Russell. Bob was a former Miss Universe Master of Ceremonies and Bob liked Dad a lot. Here was a poem he wrote in honor of my father upon Dad's passing away.

IN MEMORY OF CARL HACKELING

January 29, 1991
by Bob Russell

<u>MY OLD FRIEND</u>
What do you say when a friend departs
So long? Au Revoir? Good-bye?
I wish I had the words to say
About a friend who has gone away
Leaving us all just the other day
To look for that place in the sky.

Charlie, old pal, what a hand he had
Whatever went wrong-he could fix it
The window's jammed-this needs a crown
Got a personal problem- he broke it down
The peg is square, the hole is round
No matter how tough-he licks it.

Carl loved to laugh, enjoyed his life
'Specially his fire company
Life's give and take, his animation
The liveliness of conversation
The open door-his invitation to join the family

Family-family
Oh, what a beautiful word!
A wonderful grandpa-and his sons gave him many

Grandchildren, beautiful ones.
His boys-their wives- the good line runs
They'll be seen by the world, and heard
We're looking up, Paul!

Remind Peter to hang out the "Welcome" sign!
High up above the old front gate
The red carpet-be sure it's straight
Tell Gabriel, Blow! And play it great!
Make Charlie's welcome divine.
Just- God speed! Charlie dear, sail on Carl-
God is near

What do you say when a friend departs?
A link of a friendship strong? —
It's going to be awfully lonesome here-
But- we'll be seeing you ere long.

It was a nice tribute by a good friend. My father got to live out some of his lifelong dreams. He always wanted to own a Cadillac car and his own home. After he moved from the Bronx to Lake Tippicanoe in Sarasota, Florida, he was able to save enough money to buy his own condo. Shortly after that he purchased the Cadillac. When he bought the Caddy he said to me, "Charlie, I now have everything in life that I ever wanted!"

Carl was a handyman, and was known around Lake Tippicanoe as the man who could fix anything. He did, and in the process made a bevy of friends, all of whom loved him.

What more can a man ask for?

REFLECTIONS OF MY FATHER

There are two sides to every coin. So too, there are two sides to us, human beings. At least it was that way with my father. I loved both sides.

My father was the toughest man I ever knew. Even at the age of fifty he could do a back flip from a standing position. It wasn't that he was big. On the contrary, he was small. About five-feet-six-inches tall and never weighed more than a hundred thirty-five pounds. He learned early in life that he had to fight to survive. He was a hard worker, and as tough as they come. He was afraid of nothing and no one.

As I mentioned earlier, he didn't have much of a childhood. His father died when he was a year old and his brother was three. His mother was a young, naive, immigrant girl. They were poor and lived in a small flat in a section of New York known as Hell's Kitchen. It was a tough, mean neighborhood.

I said my father was a tough man....and he was. But he was fair and had a heart bigger than the potbelly stove and softer than butter in August. My mother on the other hand, although physically soft, had the will and determination of Attila the Hun. Raised in an Irish-German, Catholic family, her mother instilled a stoic discipline about things right and wrong. For example, men did not kiss in public. And they never kissed other men.

I remember the day I left for the service. I was seventeen, had finished high school, and joined the Navy. I was to report to the Great Lakes Training Camp in Chicago. This was the first time I would be away from home for any length of time. It marked a turning point in my life.

My family and I lived in a two story house, inherited from my grandfather on my mother's side. My uncle, aunt, and cousins lived on the ground floor with Grandpa, and my family and I lived on the top floor. A staircase ran from the vestibule to our upstairs apartment. At the top was a small landing and a door to the upstairs rooms. As I was leaving, my mother and father were standing on the landing. I kissed my mother and started down the steps. Out of the corner of my eye I saw my father step out from behind my mother and lean toward me. I knew he wanted to kiss me good-bye. I turned toward him; he had tears in his eyes. As he got to the banister, my mother quickly reached out her hand and seized him by the wrist. It was her signal for him to stop. He drew up quickly, stood awkwardly still, and waved. But I knew he wanted to take me in his arms and kiss me. As I went down the steps I thought, 'How strange. My father wants to kiss me good-bye, but my mother won't let him.' I resolved that in that moment, nothing would ever stop me from hugging and kissing my children. The memory of my father standing on that landing remains with me to this day. I still see tears in the eyes of the toughest man I ever knew.

I was standing in front of Hamburger Heaven, on Fifty-Third Street and Madison Avenue in New York City, waiting for Michael, my son. Michael worked a few blocks away. I saw him crossing the street, a big grin upon his face. As he walked up to me I gave him a big hug and kiss. Some people stared, and as they did, I thought of my father standing on the stairs with tears in his eyes over fifty years ago.

"Michael!" I said, as I looked into his smiling face, "Come here! Give your 'Old Man' a hug and kiss! Grandpa would like that!"

REFLECTIONS OF MY MOTHER

Although my father was tough, my mother, on the other hand, was a soft woman. She was very bright and finished high school in three years. She had worked as a court stenographer before she married my father. My mother loved to read. As a child I remember the closets being filled with books. She liked mysteries. But she read everything.

My mother was raised in an Irish-German, Catholic family. It was my grandmother who most influenced my mother. She wanted to protect her daughter. There were stories of white slaves and the lives of the young girls they preyed upon. My grandmother must have made a big issue of white slavers because I can remember my mother telling me of a recurring nightmare in which she is chased by the white slavers. Her home had a high front porch and many steps from the street level to the front door. My mother would scream as she tried to lift her feet to get up those steps and away from the white slavers. It seemed her feet were encased in heavy cement. Just as her fate was being sealed she would awake, drenched in sweat and trembling. My grandmother installed many fears in my mother. As she grew older, my mother was afraid of everything. She would hide in a dark closet or under a bed if there was a thunder and lightning storm. Little did my grandmother know how much damage she did by trying to protect her daughter.

But my grandmother also installed a stoic discipline in my mother about what is right and what is wrong. "You never compromise with evil" was one of my mother's favorite sayings. She was right, and every time you think differently, rethink it. Evil is the Devil's workshop. Never compromise with evil. Make it your mantra.

CHAPTER 8

OUR GRANDPARENTS: YOUR GREAT GRAND PARENTS

THERESA

The oldest people I can remember are my grandmother on my father's side and my grandfather on my mother's side. My grandfather on my father's side died when my father was about one year old. Even my father didn't get to know him. But what we do know about him is that his correct name is John Van Hackeling. He was a doctor in Holland and a pharmacist here in the States. He was killed in the military.

His wife, my grand-mother Theresa, is seen in the photo below with my Uncle John, on her left side, and my father, Carl, on her lap (the dog is unaccounted for).

Theresa Hackeling, Carl, & John

She lived a long life and used to visit her two sons and daughter (my father's half sister) during varying times of the year. Grandma never stayed any longer than she could stand us. We too were glad to see her go when her time was up. I say that with my tongue in my cheek because we children loved her and were delighted when she came to visit us. There are a good many stories to tell about Grandma, but the one I like best is her escape from Germany.

THERESA DIETRICH'S ESCAPE FROM GERMANY

The year was 1891. One winter evening, in a small farming village just outside Munich, Germany, Theresa Dietrich, age 14, overheard her mother and father talking about Tessa's (Theresa) future.

"Otto Hoffman was up to talk with me today," said Father. "He has a large farm and can support a wife and several children. He has had his eye on Tessa for some time. He is lonely since his wife died. He has asked for Theresa's hand. She will marry Otto."

"But she's still too young and she hasn't finished high school," her mother protested. "Besides, she doesn't love him."

"What does all that have to do with anything?" shouted Father. "It's settled!" He shot back as he rose from the kitchen table, indicating the discussion was over.

Father had spoken. Well, thought Theresa, I'm not going to marry that big fat old man. When her father came to her to explain the situation, she pleaded with him. "I'm not through with school yet father, and I don't want to marry that old man."

Father took the insult personally. After all, he was the same age as Otto. But father's mind was made up. It was a good match for Tessa. She would be provided for the rest of her life. He started to make plans for the wedding.

Theresa knew there was little to be gained by arguing with father. He was doing what he thought best for her and the family. But Theresa was a girl of independent character. She was not going to marry Otto. If father liked him so much, he could marry him.

As the winter was coming to a close, one clear brisk night, after all had gone to bed, Theresa stole out of the house, saddled father's best horse, and rode off for Holland. Once there she sold the horse, booked passage for America, and sent the bulk of the money that remained to her father. She kept only enough to get herself to America at the age of fourteen.

Upon arrival at Ellis Island, she disembarked and with her one suitcase started to wander to the gates that would ultimately take her into the city of New York. She must have looked like a little waif, slowly maneuvering among all those people. A large Germanic woman noticed her and asked her if she was waiting for someone. Theresa didn't speak English, and once Anna, the woman in question, figured this out, they conversed in a common language, German.

When she landed, there was no one to meet her. No one even knew she was coming. After everyone else left the dock she was alone. A small girl, with a smaller suitcase containing everything she owned. How lonely and frightened she must have been. But providence was kind to her. A large German woman, Tonda Fritz, was there to meet one of her sister's children, Anna. After collecting Anna, Tonda saw the small waif still standing alone, not a soul in the world to comfort her, looking like an abandoned child. She approached Theresa and asked if there wasn't someone who knew her, someone to greet her. Grandma shook her head 'No!'

"Then you will come with me," Tonda said. And from that moment forward, Tonda Fritz, Theresa and Anna started a lifetime of friendship that grew into a family.

Theresa grew up with Tonda Fritz, Anna, and her family in a small apartment in New York City's west side. There my grandmother went to school, learned English and helped Tonda Fritz wash and iron sheets and bedding that seemed to never stop coming into their little apartment. But it provided the income needed to support Tonda, grandma and Anna. Anna was a few years younger than grandma but they shared a room and soon learned to love one another as sisters.

As time marched on, Theresa met a young doctor named Johannas Van Hackeling. He migrated to the United States in 1897. They married, were a happy young couple and soon had a son who they named John. A little while later she was again with child, Carl (Grandpa Hackeling). Shortly after the birth of Carl, Johannas was inducted into the military. Where he went, or what happened during his time in the service is not known, but sadly, during his tour of duty, he was killed.

Theresa, being unfamiliar with the customs in this new country, did what she had to do to survive. In order to provide for her two sons, grandma, my grandma, used to scrub floors, take in laundry and sew. She worked long hours in Hell's Kitchen but didn't seem to complain. At least I never heard my father say she complained. I suppose she was grateful just to be in America.

They lived in poverty, until, years later, when John became a Certified Public Accountant and realized that his mother should have been eligible for some veteran's benefits upon the death of her husband. He applied for them and Theresa became a rich widow.

GRANDPA KEELING

In this photo, my grandfather, your great grandfather James Keeling, is on the front poach of his house on Taylor Avenue. Grandpa, as he was called, is in the center of the picture. His wife, my grandmother, Anna, is on his left, and directly behind them is my mother, Edna. My Uncle Jim and Aunt Edith are the other two in the picture. I never met my grandmother, Anna; she died before I was born, but she looks like a strong attractive woman. I know my mother loved her very much.

On my mother's side, her father, Grandpa Keeling was a big man. He was tall, six feet, and on the heavy side. He reminded me of the Captain in the comic strip The Katzenjammer Kids. He wore glasses and his hair was thinning. He walked with a cane due to an injury suffered at a fire when he was younger.

He was a Captain in the New York City Fire Department. One evening, there was a fire in one of the big factories in lower Manhattan. His engine responded and upon arriving at the scene, he rushed into the burning building with his men. After getting the fire under control, he went up on the roof of the building with his men to inspect the damage. A tall eight foot iron picketed fence surrounded the building. Each upright bar was a spike, and was held together by strong crossbars at the top and bottom. The spikes were at least 16 inches long, ending in a sharp point. As grandpa was walking along the edge of the building an explosion occurred underneath him. It hurled him up in the air and across the path that ran between the iron fence and the building. He was thrown up and across the path ending up impaled through his legs on the iron fence. There he was suspended, upside down, his legs held fast by the iron spikes which were thrusts through his thighs.

As soon as the other firemen were able to get to him they cut the metal spikes and rods and took him to the hospital, fence and all. There at the hospital they removed the spikes from his legs, but his legs were never the same after that. He needed extensive therapy and the help of a cane to get around. But he was alive. He retired shortly after this incident and lived in the house he had built years earlier. The address was 1160 Taylor Avenue.

THE GENERAL SLOCUM STORY

As a matter of interest, I want to tell you another story about Grandpa Keeling. This involves his heroic efforts to save the lives of people aboard the SS General Slocum on June 15th, 1904. The Northport Journal, a local Long Island newspaper, recorded the incident under these headlines:

The Day a Thousand Died

The day the General Slocum - bound for a picnic ground on Eaton's Neck with a boatload of youngsters - went down, they draped New York City Hall in mourning. The date- June 15, 1904- would be remembered in various ways over the years. Monuments to the dead would be erected in cemeteries and in communities from which the victims came. Articles and books would be written. Survivor associations would spring up. The captain of the ship would be dragged through the court system and sent to prison for a 10-year sentence.

And the horrible scene of an excursion boat loaded with over 1,000 passengers burning and sinking into the East River at Hell's Gate would remain etched in the memories of those who survived- as would the name Locust Grove, the picnic grounds on Eaton's Neck where the ill-starred ship was headed.

At the turn of the century, picnic groves on Long Island were important to the hard working Manhattan laboring communities. Whether at Far Rockaway or Coney Island or Glen Island or Eaton's Neck, resorts were plentiful on Long Island shores. The groves of Eaton's Neck and areas around our harbor ways - such as Valley Grove, Locust Grove and nearby Columbia Grove - were important recreational sites for city dwellers. And the paddle wheeled ships, which brought people out by the thousands for a day-trip, were an important transportation link.

The General Slocum disaster changed all that. It was a catastrophe so great, having wiped out nearly half of the population of a German community parish in Manhattan, that for many years, afterwards it was considered to have been an unparalleled event in the annals of American history.

That so many could die so quickly and so horribly on their way to a picnic not only changed the way that people perceived travel by vessel along Long Island shores, but it raised serious questions about the quality of safety equipment on shipboard, the reliability and training of crews, and the veracity of those charged with assuring such quality and reliability might be depended upon.

According to The Long Islander, the pastor of St. Mark's Evangelical Lutheran Church, a church serving a neighborhood of hard working German immigrants, had charted the 13 year old riverboat for the sum of $350 to take a group of picnic-goers to Long Island. The 1300 people aboard were mostly women and children.

The General Slocum was no cattle boat, mind you. Together with her sister ship, the Grand Republic, the picturesque paddle-boat was the pride of her steamship company and was captained by a man who had been running her from the day she had been commissioned. Pulling in to harbor, she must have made an impressive sight, with her two tall yellow stacks, banners and flags flying, her two paddle boxes, and fancy polished wood interior topped off with red velvet. Still, the ship had experienced a run of problems in recent years. According to historians, a record of groundings, mechanical breakdowns and other accidents had resulted in the ship's losing favor as an excursion boat. It was with some alacrity, then, that the crew of the General Slocum set sail with a charter from the St. Mark's Church.

By 9:40 a.m. the party was aboard with plenty of food, beer and soda. Several barrels of drinking glasses packed in hay were aboard. Professor George Maurer's German Band played a hymn as the paddleboat left the dock, and headed for Hell's Gate – the narrow channel that all ships had to pass through to get into Long Island Sound.

And it was in Hell's Gate - renowned for its powerful currents, underwater rocks, and daunting navigational demands - that disaster struck. When passengers began to smell smoke, the ship's crew began to check below. And they discovered that some of the hay in a barrel that contained those drinking glasses had caught fire. Panicked, one of the crew members grabbed the nearest thing he could find to throw on the fire and ran for help.

What happened next would figure in court battles over the next several years. But essentially, the captain and his crew - some of whom had little or no experience at sea - let things get out of hand. Confusion reigned for precious minutes as the flames grew and the crew failed to respond in an organized fashion. When the crew was finally mobilized, water hoses burst and couplings disconnected.

By now, strong winds, the speed of the boat, and the powerful current brought the situation out of control. For the next 20 minutes, panicked passengers reacted in horror as they reached for life preservers that were wired in place or so decomposed that they were useless. Lifeboats, glued or wired in place, could not be launched, and nearby boats could not get close enough to the burning vessel to help.

By 10:20 a.m. –just 40 minutes after the General Slocum set sail - she sank. And 1,021 souls expired on that fateful day.

The results of the incident were profound. The New York City Mayor decreed a 30-day period of mourning. Bands were directed to play only funeral music on the city piers. City Hall was draped in black for the second time in history - the first being the assassination of President Lincoln.

The Captain, it was later revealed, had done a pretty poor job of inspecting his ship and training her crew. He was sent to Sing Sing, convicted of manslaughter for 10 years.

Now that was the Long Islander's report of the catastrophe. My grandfather was assigned to the boats in the harbor. He directed his boat to get as close as possible to the General Slocum and then began diving into the water to pull children out of the furious currents. In and out he went, several times, until he was exhausted. The Mayor of the City awarded him a medal for his heroism. He never spoke of this tragedy, but it was one of New York City's darkest summers, and one of Grandpa's finest moments.

CHAPTER 9

FROM CIVILIAN TO MILITARY LIFE 1948-1952

Before I went into the military service, my life at home was quiet, serene and very limited. After graduation from La Salle Academy, I took a job at Stroheim and Roman, a clothing distributor in New York City. I didn't want to go away to college; in fact, I don't believe my folks thought I was capable of college work.....must have been my high school grades.

I remember my Uncle Larry asking me if I was interested in going away to college, and if I was that he would make all the arrangements. Little did I know that the school my Uncle was referring to was Lee High University, a very fine school in Pennsylvania. He even said he could arrange for me to get a part-time job while attending. What a fool I was to turn down such a wonderful offer. As I think back on that time in my life, I realize neither one of my parents ever mentioned Uncle Larry's offer. When I meet them in Heaven, if I am fortunate to make it, I want to confront them and ask why they didn't at least ask me to consider the offer. Uncle Larry was not only a fine gentleman, he was also a wonderful and generous man. No wonder my folks like him.

At any rate, I declined.

Fool, fool, fool that I was.

Instead of going to a fine university, I traveled every day of the week into the City, completed a job I was not crazy about, and went to school three nights a week at Pace College taking accounting classes. I remember bumping into Tommy Naughton, my high school best friend, and asking him what he was doing. He said he had tried out for the Brooklyn Dodgers, but didn't make the team. Tommy was a good pitcher, but not good enough for the big leagues. He didn't know what else to do and his mother was driving him crazy (actually, she was the crazy one) so he joined the Army. He would leave in two days for boot camp and then spend the next four years as a dog soldier. That wasn't for me, but it got me thinking. The Navy was offering a unique program, where you could enlist for one year active service followed by nine years of reserve duty. I thought, how bad can one year be? I could put up with almost anything for one year then be free to do my own thing. Our country was at peace with the world, and in the Navy, I might get to see some of the world outside New York and the Bronx. So that was what I did. I enlisted for one year of active duty.

GREAT LAKES, USN

I went to boot camp at the Great Lakes Training Base just outside Chicago. It was February and the winters were cold, and I mean cold.

The time spent at the training center was to get each of us in condition to perform any of the duties the Navy might require. I didn't mind the program because I felt I needed it to get myself in perfect physical condition. It was here that I met some very good friends and began my first exposure to wrestling.

While we were going through boot camp, the Navy was evaluating the battery of exams they administered to us when we first arrived at the center. On the basis of these tests the Navy appointed us for further training after boot camp was completed. I was assigned to go to radio school in Norfolk, Virginia. This was considered a plum assignment. And it was. I learned Morse code and how to send and receive it on board ship. When radio school was over, I was assigned to the USS Beltrami, a cargo ship stationed in Norfolk and getting ready for a trip to Europe and Africa to deliver food and other needed materials.

Almost immediately I started to get an understanding of what life in the Navy was like, even as a senior officer. I remember one evening I was on duty in the radio shack when an important message came in for the Captain. After I delivered it to the Captain, he asked me to sit with him for a few minutes and shoot the breeze. Sure. It was an honor to be asked by the Captain to sit and chat. We got around to talking about married life and having a family in the military.

"One of the advantages of being in the Navy and being married is that you are always home to lay the keel but never there for the launching," he said. He thought it was a benefit, not being around for the birth of your child, but as I heard him telling this to me, I saw it as a deficit.

"You mean," I said, "You are never there to see your child born?"

"Who wants to be there for that?" he responded.

We both laughed, but I was thinking, I want to be there when my children were born.

This was the beginning of my development as a maturing young man. Shortly after our return from the Mediterranean and our deployment in Rhode Island, I was discharged and sent to a reserve unit on Fort Schyler. Life was starting to settle back into the routines that I had fled just one year before, with one difference. I had joined my father in his delicatessen and found someone who had tweaked my curiosity. Her name was Mae. But also looming on the horizon was the problem with a small country most of us had never heard of before; North Korea.

The war soon broke out and before I could catch my breath, I was being recalled. This time to report for duty aboard the USS Antietam, a ship of the line being outfitted in the Philadelphia Naval Yard. It would be the first aircraft carrier with a canted deck. That is a deck that was capable of putting aircraft into the air while at the same time allowing aircraft to land on the deck. But for me it meant that as long as we were being outfitted with the new deck, I would be able to have liberty at least three out of four weekends each month. That meant I could go home and see Mae. The only time we were not together was when she wasn't free because of classes or hospital work. They worked the girls unmercifully at St. Catherine's, both day and night.

Once the ship was declared ready for sea duty we had to take the ship on a shakedown cruise. Work out all the bugs that unfortunately crop up no matter how hard you try to eliminate them. Our shakedown cruise was to be conducted in the Caribbean Sea.

We were deployed for three months during which time we got the ship in tip-top shape. Not that we were so busy that I couldn't write to Mae, but the truth of the matter is, I was too lazy and kept putting it off.

I'll do it tomorrow, or I'll do it later. Always an excuse not to write. But before I knew it, the three months were up and we were heading home. Now it was too late to write. "Oh well!" I thought. "She probably doesn't even remember when the last time was we dated. Oh! Yea! Was I in for a surprise! Couple this with my getting an appointment to the Naval Academy, you can see that I was starting to reach the point of having to make some mammoth decisions.

CHAPTER 10

ACADEMIC LIFE 1952-1956

PLEBE YEAR

With the Korean War in full swing, the chances of my getting out of the Navy were slim. If I turned down the appointment to the Academy I would surely be sent back to sea duty as an enlisted man. This helped me make my decision. It wasn't that I was completely unhappy about going to the Academy; in fact, I was short of looking forward to being the first one in my family to become an officer in the United States Navy. Therefore my decision to accept the appointment to the Academy was made for me.

I was delighted to leave the ship in Miami after having spent the last month on mess cook duty. I headed for my new assignment at the Toll Preparatory School in Bainbridge, Maryland. School had started in June and the students were already through some of the books I was supposed to study. The officer in charge gave me a full complement of books and notes and told me to do the best I could, and they would do what they could to bring me up to speed.

My roommate was a boy by the name of John Cavanaugh, of the Cavanaugh's of Philadelphia. His father was CEO of the

Pennsylvania Rail Road, and member of the Board. John was bright and told me he had two things he was going to accomplish. First, he was going to be the first string kicker for the Navy football team, and second, he was going to become The Chief of Naval Operations, the highest position in the Navy. Not bad for a kid just out of high school. We'll follow John's progress as he became my roommate for the first year at the Academy.

Since I arrived at school rather late, there wasn't much I could do other than hole up in my room and study day and night. This must have impressed the instructors because before long they were calling on me and trying to bring me up to date in the areas I needed the most help. As it turned out, John Cavanaugh was not only extremely bright, but his favorite field was one in which I lacked the most skill, English and English Composition. John told me he would coach me and if I listened to him I would pass the English part of the exam with flying colors. He was right. When the results of the exams were published, John stood number one and I stood number two. I didn't mind being number two, and am grateful to John for giving me the background I needed to get there.

While I was at the Tome (US Navy Prep School), I was very busy trying to cram all the work I had missed into my head. I knew it was a great opportunity I had before me and I didn't want to screw it up. So I would get up at five thirty every morning, get dressed and jog over to the base house of worship and attend the six o'clock mass. I was calling on everyone I knew who could help, and I knew I was going to need God's help or I was sunk. Every morning, I went to mass and communion and asked God for the wisdom to pass these exams.

I didn't know it at the time but I was being observed by one of my classmates. His name was Hollis Robertson. Hollis was one of the nicest men in the class and acted every bit like a gentlemen. Not the quality sailors are expected to have. But Hollis had it. He approached me toward the end of our training and asked me why I went to church every morning. I explained that I needed all the help I could get and this was a solution that required divine help.

It must have triggered something in Hollis's head or heart but the next time I saw Robbie he asked me if I would be his Godfather at his baptism. Naturally I was honored and before we went into the Academy, Robbie was baptized a Catholic. Hollis went through the four years, graduated, married his high school sweetheart, was commissioned in the Navy and achieved the rank of Captain before his retirement. This was and still is a great achievement.

Once the decision was made that I was going to remain at the Academy it became a contest between me and the upperclassmen as to whether or not I could take their crap. During Plebe year most of the harassment was done at the dinner table. Usually they would ask about five or six questions per upperclassman. You either knew the answer or said, "I'll find out, Sir." You were required to have the answer at the next meal. If you didn't have the answer you would be told to 'Come around' which meant you would report to the upperclassman's room immediately after dinner that evening or the upperclassman could tell you to 'shove out' which meant you pushed your chair out from under you and tried to eat in that not very comfortable position. We learned it was easier to get the answers to their questions rather than go hungry every meal.

Both John and I passed all the exams and were qualified for entrance into the Academy. All that remained was to get an appointment to enter with the Class of '56. This was accomplished and both John and I went into the Academy for our first summer before the upperclassmen arrived back from their cruise. When they did arrive back from their cruise and summer leave, we knew we were in for at least one year of harassment before we became upperclassmen.

The way it worked at the Academy was there were basically two classes of midshipmen. The Upperclassmen, consisting of First classmen, men who have been there three years and were now in their fourth year after which they would be commissioned in one of the services; Second classmen, midshipmen in their third year at the Academy; Third classmen, midshipmen who had just completed their first or Plebe year at the Academy and who were now considered Upperclassmen and no longer Plebes. Finally, that left only us, the new class of midshipmen who would be starting our first year as midshipmen and who were ready to be broken down so as to lose our ego's before the upperclassmen had three years to build them up into officers who not only knew how to give orders, but more importantly, know how to take orders and carry them out to the best of their abilities. The system worked fine if you knew how to work within the boundaries described by the upper classes. I decided I would go with the flow and try to get along with everyone. Only one time did that fail me.

We were at a football game, Navy vs. Maryland. I had sent Mae tickets so I knew she was somewhere in the seats directly behind the corpse of midshipmen. As the game started, I tried several times to turn around and see if I could find her. This must have annoyed the Third class middie who was right behind me and so in a not-too-nice a manner he shouted in my ear that I was to turn around and pay attention to the game. All of a sudden a big play happened and all the midshipmen jumped to their feet and were shouting. It was a good time for me to turn around and look for Mae, which I did. As it turned out, the Third class middie behind me was short and I of course was tall. So he missed the play. He was so mad that he punched me in the shoulder and yelled something at me. Well. Although there is plenty of harassment at the Academy, one thing you are not supposed to do is hit anyone. I looked at this middie right in the eye and told him if he did anything like that again, I would put him under the stands and pound him to dust. A First classmen observed the entire episode and intervened. He told me to turn around and then he proceeded to chew the ass out of the Third class middie. I continued to look whenever I liked after that and smiled often at my adversary. When I got back to the Academy, I was told to report to my Company Commander who asked for a complete explanation of what went on. I told him, he listened, told me to return to my room and I never heard any more about the incident.

Now John was not as accommodating as I was. As a matter of fact, John was stuck on the fact that he was a child of privilege. He felt he didn't have to take any gruff from anyone. I told him from time to time to stick his ego in his back pocket and not mouth off to upper classmen or he would be headed for trouble. After all, he only had to swallow their crap for one year. John pooh-poohed me and went his own way. One night he was coming back from a liberty he was not entitled too and was caught by the officer on duty. That was bad enough, but when the officer, a Marine Major, started to question John, he had the balls to ask the Major if he knew who he was. The Major told him he didn't give a rat's ass who he was and if he said anything else, he would be on his way out of the Academy. Naturally John pursued the discussion and found himself in the brig.

In those days, the fifties, the brig was an old Spanish galleon that had been captured during the war with Spain many, many years ago. It served as a brig and it was here that his mother visited John. I was on duty the day his mother arrived in a big limo. She emerged from the car in her furs - it being February - and walked up the steps to the rotunda where the officer of the day was on guard. When I saw it was Mrs. Cavanaugh, I informed the OD (Officer of the Day) that John was my roommate and maybe I could help Mrs. Cavanaugh. I explained to her that John was not in his room and gave her a modified version of John's escapades. She was not at all troubled and asked what she could do to take John home. Arrangements were made through the Admiral's Office and when I came back into my room there was John packing his belongings. When I asked him how he was going to become Chief of Naval Operations from home, he thought for a moment and replied, "I think instead I'll become the Secretary of the Navy. That's an appointed position."

That was the last I saw of John. I liked him and wish he had stuck it out. I wonder where he is today.

MARRIAGE

Life goes on, and before you know it, you are making decisions that will affect the rest of your days. The four years at the Academy seemed like an eternity while I was going through them. But once they are done and the final chapter is written then you look back with melancholy and realize how fortunate you were to have completed four years at one of the finest institutions in the world. You hope you have made friends who will be your support throughout your remaining years. And finally, you are free to marry.

Mae and I decided we would marry during the Christmas of my senior year. We were married in St. Philip and James Church in the Bronx, just a few blocks from Mae's home. Father Raphaelite was the presiding priest and he agreed to suspend the announcing of the bans before the wedding. He was a gem of a priest, a good friend of the Corry's, and a special person in our lives.

We were married at the ten o'clock mass and after pictures were taken, we adjoined to Mayer's for the open bar and festivities. It's strange how things play out. We weren't sure Ron would make it to the wedding on time so Walter was chosen to be my best man. While we were in the back of the church, you would have thought Walter was the one getting married. Water literally ran off his hands and he shook whenever he was asked if he had the ring or if he knew his part. As it happened, Walter did just fine, despite the fact that he and Jackie were the only two left at the bar when the bachelor party was called to a close the night before.

The mass was fine and the vows must have been great because I don't remember anyone complaining about them. There was a moment when the tension hung in the air like a spider web encircling everyone in the church.

"Is there anyone here who knows of any reason why these two people should not be joined in Holy Matrimony?" You could hear a pin drop. But no one spoke and the mass and marriage ceremony came to a peaceful close.

We had snow flurries right after the pictures were taken, but that didn't dampen our spirits one bit.

Mae designed her dress and had it made especially for her. Beautiful; isn't it? Susan, our first daughter, was able to wear it on her wedding day, and Maureen, our second daughter got to salvage the crown.

Our wedding cake was three tiers high and each tier was held up by a series of swans. There must have been at least a dozen or more to hold the cake.

I never thought to thank my father for all the spade work he did for me prior to the wedding. Although he couldn't try on my tux, he did everything else. He arranged for a room at the Grand Concourse Hotel so Mae and I wouldn't have far to go after the wedding reception, and kept it a secret so no one could pull any dirty tricks on us on our first night as husband and wife.

He arranged for his car to be in tip top condition so we wouldn't have any trouble getting to the Pocono Mountains the following day. I had to borrow his car for transportation, and never thought about how he was going to get around. Thanks Dad. You were great.

After the wedding, before heading to the hotel, we stopped at Mae's house and opened the gifts. I remember Mae saying as she looked at a check in her hand, "Will you look at this… someone made a check out to your parents, Mr. & Mrs. Hackeling."

It even took me a few minutes to get used to the new name. The following day Mae and I started for the Poconos. We didn't have many days left and we didn't want to waste any. They were precious days. We wormed our way around the mountains until we found Paradise Valley Lodge. The lodge was run by a delightful couple by the names of Paul and Mae Asuer.

At first we thought we were the only couple there but it turned out there was another couple. Except for them, we had the place to ourselves. It snowed at night, but it was cozy … just what you want on a honeymoon. With our little fireplace and plenty of blankets we were perfectly comfortable. Another thing the Asuers did to make their guests feel at home was to put a copy of their Little Blue Book in each room. It was basically SEX 101, with diagrams and photos to make sure everything went in the right place. It was a good book and I'm sorry we lost it. It was a primer for all newlyweds.

The first day at the lodge we slept in, but on the second day we arrived in the dining room just as breakfast was being served. It was memorable because we were trying to act the part of an old married couple but things quickly fell apart. Mae gave us away. As she was pouring the coffee from the urn to her cup and saucer, she made one little mistake. It wasn't long before she realized her mistake. Mae Asuer saw what was happening and lightened the event by commenting, "It works better if you put a cup in the saucer first, Mae."

Everyone laughed and Mae turned bright red. I tried to relive the pain Mae was experiencing by saying, "Oh! It's OK. We've just been busy lately."

"I guess so," Mae Asuer replied. "It's your honeymoon."

The Asuer's had a beautiful spot. They had the main house attached to the lodge which housed the kitchen, the dining room, and the reception area where they has wine and cheese every afternoon around four o'clock. Outside there were several cabins in the woods, furnished with a fireplace and all the wood you could carry. Very cozy. We were housed in the cottage entitled 'The Oaks." It was just off the pond which was frozen solid and great for ice skating. I was surprised that I was able to stay up on the skates, but Mae couldn't. With the help of a chair, however, she was able to get around. It didn't make for the best skating, but it did help to convince Mae there was a better place inside 'The Oaks."

When our time was up, we left The Oaks and promised to return as soon as possible. We did return, but it was twenty years later. However, when we went inside the barn, which had been converted to a general store, we walked up to Mae and she greeted us by saying, "Hi! Mae and Charlie. How the hell have you been?'

"How did you remember our names?" I inquired.

"Who could forget Mae pouring her coffee into an imaginary cup!" was her reply.

Well we had a wonderful time talking to Mae, but unfortunately, Paul was suffering from Alzheimer's disease and didn't remember much. It was a sad ending to a wonderful couple.

When Mae and I first honeymooned in the Poconos, so many years ago, I remember saying that I thought the life the Asuers were leading would be a wonderful way to spend our life. At least the kids would be free from the influence of drugs and other undesirable practices. But the truth of the matter is there is probably no place that is completely safe. You do the best you can and leave the rest to God.

AIR FORCE

Graduation from the Academy was in June of 1956. I struggled with the decision of whether I should go in the Navy or the Air Force. I wanted to be commissioned in the Air Force and not the Navy for one simple reason, Sea Duty. Those who were commissioned in the Navy were assured of being assigned sea duty, which meant being away from their families and at sea for at least six months. Not a good way to start a marriage. I realized early in my life that I would marry and raise a family. I couldn't see myself being away from my family any length of time, playing war games while my wife struggled with the job of raising our family. Now that I had met this girl, Mae Corry, I knew I could never be happy being away from her any length of time. For me, the decision became simple.

We were assigned which branch of service we would serve in by luck of the draw. Every graduates name was entered in a barrel and drawn blindly one at a time. If you drew a low number, you got to pick your branch of service before the rest of the classmates. The Air Force was entitled to 25 percent of the graduates since they paid 25 percent of the cost of educating the graduates. If you drew a high number, you got to pick last and the chances were good that the quota for the Air Force or Marine Corp was already filled. The problem was, the drawing didn't take place until after Christmas leave. That meant the last chance you had to affect the outcome of your life was over Christmas leave. I drew a number 26 in the lottery which meant the Air Force was a sure thing.

TUCSON, ARIZONA

After graduation Mae and I drove to Tucson in our newly acquired red and white Plymouth. Talk about being stupid. Here is how we decided to get to Tucson. We would head south until we were parallel to Atlanta, Georgia on the Gousha Road Map. There we would turn west, and once we hit Atlanta we would look for Bob Hammond and his wife, Shelby. Remember, we were young, indestructible, knew everything and had the world by the ba__s. That worked out fine. We found Bob, nestled in his mobile home, with room enough for at least two people. He invited us to stay because he wanted to take me to his Air Base and give me the royal tour.

I should have taken the clues he dropped occasionally and realized that married life was not the life for Bob. For example, when we got to the base and were inspecting his plane he explained to me that there was a side pocket on each of the planes that served the purpose of holding your wedding ring when you traveled any place away from home. The second big clue came that night when Bob insisted we play bridge. I explained to him that I had a smattering of knowledge about the game and Mae knew nothing about it.

"Don't worry", Bob explained, "you'll pick it up as we go along."

Well, what Bob neglected to tell us was that he was a very serious bridge player, and didn't tolerate mistakes, from his wife or others. Now all during the night as we played the game Bob was constantly correcting or scolding Shelby, his partner. It was almost at the point of murder when finally we suggested changing partners. Remember now, Mae and I still thought of the game as a game. Nothing more. But not Bob. Now Bob had a chance to play with Mae as his partner. The bidding for the hand we were about to play was definitely in Bob's and his new partner, Mae's court. Bob kept bidding clubs, Mae kept bidding spades. When they finally got to the sixth level, Bob said, "All right, I'll play it in six spades. Put down your spades."

Mae smiled and said to Bob as she laid down her hand, "You're going to like what I've got."

With that, she laid down the six clubs, smiled and said to him she was void in the other black suite. I thought Bob would have a hemorrhage. He jumped out of his chair, threw his cards up in the air and couldn't speak for what seemed like eternity. I thought he was having a stroke. When he finally calmed down, we all agreed it was time to go to bed.

Mae and I quietly giggled during the night every time we thought of Mae's hand full of clubs and Bob's hand full of the remaining clubs.

"I warned him we were novices at this game," I said to Mae and followed it with hysterical laughing.

Oh! By the way, we left the next morning and continued our trip west.

NEW YORK TO TUCSON

As my thirty days of leave were coming to a close Mae and I continued our trip from New York to Tucson, Arizona. Here we stayed …me going through flight training and Mae getting ready to deliver our first child, Stephen. That was a traumatic period in our lives because once Stephen was delivered we were never sure whether he was going to live or die.

STEPHEN'S BIRTH

Since we arrived a few days early I suggested we go up to see the Grand Canyon. I didn't think it was very far from where we would live. But it was. And it was a long hot trip. When we finally arrived at the Canyon, I couldn't wait to get out of the car and walk to the edge of the viewing area. Remember now, Mae was seven months pregnant, hot, cramped and not in a very good mood. I got as far over the railing as I could safely go and was astounded by the beauty of the sun going down on the Canyon.

"Will you look at that?" I shouted to Mae who was still sitting in the car.

Mae took one side view look out her window and replied, "Yep! It's a big ditch!"

…End of conversation.

I didn't know there was a disease called morning sickness and that sometimes, it lasted all day. Remember, there were no girls in my family. Mae had a good dose of the sickness and was in no mood to walk around in the desert. That was the end of our Grand Canyon Tour.

Stephen was born a few weeks after we got back from our trip. He was two months premature and the doctors at the hospital didn't give him much of a chance of living. He was afflicted with what is known as a Hyaline Membrane. In short, his lungs had not fully developed and his chances of survival were limited. The way it played out was Mae and I had gone to the base hospital to check in and start preparing for our blessed event. The night before we were watching the Jackie

Gleason show on TV. I can't remember the show but I do remember it was hilarious. Mae and I were laughing so hard we were doubled over. All of a sudden Mae excused herself and went into the bathroom. She came out a few minutes later, sat down next to me and said her water had broken. Remember, this was a new experience for both of us, and we had no one to lean upon.

"So what does that mean?" I asked her.

Since she was a nurse I assumed she knew everything, medically at least. You know what they say about assuming! Mae really wasn't sure what it meant, but felt it was the beginning of our baby's birth. The thing that confused her was there were no contractions. We quickly started to count fingers and realized that couldn't be it since she was just entering her seventh month. Since the following day we were scheduled to see the base doctor we decided to wait it out until the following day. Believe me, we were first in line to see the doctor the following morning. After the doctor examined Mae he said it was too soon for her to deliver but if it made her feel better she could spend the rest of the day in the hospital. We spent the next few hours getting Mae comfortable and I stayed by her side and held her hand. She slept for a couple of hours. When she awoke she was perspiring and just felt horrible.

"I think I'm going to have this baby," she kept repeating.

In order to comfort her we went back to the doctor's office and I told him of her concern. His response was, "Oh! She's just a first time mother and they're not used to pregnancy. She'll be fine. Just take her home and let her rest."

By the time I got back to where Mae was confined, I knew something was wrong. She looked terrible. Sweating profusely she was turning from side to side not being able to find a comfortable position and sometimes talking incoherently.

"Please," she asked me as she clung to my arm, "Make them come in here, I'm going to have this baby."

After reassuring her that the doctor said it was first time jitters, I said I would get him to examine her before he left for the day. Back again I went to see the doctor. I pleaded with him please come and check her out if for no other reason than to appease me. OK! With the doctor in tow I marched back to the dorm where Mae was housed. The doctor gave Mae his best,

"Now, now, dear. You are not going to have this baby today."

With that he pulled the curtain hanging around the bed so as to leave me outside while he examined her inside. Within seconds the curtain parted exposing the doctor's head and he yelled to no one in particular, "Nurse! Nurse! Get in here in a hurry. I'm going to have to deliver this baby."

All hell broke loose. Nurses, corpsmen and doctors seemed to appear out of nowhere. I was shuffled out of the ward and into a waiting room. Stay here, I was told. We'll call you when we need you. As if I was going to be of any help to anyone. At this point, after a night of no sleep and a day of running back and forth from Mae to the doctor and vice-versa, I was ready for a week of rest and relaxation. But that was not to be. I waited four hours with no word as to how Mae or the baby was doing. All they could tell me was they were in the operating room, and they would tell me something as soon as they were able. At about nine o'clock that night an incubator came running through the waiting room with two nurses attached. I caught a brief glimpse of what was in the incubator. It looked like a small monkey lying on its side and covered with blood.

What's that?" I asked one of the nurses.

When she responded it was the Hackeling baby I almost keeled over. But I knew Mae was going to need me to hold up since we had no family or even close friends to lean on. I discovered the baby was being taken to the incubation portion of the hospital. I followed until we were let into a small section of the hospital next to Dr. O'Donnell's office. He was the head pediatrician. Right now he was bent over the small incubator that housed my baby and examining him closely. When I approached him and told him who I was he took me by the arm and led me into his office. Here he explained to me the problems we were going to have with the baby. The baby, being almost three months premature, had not had time to expand and fill both lungs. As a matter of fact the baby was breathing on a half of one lung. How long it would take for the remaining lung and a half to open up was anybody's guess. Most of the time the children die. Usually it took ten to twelve days before knowing if the baby was going to live. You can imagine the shock I got. I didn't know what to do or say. I asked the doctor if I could see my wife. He assured me I could and the next thing I knew I was next to Mae assuring her the baby was fine. I didn't want to lie to her but I didn't think she was strong enough to receive such bad news. At least not right away. About two in the morning Mae fell asleep and I decided to go home and get a little shut-eye myself. Before leaving I saw the doctor and told him what I had told Mae. I asked him if they could hold off any bad news until I returned which I said would be at five that morning. He said no problem…but that wasn't the last of it.

The following morning, good to my word, I arrived at the hospital. I quickly found Mae's room and entered. Nobody had to tell me-I could see it in Mae's expression-someone had told her the bad news. I went to her and she collapsed in my arms in tears. I found out later that shortly after I left the hospital last night the doctor came into Mae's room, turned on the lights and announced, "I'm not the only one who's going to worry about this child. You might as well join me. Your baby stands about one in one hundred chances of making it."

With that he turned on his heels and left Mae bewildered and in a state of shock. When I arrived and asked to see him, he put up an x-ray of the infant's lungs. They were mostly closed. He went on for several minutes using his big medical terms and leaving me in the dust. Wait a minute, I asked him, what does all of this mean as far as the baby is concerned. He halted his speech, looked down at his shoes and said rather mournfully,

"It isn't good. He stands about one chance in a hundred of making it. Other than keeping him under observation there isn't much we can do for him. If he's strong enough, he may pull though."

What Mae and I didn't know was the doctor himself was suffering from a debilitating disease. This was reflected in his bedside manner. Stephen was kept in an oxygen tent for about three weeks, and after Mae was released from the hospital, she and I went over to the hospital for the daily report every day. Every day they told us the same thing. "If he makes it through the night he should be better by morning." But each morning brought the same results. "He's not out of the woods yet, but he's looking better."

To me he looked like a dried up frog. But to Mae he was the most beautiful baby you had ever seen. We prayed a lot for the next couple of months. We learned a lot about the power of prayer.

"Please dear God, let him live."

It was very uncertain, but by the time Christmas rolled around, Stephen had rallied, beat all the odds and was developing into a husky baby boy who never shut his mouth.

The hospital agreed to release him to us when he was about four and a half pounds. Mae assured them that he would get the best care since she was a nurse. And the best he got. Every time he opened his mouth Mae put a bottle in it and held him in her arms. He flourished and started to talk up a blue streak. Very different from today, you can hardly squeeze a word out of him.

This all was taking place while we were in Tucson, Arizona, and I was in flight school training. While in flight training we trained on the Air Force T 28's and T 34's. The T 28's were big single engines trainees that sounded like a railroad train coming through your living room. The T34's were single engine jet trainers and were fun to fly. And both were safe. But no matter how safe they were, they still had to be handled carefully. It was always on my mind that no matter how good I became in handling these planes, I could make a mistake and that could cost me my life. Most of the trainees weren't married and they loved the thrill of projecting themselves high into the air and practicing barrel rolls, spins, drop offs, and other maneuvers that were really necessary in order to be considered a good pilot. Me? I worried every time I got into the cockpit; will this be my last flight? I soon realized, flying was a young man's game, and although I was only twenty six years old, I was overly concerned about Mae. I was already too old for this game.

Halfway through our training in the T34's Mr. O'Connor, who was my flight instructor, climbed out of the plane after we landed and said, very seriously, "Charlie, didn't you feel the plane shutter during the last force landing?"

"No! I replied, "I thought I had made a great approach to that empty field."

Mr. O'Connor said, "Charlie, you don't have a feel for the plane. Oh! You'll graduate from flight training, but I predict that someday you'll kill yourself."

In training we also learned that, unfortunately, in the class before us they had a bad accident and lost one of the trainees. It wasn't a good idea to showcase the accident for the wives of the incoming cadets as it meant any one of them could be next. Naturally, each of us undergoing flight training took out as much life insurance as the insurance companies would issue, but that wasn't much. All I could think about was whether the insurance company would pay off if I bought the farm. I tried to imagine how Mae would get along with Stephen and no husband. Even if the insurance company did pay off, it wouldn't be enough. Believe me, it isn't a good way to learn to fly when these are the thoughts that fill your head day and night. Flying airplanes is dangerously fun, but fun wasn't exactly what we were looking for. At any rate, we were trained and qualified in the T28's and T34's but since Mae and I couldn't come to an agreement on the flying issue, I wound up going to Guided Missile Training in Denver, Colorado.

COLORADO

That was enough for me. Flying was not my cup of tea. I was destined to get out of flying. Next stop was Guided Missile training at Lowry Air Force Base in Denver, Colorado. We spent nine months in Missile Training in Denver.

The trip across the Rocky Mountains was uneventful, except for those occasions when Stephen decided it was time for a big poop. I can tell you that as an environmentalist, it broke my heart to heave those stinky diapers, loaded with poop, over the side of the car and down the mountain. I heaved them as far as I could and hoped they would quickly disintegrate.

Once we reached our new location in Denver we started to enjoy the snow and dry air. The air was so dry, that as long as the wind was not blowing, you could be outside in just sweaters. We took advantage of the nice weather and went skiing and sleigh riding. Mae was in no condition to ski since Michael was protruding a foot and a half in front of her spine. We soon got settled in our quarters and things started to pick up.

MEET DIPPY

We were assigned government quarters; the bottom apartment in a four-plex. Lucky us, we were underneath a Captain and his new bride, a seventeen year old moron. They had a child the same age as Stephen so we thought baby- sitting would be no problem. Not so. We soon learned that rules had to be declared and followed.

One morning, about ten o'clock, Dippy, as I called her, leaning out of her upstairs window with her massive boobs hanging out, asked if we could baby sit for her and her husband while they went to the commissary for food. We obliged. About one o'clock that afternoon, when they still had not come back from the commissary, we became concerned. We went up to their apartment to get a bottle for their little boy. We no longer had to wonder why we had a roach problem we couldn't control. Every glass and dish, spoons, knives and forks were piled up in the sink, not yet washed. I mean, everything they had to eat off of was dirty and not cleaned. I wouldn't care but they had a brand new dishwasher installed by the base commander. We went to the pantry to find it stacked full of bags of garbage. Again, no excuse for not putting their garbage out since they picked up garbage twice a week.

We returned to our apartment in the state of shock. We gave the poor baby one of Stephen's bottles but that didn't seem to satisfy him. He hollered the entire afternoon. At supper time, when they still had not returned home, we were sure something awful had happened to them. We washed both children and put them down for the night. We had to put them together since the now famous couple still had not returned. When we went up to their apartment again to get a diaper for their little boy we found not a single clean diaper in the entire apartment. They had a year's worth of dirty diapers in every corner of their baby's room. It smelled atrocious. We wonder how they lived like this. We were starting to panic since they still had not returned home or called. There was no excuse unless they both lay dead on gurneys in some hospital.

A little after midnight the Captain and Dippy arrived home, laughing and acting as if nothing had happened. We were furious. There was no apology, nothing. They said that instead of getting groceries that morning they decided to go to the track and make a day of it. Remember now, he was a captain and I was just a lieutenant. Their baby was fussing and when we told Dippy he cried all day and this was unlike him since we never heard a word out of him prior, Dippy informed us that she puts a spoon full of a narcotic in every bottle and he goes right to sleep. Mae and I nearly fell over. When Mae told her the implications of what they were doing they became very defensive. I was so mad it made no difference. I read the riot act to them and told them we would no longer baby sit for them. He decided to punish me by refusing to take his turn cutting the grass around our apartment. What a nit.

Anyway, I kept myself busy by going with Captain Murphy to the dump. It seems every week the base discarded their worn out furniture and goods by dumping them. Many of the items were still in good shape, or easily fixed up, and we made ourselves comfortable taking what we needed. It was fun putting things back together and building new items. For the first time in our military career, we were housed properly with furniture, thanks to the dump.

When school ended everyone was reassigned but me. Per Air Force policy, I wouldn't be reassigned me until Michael was born. But they had to find something for me to do.

The Captain in charge of reassignments asked me, "Have you ever been exposed to the Court Marshal Procedures?"

"Yes," I answered.

"Good, you'll do fine. We need you to fill in as defense council for a guy we want to put out of the service."

SERGEANT GERARD

Since I already had experience serving on the Court side of a Court Marshal they thought it might be appropriate for me to view things from the other side. I would serve as the attorney for the defendant. The first thing I advised him to do when we met was to hire a real attorney, one versed in military law. He declined. Here was the background of Private Gerard.

Sergeant Gerard was stationed in Germany with his wife, his son and his daughter. His son contracted tonsillitis. He went into the base hospital for the operation and although the operation was successful, the boy died. Grief stricken, the family was shipped home to Denver, Colorado where they were able to bury their son.

While they were in Denver, Sgt. Gerard's father, sick with cancer, died. When he did he left an estate full of unpaid bills and no money. Sgt. Gerard was able to borrow enough money to give his father a proper burial. But by now his wife's health was deteriorating and she was acting in a strange manner. For example she was buying furniture they didn't need, spending money they didn't have and acting strange in other ways, all of which put them in financial distress. He, of course, started drinking. This didn't help.

While all of this was going on the sergeant began to drink heavily. He became involved in several bar fights and was court marshaled, reduced one rank to Corporal, and fined $500.

Struggling to make the required payments, and dealing with his wife's continuing decline in health, he was barely able to hold his life together. He drank more.

His daughter became ill and the doctors at the base hospital decided it was best to operate to find the cause of her illness. Corporal Gerard cautioned the doctors that his daughter was a bleeder and to pay close attention to her after the operation. They didn't and she died of a loss of blood.

Now his wife went completely crazy. Corporal Gerard found solace in the bottle and this caused him to engage in more fights and more court marshals. He was broken again and this time to the rank of private. Now recognize every time Gerard was demoted, he lost more of his pay. His inability to pay his debts was overwhelming. He started to drop out of life.

Now after another drunken fight he was before the court, the charge being he should be discharged dishonorably. If this happened he would lose all his benefits including his right to keep his wife in the base hospital. In my view, this couldn't happen. Why? Because we, the Armed Services had helped to cause this terrible problem, and merely throwing him and his family out in the street was unfair and inhumane.

I dragged out the code of military justice from the library and started to go through it page by page. Unfortunately there was nothing that pertained to my situation or would help my client except one paragraph I found that stated, "If a service man had at least ten years of honorable service, and it then became necessary to discharge him dishonorably, he should be considered for a discharge for the benefit of the service, not a dishonorable discharge." Private Gerard had fourteen years of honorable service. This would at least allow him to keep his benefits and keep his wife confined where they could help her.

I met with Gerard one afternoon and it was evident that he had already been drinking. I advised him of the date of the court marshal and the time, 11:00 am. I asked him to please show up sober. He said he would and I went back to the code of military justice to see if I could find more help. Nothing!

On the morning of our hearing, I arrived at 10:00 am and waited with my heart in my throat. Would he show? At 11:00 our case was called and I had to ask for an extension since he had not shown up. Fortunately, we were granted an extension until 1:30 pm that same day. The court went out to lunch. I waited on pins and needles, trying to reach Gerard by phone, to no avail. At 12:30 Gerard appeared, drunk, and hardly in condition to take the stand. I cleaned him up and said that if we stood any chance of getting any mercy he would have to sit at our bench, be quiet and make no noise. Try to act sober.

At 1:30 pm the court reconvened. I described the conditions that had affected my client and his state of mind. I described his broken heart every time another calamity occurred. I asked if the court couldn't, in its mercy give

Private Gerard another chance and rehabilitate him rather than discharge him. If, however, the court felt it had to discharge Gerard I asked they consider the article concerning his 14 years of service prior to these catastrophes.

I returned home that day feeling deflated and depressed. However, just as I arrived at home the Colonial in charge of the Court called me to say he felt I had done a wonderful job defending Gerard, and although they couldn't keep him in the service they would discharge him under the clause I brought to their attention. Half a battle won.

I met with Gerard and informed him of the Court's decision. In addition I suggested he get a real attorney and try to fight the decision. He shook his head 'no', said thank you and quietly walked out the door. I felt bad for him, but at least his family, what was left of it, would get the benefits they desperately needed.

During all of this and before our next move to Florida, the best thing that happened to us was Michael. Our biggest concern with Michael was if he would ever grow any hair. At this point in our lives we had two boys. Life was grand!

CHAPTER 11

LIFE IN FLORIDA 1956-1960

From Denver we were finally assigned to Eglin Air Force Base in Florida. I was assigned to the Research and Development Division. Florida was a great place for Mae and the children to enjoy the beach and sunshine.

BIG SNAKE

After checking in at Eglin and getting to meet my new boss, Colonel Vanderhoven, we were relaxing in his office when a base emergency arose. The sirens went off and my new boss asked me, "Want to see some action?"

"Sure, why not!" was my answer.

Together we jumped into his jeep and headed out towards the family quarters, following the fire trucks.

"We haven't had this much excitement in quite a while," the Colonel said.

As we flew over the empty fields trying to outpace the engines I noticed we were headed toward the buildings where we were assigned our quarters. To my dismay, there, in the middle of our backyard was the Fire Chief, the Base Commander, the head of the medical department and an assortment of Colonels, Light Colonials, Majors, Captains, and no, I repeat, no Lieutenants. None but me…I was the only Lieutenant on the base.

I jumped out of the jeep as soon as Colonel Vanderhoven brought it to a stop and ran to where Mae was conversing with a member of the medical staff. She had Stephen and Michael both by the hand explaining something to the Lieutenant Colonial who had a long stick in his hands.

"What's the problem?" I asked Mae.

"Well, remember this morning you warned me about the snakes here in Florida and how I had to be very careful to check the yard before I let the children play outside?"

"Yes!" I replied.

"Well, I was going to put the children in the area you had enclosed so the boys could get some fresh air and let off some of their excess energy and at the same time put away our suitcases which were on the back porch. I opened the door leading to the underside of the house and I started to put the cases in when I saw a gigantic snake under the house. I grabbed the kids and ran back into the house and called the Base Commander."

"Well, that was fine, but something like this isn't the job of the Base Commander. Just look at what you attracted," I said.

At that moment, one of the airmen came up to us with a ten foot rod and a clamp for seizing and holding the snake.

"Is this long enough?" he asked me.

I had no idea but thought I ought to go with him to the opening under the house. By now, we had the entire fire department with all their equipment, the Air Police with their cars and guns, the Base Commander and his entourage, as well as my entire department. Oh! We had also attracted all the neighbors and their friends. It looked like a hundred people. And did I mention there was only one lieutenant in the entire company? Me.

I quietly slid up to Mae and said, "Mae, check around and see if you can find even one other lieutenant. I suspect I'm the only one on the base. Lucky me, I can get to empty cigarette butt ashtrays and empty beer bottles."

At any rate the sergeant and I headed over to the opening to the crawl space. Very gingerly we peered into the darkened space. Now everyone was crowded around the sergeant. Gingerly he passed the pole into the open space. Remember, here in Florida we had rattlesnakes, cottonmouths, king snakes, coral snakes, etc. You name it, we had it. The week before we arrived on base a six foot rattler had been found beneath one of the other houses. Believe me, we were careful. Every time the sergeant jerked the pole every one behind us jumped back.

"I think I see him said the sergeant. He's a big one. Looks like a cotton mouth."

"Be careful," was all I could say to him.

And then he jumped. He made several attempts to grab the snake, but each time the snake managed to wiggle free of the clamp. Finally the sergeant got a good hold and started backing out bringing the pole out from under the house. As he backed up, everyone else backed up too. At last the snake came clear of the door and out into the daylight. He was big and heavy. He was almost five feet long and four inches in diameter. There was only one problem. He wasn't a snake. It was a broken off root from one of the surrounding trees.

"Is this the snake?" the sergeant wanted to know.

"Well," Mae stammered, "he sure looked a lot meaner under the house."

By now everyone was laughing and passing jokes back and forth.

"Oh!" I said to Mae, "This is a great way to start off my career here at Eglin. I had better go over to the Base Commander and apologize.

We spent three years in Florida at Eglin Air Force.

A GIRL

The next few months were spent quietly trying to integrate into base society. We had some really fine friends who lived in the house next to us, and some unique friends behind and around us. The O'Sheas, a family with seven children, lived next to us. Tom O'Shea was a survivor of the Bataan Death March in the Philippines. Tom was captured by the Japanese and sent to a concentration camp in Japan. On the way from Bataan to Japan, he was sunk three times by US Submarines. While in a Japanese concentration camp, Tom was exposed to everything from disease to starvation. Brothers fought over a fish head. Tom never really recovered from this experience.

When Tom was returned to the States after the war, he was assigned to the Air Police and saw most of the underbelly of society. As a result he was not a very happy camper. His wife, Rose, on the other hand, was the kindest person you could ever expect to meet. She understood Tom and supported him in every way possible but they were a most unusual couple.

As we were adjusting to the weather, we were blessed with the arrival of a baby girl, Susan. Susan arrived and introduced me to the world of girls. Remember, I was disadvantaged as a child. I had two brothers, but no sisters. Girls frightened the daylights out of me. But Susan taught me there was nothing to be frightened about. With proper feeding, sleeping, and attention they were a pleasure to live with.

At this point we had Stephen, Michael, and Susan. We thought our family was just right. On the face of it, everything seemed nice and balanced. It wasn't really! On one specific morning, son #2…Michael, proved this to us.

MICHAEL'S EARLY MORNING BREAKFAST

One morning we awoke to a new nightmare. It seems that Michael had awakened earlier and feeling hungry, he decided to fix his own breakfast. Believe me, it wasn't often we got to sleep in, and why we picked this morning to stay in bed I will never know, but it was a disastrous decision. When we finally arose and entered the kitchen we found Michael up on the top shelf of the cabinets, sitting in the closet eating Cornflakes, from the box.

He had emptied the baby formula from the refrigerator onto the kitchen floor. These were the bottles that Mae had spent the better part of last night making. In those days, which don't seem so long ago, we had to mix up and make formula; it didn't come ready made. In addition to the formula mess, Michael had performed surgery on the new couch pillows with our newly acquired steak knives. Michael had also managed to put Mae's new lipstick in the peanut butter and jelly jar and was feeding this to the baby. Grapes and bananas were also on the floor and in the baby's breakfast plan. Somehow, Michael had found a way to unlock the hooked cabinet doors.

I quickly found a way to dress and run off to work. Mae, in the meantime, had the dubious distinction of cleaning up not only Michael, but also the baby and the house. Now Mae was about seven months pregnant and our government quarters were such that when the door to the back porch closed, it locked and could not be opened from the outside. After Mae cleaned up the mess and got the baby changed, she headed for the clothes she had left outside in the back still in her baby doll pajamas. This spelled disaster.

Oh! Oh! She forgot to unlock the back door before stepping out. The door closed and locked. Oh, well! No real problem, Michael was just on the other side of the door and Mae felt sure he would unlock the door. Wrong.

"Michael! Open the door for Mommy, please!"

Michael wasn't talking yet, but he understood everything you said to him. He looked Mae straight in the eye and shook his head, 'No' . . . with a big grin on his face.

Michael thought Mae was playing a game with him. Only now, the men on the base were starting to drive across the air field to the business side of the base. Mae was thanking God that she was on the backside of the house and not the front. She was also grateful for the big rhododendron bush beside the rear door as it provided some coverage. Again, she pleaded with Michael.

"Please Michael! Mommy is not playing. Open the door!"

Michael's grin grew wider by the minute. "No!"

When Mae would try to talk to him he would run from the porch into the living room and hide. No matter how much Mae tried to convince Michael she wasn't playing, he wouldn't hear of it. He thought it was fun. Mae noticed the bedroom window adjacent to the stoop was open. She would have to pull off the screen, climb up on the porch railing and ease through the open window. She was athletic, so she thought she could do it. No problem for a girl like Mae. She climbed many a fence in her youth. I have to admit she must have been quite a site trying to climb up the handrail on the porch, but her guardian angel must have been working overtime, because Stephen awoke, came out on the porch and opened the door just as Mae was about to haul her seven month belly over the porch rail.

God had delivered one miracle; dare we keep our fingers crossed and await the next one?

APPENDECTOMY

It was a fine December day. I had just finished my shower and was getting dressed for duty when I felt a twitch in my stomach. It wasn't all that bad, but it was painful enough to make me sit down on the edge of the bed and try to get my wind back. For a moment I thought I might be having a heart attack. But this was more like a tummy ache. Not a heart attack. Not that I've ever had either one. I sat for a few minutes and collected my thoughts. No it's not a heart attack, or even a stroke. It seems to be subsiding anyway. There, I'll be fine in a few minutes. I went into the kitchen where Mae was feeding the baby. By most people's standards, any one of the three children at the table could be called the baby. All three were still in diapers. Although Stephen, the oldest, was just about to give them up and graduate to big boy clothes. What a relief. Do you know how much diapers cost? And remember these were the days before disposable diapers were invented. I mentioned to Mae the stitch in my side and she told me she didn't have time for a sick husband. I had to get healthy, and do it in a hurry. She asked if it hurt now. I told her no, but it could come back. Come and see me when the pain comes back was her reply.

So off I went to my job. It was on the opposite side of the base and I had to go pass the dispensary on the way. Why not stop in and get something for the pain just in case it comes back. Good idea I thought. So I stopped at the dispensary, signed in, and took a seat. All right, I'll be a little late for inspection, but I had a good excuse. I waited about forty-five minutes. Time was really getting away from me so I thought I'd just ask for a few aspirin and be on my way. "No can do," said the guy at the desk. "You signed in; you have to be seen by a doctor."

But I'm feeling much better, I said.

"Too bad....you must see a doctor. As a matter of fact, here's the doctor now."

After a quick examination the doctor told me I could go as soon as they performed this one blood test, just to rule out appendicitis. Fifteen minutes later, the pain had disappeared completely. In fact, I was feeling pretty good. In walked a corpsman with a pan of hot water, shaving cream, and a razor.

"What's that for?" I asked.

"I have to prep you for surgery."

"Prep me for surgery, what are you talking about. I'm just waiting for the results of my blood test so I can go to my duty station."

"Good news," the corpsman replied. "The results of your blood test are back. You have appendicitis. We're going to operate in just a few minutes."

Wow! You can imagine how confused I was by now. I was feeling pretty good and eager to get back to my duty station and the next thing I knew was I being prepared for surgery.

"How long will this take?" I asked.

"Oh! Not long. We'll have you in and out before you know it."

Next he was to shave my private areas.

"Hold on just a minute," I said. "I think I'm capable of shaving off a few hairs in these sensitive areas."

"Yes! I'm sure you are, but you can't do it as quickly or as thoroughly as I can. Roll up your night shirt."

No sense in arguing with the boss. Especially since he will soon be hovering over me with a scalpel. Before I knew what was happening to me I was wheeled into the O.R., put under the lights and sent off to *lala land*. There was little or no time to call Mae. I must admit I was worried about being late for muster at the flight line more than about calling Mae. I guess I assumed I would have the operation and be out in about an hour. Big mistake. Have you noticed I seem to have made a good many 'Big Mistakes?'

As I was coming out of the O.R. a nurse was leaning over me with what looked like a red pepper in a plastic jar.

"We got it just in time," she was saying, "much longer and you would have been a goner."

That wasn't the worst news I was to receive that day. Immediately after the nurse I saw Mae, in tears, leaning over me and saying, "How could you? You could have died?"

"Gee! Thanks! I'm not quite sure what they did to me. Can you check and make sure they didn't take any of the important parts off?"

I hadn't realized what the impact of a phone call to Mae from the Sick Bay would have, but it shook her up pretty badly. For that I am truly sorry. As I think of it now I realize how unfeeling I was to put her through this. Here she was with three children and no one to help her because no one, not even me, really knew how serious this operation was. I spent three days in Sick Bay and finally they discharged me to finish recuperating at home.

But that isn't the end of the story. After three days at home recuperating I developed a massive infection in my stomach and popped three stitches at the top of my seven inch incision. It happened one morning when I awoke and asked Mae to check me because I felt warm and wet under the covers. Mae removed the covers and was astounded at what she found. The three top stitches of my incision had popped open and blood and mucus were pouring out of the rather large hole. As Mae pressed on my stomach, the fluids came out in torrents. Mae was furious. She packed me up and took me back to the hospital and into the doctor's office without an appointment. She asked the doctor what antibiotics he had given me and when he said none, he didn't believe in them, she threw a fit. She ended by telling him he was too young not to believe in antibiotics. I thought we were destined to spend the next few weeks in the guardhouse. But cooler heads prevailed and I was discharged from the sick bay and sent home to recuperate once again…this time with antibiotics.

While waiting for my wound to heal, time was beginning to draw heavy on my hands. Christmas was approaching and I wanted to give Mae something meaningful.

GET OUT OF GEORGIA

In 1956, driving from Florida to New York in December was an adventure. Add to the journey three children under the age of three, and you have the ingredients for an unusual excursion.

I was recovering from an emergency appendectomy and was resting in a living room easy chair, watching the children. Stephen and Michael were playing at my feet, and Susan, the baby, was in the playpen. Mae, my better-half, was preparing dinner in the kitchen of our government provided quarters, while the radio was playing Bing Crosby's, "I'll Be Home for Christmas." This would be Mae's first Christmas away from her family. After dinner, Mae and I huddled around the small kitchen table.

"What do you think about driving home for Christmas?" I asked.

"Really?" Mae asked, as her eyes brightened. "No," she continued, pensively, "You aren't ready for such a long drive."

"I think I'm well enough to make the trip," I replied. "As long as I don't have to lift anything heavy I'll be fine."

For the next twenty minutes we debated the advantages and disadvantages of attempting such a trip. Mae was uncertain, but the more we talked, the more I liked the idea. We were getting no-where, so I finally said, "Let's use the Ben Franklin method to decide."

I took a plain piece of paper, folded it in half, lengthwise, and, on the left hand column listed the reasons to stay. On the opposite side, I listed the reasons why we should go.

REASONS TO STAY:

1) I had not completely recovered from my emergency appendectomy of 10 days ago. The surgery was a success, but because of the infection, a drain was still in place.

2) The weather up north was predicted to be bad. Snow.

3) It was a long trip to make with three young children.

4) We really didn't have sufficient winter clothing.

REASONS TO GO:

1) We could be with our families for Christmas.

We studied the list dejectedly, looked at each other, and looked at the list again. I finally broke the ice, saying, "Obviously the reason to go far outweigh the reasons for staying."

A grin spread across Mae's face. "Are you sure?" she asked, afraid the answer might be other than yes.

"It's six-thirty," I said. "You pack. I'll clear the paperwork with my commander, fix the car so the children can sleep in the back seat, and we'll be on our way by eight."

So, with a few grunts and many groans, I prepared the car for the journey; front seat slid full forward, suitcases on the floor behind the front seat, even with the back seat cushion, a single piece of plywood stretched across the rear seat and over the suitcases made a handsome, platform bed. Plenty of blankets and pillows made the bed soft and comfortable.

I returned to the house and said to Mae, "It's cold, but we should be warm enough in the car once the heater is running."

As we left the base that evening, it was with the intention of driving all night and the following day. We realized it would be a little uncomfortable, but the inconvenience was worth the reward at the journey's end. We agreed Mae should take the first turn driving. She would drive until midnight. I, assuming the role of navigator, guided us off the base, through the twin cities of Crestview and Valparaiso, and north by east toward route 110, the main highway north.

"Now don't forget," I cautioned, as I tried to adjust myself to a comfortable position, "follow the sign to route 110. If you miss the highway, and I fall asleep, wake me. Just remember, always keep going north."

"O.K.," said Mae, "now you get some sleep."

I tried to doze, but since I was unable to stretch out, the awkward position caused pain in my side and made sleep fitful. The hours dragged on, 9:00, 10:00, 11:00, finally, midnight. Mae woke me to take over. I welcomed the chance to change positions.

I opened the car and walked around to the driver's side. Mae moved across the seat to the passenger's side. With the doors open, the warm air flooded out of the car, and the temperature dropped several degrees. Mae expressed concern that the children might catch cold.

"It's too cold to open the doors," she declared, shivering and turning around to make sure the children were bundled under the blankets.

"Well," I sighed, "we won't change seats that way again. From now on, the doors will stay closed! We can switch seats by maneuvering over each other. Even if I do have a pain in my belly," I added sheepishly.

With me behind the wheel, Mae felt more confident and at ease. She cuddled up next to me, but I was quick to caution her not to lean too heavily on my side.

"Ooh!" she exclaimed, "I almost forgot. How is your side?"

"I know it's there," I returned and smiled at her. "Now try to get some sleep."

Time passed slowly as we drove silently northward. We passed through one small town after another. At three in the morning, Mae awoke, and asked me if I would like her to spell me behind the wheel. I felt she hadn't enough sleep, but she assured me she was wide awake. We were passing through a quiet, sleepy little town in Georgia. The car came to a halt near the curb on a quiet tree lined street.

"This time," I said, "we'll stay in the car and make the shift."

"How?" asked Mae.

"You'll see," I answered.

Cautioning her to be careful of my incision, I gave the following instructions: "I'll slide over to the center of the seat; you do the best you can at standing up and moving over on top of me. When you're over me, I'll slide under you, to the passenger side."

It all made sense to me. One, two, three and the maneuver would be over. It was anything but a graceful move, however, especially with the front seat of the car fully forward. With a little discomfort, I slid from behind the wheel to the center of the front seat. Mae raised herself into a squatting position, head bent forward, struggling to stay up. Inch by inch, she maneuvered her body directly over me. She had to hold the rear view mirror with her left hand, and the back of the front seat with her right, while she stood in a crouched position. Progress was slow, and I was starting to breathe heavily as I tried to bring my head under Mae's right arm. My side was beginning to throb. I was starting to think this was a bad idea. Mae squeezed and pushed her body as far forward as the dashboard and windshield would allow. She tried to slide under the steering wheel, but there just wasn't enough room to complete the move. We were stuck. I couldn't go right. Mae couldn't go left.

"Hurry up," Mae giggled, "I can't stay like this forever!"

"Wait a minute!" I said, the sweat beading up on my forehead.

I was using her waist as a lever to pry myself free and move across the seat. Mae's legs gave out at a crucial moment, and she sagged into my lap.

"Oooooh!" I groaned, and, knowing how best to get her off my lap, I goosed her. Mae jumped up, hit her head on the roof, and settled back in my lap again.

"Oooooh! You . . . you . . . fresh thing!" yelled Mae, as she tried to return to the crouched position hitting her head in the effort.

After a few groans, I asked, "Are you all right?"

"Little do you care," came Mae's response, "all you care about is your tummy. What about my head?"

"I do care about your head," I said, offended, "but I can only take so much weight on my belly."

"Are you saying I'm fat?" Mae blurted out.

Not being a total fool, I responded, "Of course not," and tried raising Mae up, just a little.

With Mae in the air again, I managed to break free and slid to the far side of the seat. A great sigh of relief ushered from my mouth as I straightened myself. Mae slid behind the wheel.

"You are fresh!" she snapped with half a smile on her lips.

"You know you're not exactly a light weight," I replied. "It will be a miracle if I get to New York in one piece, if you keep sitting on my sore stomach."

"What could I do," Mae replied, "I couldn't hold that position forever."

Mae giggled, but her laughter ceased as the headlights, from a car diagonally across from them, suddenly came on. I was immediately alarmed. We were in a strange town; in the middle of the night; not a sign of life anywhere. If only I was behind the wheel. Blinded by the bright headlights it was impossible to see who was in the other car, or what make of automobile it was.

"Start the car, and let's get out of here," I said, as I leaned across Mae to make sure the door on her side of the car was locked.

"Who are they?" Mae asked.

"I don't know. They could be kids, or at the very best, cops. Let's move."

Mae put the car in drive and pulled away from the curb.

"Stay on the road and don't exceed the speed limit," I cautioned, "just in case it is the police."

I looked out the rear window as the unmarked vehicle made a turn and started to follow us. Mae's eyes fixed on the rear view mirror.

"Don't worry about them!" I snapped, obviously uneasy, "Keep your eyes on the road and stay within the speed limit. They may be kids, looking for a little excitement," I repeated. "Just do what I tell you."

After a short distance, a siren and red blinking light ushered forth from the trailing car. I breathed a sigh of relief.

"It's the police!" I said to Mae.

Mae responded somewhat annoyed: "Haven't they anything better to do? What do you think they want?"

"Just pull over," I said, "after all, that wasn't exactly a ballet we were doing back there. They probably think we're lovers."

Mae gasped. "Lovers?" she snapped, "With three children?"

"Calm down Mae," I cautioned, "They don't know we have three children."

Mae pulled over and rolled down the window, awaiting the arrival of the State Trooper. As he came up to the driver's window, Mae asked, "Is there something wrong officer?"

"Let me see your license and registration," he barked, as he passed his flashlight across our faces, blinding us both. This, and the tone of his voice, angered Mae.

"What were you doing back there?" he wanted to know.

"We were just switching seats," I said, as Mae went through her purse for license and registration.

"We're on our way home for Christmas," I continued, hoping to strike some spirit of fellowship in this guardian of the law.

"I know what you must be thinking, Officer," said Mae in a very sarcastic tone of voice, "but if you'll look in the back seat you'll see we're not lovers."

With Mae's sudden outburst, I looked like I was going into shock. I wanted quiet from Mae. I wanted to handle this.

"Make nice," I whispered to Mae.

The officer flashed the light into the back seat and observed the three children, sound asleep.

"You see," continued Mae, as she handed the officer her license and registration, "we're on our way home to New York for the holidays, and . . ."

Mae broke off as the trooper, taking her license and registration, abruptly walked away from her and went to the front of the car.

"That's very rude of him," she snapped. "Who does he think he is, walking away like that!"

"Be quiet!" I cautioned through clenched teeth, "Remember, he is the police."

The trooper stood, illuminated by the headlights, checking the license and registration with the plates on the car. My previous tour of duty was in Virginia, so I retained my Virginia plates. Mae had a Florida license. I realized we were in trouble, when I noticed the trooper switching his flashlight from Mae's license to the car plates, to the registration card. Back and forth, back and forth went the flashlight beam.

"He's confused." I whispered to Mae. "Your license is from Florida and the plates are from Virginia. He's confused."

With the window open, and the temperature in the car dropping, Mae was getting cold. She whispered to me: "What's taking him so long? I hate it when someone walks away from you while you're talking to them!" Mae is not one to be trifled with when treated rudely.

"I know," I replied, "but you have to excuse him, he's confused. And if he's confused now, wait until he asks for my license. That should make him real happy!"

The officer returned to the window, and, as I predicted, said, pointing to me with his light: "Let's see your license."

I, having retrieved my license in anticipation, handed it to the officer and tried to explain: "Officer, I know there's liable to be some confusion over the differences in licenses and plates, but ..."

It was my turn to be interrupted.

"Shut up!" said the trooper. "When I want an explanation, I'll ask for it."

Mae was starting a slow boil. The trooper grabbed my New York license and began to examine it. He looked more puzzled than before, and, dropping his hands to his side, sighed:

"What the . . . ! What the . . . ! How come, he finally said, "you have a New York license, she has a Florida license, and you're driving a car with Virginia plates?"

"Well that's easy to explain," I said, as I gingerly leaned across Mae's lap and started to give my explanation. Mae, getting more annoyed by the minute, interrupted:

"We're in the service, on our way home for Christmas, and it's getting cold in here."

With my left hand concealed, I grabbed Mae's thigh and squeezed, signaling, 'Be quiet!' Mae's face instantly turned to look me directly in the eye; had the daggers she shot at me been real, I would be impaled on the far side of the car.

"You see Officer," I continued, trying to shed light on what was obviously a confusing situation, "I've had a New York license ever since I learned to drive. I grew up in New York. We were stationed in Virginia last year. We're currently stationed in Florida, where my wife got her license. I know it's a bit confusing, but it's all in order."

"It is huh!" said the trooper. Still puzzled, he mumbled, "I don't know?" and returned to the front of the car to reconsider. Again the flashlight beam went back and forth.

Mae was no longer annoyed. Now she was angry; not just at the trooper, but at me for squeezing her leg and trying to silence her. Mae was not going to be silenced. The temperature of the car was dropping, but Mae's temperature was rising. She decided she would deal with the trooper first. She rolled her window down, stuck her head out, and yelled at the Trooper standing in front of the car:

"When you decide what you want to do, rap on the window. It's getting cold in here!" and with that, she raised the window.

I went into shock. I couldn't believe what I had just heard. "If you don't shut up," I said between my teeth, "we'll all wind up in the jug, instead of going home."

"Well, what's the matter with him?" screamed Mae. "Can't he see we have children in the back? Is it so hard to believe people go home on Christmas? And besides, what do you think you're doing pinching my leg?"

Knowing that discretion is the better part of valor, I said: "I'm sorry, honey, but you'll have to admit, a Florida license, a New York license, Virginia plates, and it gets confusing. Now just be nice and I'm sure we'll get out of this. OK?"

"Nice! I'll give him nice," exclaimed Mae, "his manners need improvement."

"OK!" I returned in a panicky voice, "but let his mother do it. Not you. This is not the time to get on his bad side."

The trooper returned to the car still shaking his head. Mae refused to roll down the window until the trooper requested it.

"Roll down the window," I said.

"No!" Mae replied, in a pout.

"Roll down the window," I pleaded.

"No!" Mae repeated, and looked me in the eye. "Not until he asks for it."

The trooper rapped on the window with a knuckle, still mussing over the paper work in his hand. Mae lowered the window, slowly, as I held my breath. The trooper leaned over, looked again in the back seat, shook his head and said to Mae:

"Look lady, this is too confusing. Here are your licenses. Get out of Georgia." Then he added, half smiling, "And don't change seats again."

"Thank you, and Merry Christmas." I rushed to say, hoping Mae would remain silent.

Mae started the car, eased out onto the road, and headed north. She was not amused, but at least we weren't headed for jail. Still annoyed at me, Mae noticed a broad grin spreading across my face and asked, in a terse way,

"What's so funny?"

I started to laugh, "Imagine, a New York license, a Florida license, and Virginia plates. On top of that, I can just imagine what he was thinking when he saw us doing the front seat boogie-woogie. It's no wonder he was confused."

Mae started to laugh and added, "You don't really think he would have arrested us, do you?"

"No," I said, "But they don't much like Yankee's down here. Can you imagine what the folks back home would think if they heard we were arrested for indecent exposure?"

CATHOLIC CHURCH

As Mae and I continued our trip north, we put the incident with the trooper behind us. I dozed as Mae continued to drive during the early hours of the morning. About five thirty, her eyes getting heavy, she nudged me.

"I'm getting tired," she said.

I started to stretch; as I did, the wound in my side tightened and pulled against the stitches. I bolted upright in a jerky motion, ceased the stretching and moved to a more comfortable position.

"Let me have a cup of coffee, and then I'll take the wheel," I said.

I finished the coffee and Mae pulled the car over for the now infamous front seat boogy-woogy.

"Are we still in Georgia?" I asked with a devilish grin.

Time had healed Mae's annoyance at me. "Yes! But I don't care," she giggled, as she kissed me on the cheek.

"Make sure there are no cops lurking in the shadows," I said. We laughed, but looked front and back before changing seats again. This time the maneuver went a little easier.

I felt better, sitting behind the wheel. Mae checked the children, adjusted the blankets, and then, pulling her feet up, crawled under her winter coat and leaned over, resting her head on my thigh. It was time for Mae to sleep.

"Now don't forget," I said as I tried to adjust to a more comfortable position, "get as much sleep as you can before the children wake up."

Mae dozed and I continued to drive into the early hours of the morning. About seven-thirty, my eyes getting heavy, I nudged Mae.

"I'm getting tired," I said.

Mae realized she had slept solidly for the last two hours, responded with love and a kiss on my nose as she whispered, "Keep driving, I'll do my penance when we get home."

I continued command of the wheel. Towns slipped silently by one after the other. We were in South Carolina as the sun came quietly over the horizon. It was going to be a clear cold day. I felt better with the sun up and was looking forward to a good hearty breakfast. Mae awoke.

"What time is it?" she asked.

"About eight-thirty," I answered.

Mae smiled, turned and checked the children. They were still sleeping. She and I talked in whispers, allowing the children to continue their slumber. We discussed where and when we should stop for breakfast and church. After all, it was Sunday. Mae never missed Sunday services. We checked the map and noticed that the next town was only a short distance away. The town looked big on the map. A Catholic church was sure to be there. We would arrive about ten o'clock, have breakfast, go to church, and be back on the road before one o'clock. Sounded like a good plan.

As it happened, at ten o'clock, the town we entered was a lovely, old-fashioned, southern town. A church, which was by far the largest of the buildings, was on one corner, and sat diagonally across from a small country kitchen.

"There's a church," said Mae, "but it's not Catholic. There's no cross on the top," she continued, disappointed.

I replied, "But there's a diner directly across from the church. We'll eat anyway. It's early and nobody's awake. We can feed the kids in their pajamas, and they won't dirty their clothes. We'll ask the waitress for directions to the closest Catholic church."

I parked the car directly in front of the little diner. A large bow window, with the only view of the street had the words painted, in bright yellow letters, 'Aunt Sarah's Kitchen'. I felt a friendly affection for the little breakfast shop. I could smell the bacon, eggs and country grits. I was hungry.

We climbed out of the car disheveled, looking like we had just rolled out of bed, which was pretty much the case. Into the small quiet shop we tumbled, all five of us. As we entered, immediately to our right, and partly projecting into the bow window was the only large, round table in the establishment. Mae, the children and I seated ourselves around the big table. Here we were not only comfortable, but commanded a terrific view of the main street. The waitress ambled up to this party of vagabonds, opened her order pad and asked with a smile upon her face,

"What can I get you folks?"

After glancing over the menu, I gave the order. Cornflakes, bacon, scrambled eggs with grits, English muffins, milk, juice and coffee. My appendectomy had little effect on my appetite. I relished the thought of bacon, eggs and grits. I turned to the children and told the two older boys, that for the first time in their lives, they were going to get a southern specialty, grits.

I raved about grits, knowing that unless I prepared the children, strange food would be unacceptable. Mae busied herself getting the children settled; removing their heavy coats, straightening their pajamas, and washing the sleep from their eyes with a napkin dipped in a glass of water.

The juice and cornflakes arrived just as the morning toiletry was complete. Breakfast proceeded normally until the arrival of the bacon, eggs, grits and muffins. With their arrival, the bells in the church across the circle started to ring. They were loud and sharp, and startled the children. The expression on the children's faces asked, 'What's happening?'

The doors of the church flew open, and the congregation began to emerge. It was evident that the waitress and cook in Aunt Sarah's, were not the only people awake in this town. Early services had just concluded, and the entire congregation appeared headed for Aunt Sarah's Kitchen. People began to enter the little shop. Before long it was overflowing. As people entered and chose their tables, they had to pass the only large, round table in the place. As they did they looked down their noses at the crew assembled there, as if to say, 'Who are you, and what are you doing at our table?'

Mae whispered, "Charlie, we look terrible! Let's get out of here. I feel like a slob. Look at the way these people are dressed."

"Are you kidding," I said, startled. "We haven't had our breakfast yet."

The town's folks were dressed in their Sunday best. Women were showcasing mink coats. Every woman wore a hat, fashionable for the time. Men wore black suites, ties, hats and overcoats. They all looked freshly scrubbed and perfumed.

"Just act natural," I whispered to Mae under my breath, "after all, they're not traveling with a car load of kids."

With all the commotion taking place, Mae and I had neglected the children's table manners. The children, realizing there was no more fun in watching the crowd, went back to breakfast with a vengeance. The cornflakes were finding their way to the floor in large groups of soggy flakes, surrounded by an ever increasing sea of milk. Juice glasses were fun to turn upside-down.

Susan turned a full glass of water upside-down on her head, evidently impressed by the display of fancy hats. She gasped with shock when the cold water cascaded over her head and down her face and neck. She got mad and thus threw the eggs, like the cornflakes, to the floor.

As the noise level rose, so did Mae's anxiety. In an attempt to bring order to their table, Mae introduced Susan to the grits. Preoccupied with the noise and the behavior of the children, and being unfamiliar with the heat retention properties of grits, Mae put a spoonful into Susan's mouth. When the grits hit Susan's tongue, her eyes opened to the size of golf balls. She let out a scream that curdled the milk in my coffee. The last thing Mae wanted was to call attention to our table. But it was too late, the damage was done. Susan was unrelenting in her screams.

I snapped at Mae, "What's the matter with you. Didn't you check the grits before you gave them to her?"

"Don't make a scene," Mae growled back from between clenched teeth.

"Make a scene," I replied in a sarcastic way, "You're kidding me."

Mae was trying to calm Susan, who was intent on convincing the entire town that child abuse abounded in this family. Like Keystone cops, both Mae and I were trying to comfort

Susan. We reached for the same glass of milk and managed to tip it into Susan's lap. Susan interpreted this as an attack and responded in kind. This time her screams put my hair on end. The breakfasting congregation now focused complete attention on the frantic family.

Recognizing she could not console Susan, Mae told me to get the check and, "... let's get out of here."

"But I haven't eaten yet!" I protested.

"Stick it in your ear!" Mae retorted, and picking up Susan retreated out the door and toward the car.

"But, but ... what about breakfast?" I continued to lament.

"And don't forget to get the address of the church!" Mae hissed back as she left the shop.

They were already the center of too much attention, but more was still to come. While trying to pay the bill and get the jackets on the boys, I asked the waitress in a whisper:

"Where's the nearest Catholic church?"

"The nearest what?" asked the waitress in her best little southern drawl.

"Church? Catholic church?" I repeated and seeing that I was still not understood, added in a louder tone, "Roman Catholic church?"

The girl turned and called out, in a loud shrill voice, to a uniformed policeman sitting at the far end of the kitchen,

"Clem, you ever hear of a Roman church?

"Roman Catholic church?" I interjected.

The waitress repeated, louder than before, "A Roman Catholic church?"

Turning in his seat, the massive police officer responded, "Ya! I think thar's one, bout a hundred miles up the road apiece."

A hush fell over the entire restaurant. Everyone focused on me. Looking sadly at my breakfast, which had arrived during the melee, I quickly stuffed four biscuits and several slices of bacon in my jacket pocket. Then I tried to ease an 'over easy egg' on to an English muffin. I had to leave it when the yoke broke as I tried to squeeze it into the other pocket. Disappointment filled my face. I gulped down the remainder of my coffee, took the boys, one under each arm, and scurried out of the shop as fast as my legs would carry me. The only noise audible in Aunt Sarah's Kitchen was the noise I made tripping over a chair as I made my exit.

Mae was standing by the car trying to console Susan.

"Open the dam door!" she ordered.

I knew this was not a good time to discuss her use of profanity. Once opened, the children returned to the makeshift bed, Mae and I jumped into the car, started the engine and quickly left town. As I was trying to extract a biscuit from my coat pocket, Mae asked, in a not so pleasant tone of voice, "Where's the church?"

I looked at her, raised an eyebrow and said, "Bout a hundred miles that-a-way!"

Thus ended our visit to Aunt Sarah's Kitchen. I can still taste the over easy eggs on my English muffin.

HOUDINI

Ever since Mae and I became parents, it had fallen into the realm of my responsibility to fix whatever broke. Mae had her hands full with two boys and a girl, all less than five years of age. We were both new to the game of parenting, but we relished each new episode. And I enjoyed the role of Mr. Fix-it.

There were times I fixed the boy's hats so they looked like real cowboys, times when I fixed the plastic punching bag, the electric trains, and the lights on the Christmas tree. Regularly I fixed the TV focus, patched torn books with Scotch tape, fixed Susie's dolls and animals with thread and needle, fixed broken airplanes, ships and soldiers. The kids and I would replace light bulbs in lamps together. They thought I actually repaired the bulbs. To them, I was Edison. I'll have to admit, I didn't do anything to convince them otherwise. After all, I was their father. Besides, these were easy jobs. But a broken balloon, this was something else.

DADDY CAN FIX ANYTHING

That's right, fathers can fix anything! How do I know? Simple, I'm a father. Whenever something goes wrong that needs fixin', you don't see a child running to Mom. They run to Dad. Why? Because fathers can fix anything. Let me give you an example:

Some years ago I was a young and powerful father. In the eyes of my three children, I ranked right up there with Houdini and Superman. One day the children were playing with balloons. Mickey Mouse balloons. The old fashioned type, made of rubber. Of course you know what happened! One of these co-fangled, light weight, happy-faced balloons popped. It was Michael's balloon. Michael, age three, shocked by the 'pop', and startled by the disappearance of Mickey, screwed up his face and began to cry. Stephen age four, the oldest, took Mike by the hand and led him into the kitchen where I was reading my paper and enjoying an after-breakfast cup of coffee. Susan, age one, crawled behind.

"Don't cry Mike," Steve was saying, "Daddy will fix it!"

"What's the matter?" I asked. Having heard the 'Pop', I knew already there was no hope for Mickey.

"Mike's balloon broke!" Steve announced. "Show him, Mike!"

Michael, a man of few words, held out his hand to reveal a limp and wrinkled piece of damp latex, dull red in color, looking mighty sick. Tears were running down Michael's face and he said heart-brokenly, "My bawoon bwoke!"

I took the exploded rubber bag of air and examined it carefully. Mickey had expired. No amount of glue or tape was ever going to put him together again.

"Looks dead to me," I said.

Mike started to cry again. Big giant tears.

"Don't worry Mike," Stephen said again, "Dad will fix it!"

"Suppose I fix it tomorrow," I said, hoping for an opportunity to buy another balloon.

"No Daddy," whined Michael, "Fix it now!"

Poor Michael! . . . Poor Daddy!

"But Michael," I asked, "How? The balloon's broken. It went to balloon heaven! Daddy can't fix it."

Stephen looked at me with the faith of the Pope, and said, "You can fix it Daddy. You can fix anything."

Silence followed. I suddenly became aware of four sets of eyes staring at me; Stephen, Michael, Susie and Mae's. Startled, and humbled, I turned to Mae and said, "Honey, did you tell them ...." I started to ask Mae.

"Noooo! . . . But they must have gotten the idea from someone," Mae quickly answered.

"Stevie," I asked, "Who told you Daddy could fix anything?"

"Yes you can Daddy! You can fix it!" he answered, shaking his head in the affirmative. "You can fix anything! Fix Michael's balloon!"

Silence again fell over the entire kitchen. Mae and the children stared at the broken balloon, then at me, then back at the broken balloon. Mae quickly realized my predicament and tried to change the subject by announcing, matter of factly, "Louise Smith had her baby last night. Eight pounds, seven ounces."

Wow! I thought, eight pounds and seven ounces . . . some baby. As I pondered the size of the baby it dawned on me a baby was my solution.

"That's it!" I shouted and nearly jumped out of my seat. The crisis is over. An idea has hatched.

"What are you talking about?" Mae asked.

"The baby," I repeated, "the balloon is going to have a baby."

Mae grinned and stooping down to the children's level said, "Would you like to see Daddy help the balloon have a baby?"

Their faces lit up. They smiled and turned to one another saying,

"Yeees! . . . Yeees"

It was time for me to go into my act. It was time for Superman. For Houdini. And I rose to the occasion.

"You see," I explained, "the balloon isn't really broken. It's just sleeping. It's getting ready to have a baby"

Spreading a thin section of the broken balloon over my lips, I sucked in a deep breath and, with a quick twist of the loose ends, captured a small and tightly packed baby balloon. A rubber band sealed the opening. Probably wouldn't last long, I thought, so I have to prepare the children for the worst. I explained the baby was very young and needed plenty of sleep; it would soon go to bed and disappear to join its mother. But for now they could play with it.

Michael beamed as I placed the baby balloon in his hands. He held it like a china cup and his eyes were wide and smiling. Steve and Susie, fascinated by the birth, hovered around Michael, each wanting to get a better look at Daddy's creation.

"See," Stephen lectured Michael and Susie, "Daddy can fix anything."

The children returned to the living room with their new play toy. I relaxed, puffed up with confidence and a renewed sense of importance. I was Houdini. As I leaned back in my chair to sip my well deserved coffee, I heard, emanating from the living room that all too familiar sound . . . 'Pop!!! . . . Pop!!!

MOM'S & DAD'S VISIT & BURNED ROLLS

Although we were married since last December, and it was now the end of September, we were still newly-weds, in the service of our country, and stationed fifteen hundred miles from home. My parents were coming to visit us. It would be nice to see them and Mae would have a chance to show off her culinary skills. After all, doesn't every new wife want to impress her mother-in- law?

My folks, who had never flown before, arrived early in the afternoon. We knew they would be tired after the long trip so we decided to have dinner at home. Mae prepared a nice roast beef, potatoes, string beans, a nice salad and dessert. Oh yes! Rolls. Baked rolls . . . right out of the oven. Mae was determined to impress my mother. When dinner was ready, Mae called us all to the dining room table and dinner was served. After grace, the roast was removed from the oven, and while I sliced it, Mae put the rolls in to bake. Not having seen each other for some months, we gathered around the table, eager for information about the rest of the family and all that was going on at home. The conversation was lively and the food tasted delicious. Suddenly Mae yelled, "Oh! . . .!" jumped up and raced for the kitchen.

Too late, a black cloud of smoke herald the arrival of the rolls. Burnt. But just barely. Mae looked on the verge of tears as the rest of us rushed into the kitchen to see what could be salvaged.

"They're ruined," she cried.

"No they're not," snapped my father coming to her defense.

"They're fine. I like my rolls dark."

Mae was partially consoled as we all returned to the dinner table and completed dinner. Dad ate four of the burnt offerings. Nobody else ate any. He kept repeating, "I like my rolls dark."

For the balance of the week of my parents' visit, Mae entered on a crusade to serve a supper with rolls of a golden brown shade. But each night the results were the same. Burnt rolls. And each night my father would go through the same refrain.

"I like my rolls dark."

The only problem was, each night the rolls seemed to get darker. I was starting to think a demon controlled our oven. By the end of the week, Mae was ready to give up on rolls. My father never failed to come to her aide and consume at least a couple of the burnt rolls.

Their vacation being over my parents climbed aboard the plane and headed for home. That night Mae prepared dinner and, as on the previous evenings, burnt the rolls. As she was removing them from the oven and heading for the garbage can I stopped her.

"What are you doing" I asked.

"I'm going to throw them out!" she said as a matter of fact. "What do you think I can do with them," she asked annoyed.

"Give them to my father," I replied. "He likes his rolls dark!"

We decided that was just what we would do. We found a small box, put the burnt rolls in, wrapped the package and mailed it to my father. It would arrive soon after he and my mother arrived home.

A couple of days later, the mailman, who had been delivering my father's mail for the last twenty years, rang the bell.

"Charlie," he said, "The kids have sent you something, but I think it's broken. Listen to it," he continued as he held up the box and rattled the contents.

"Sure sounds broken," replied my father as he took the box from George.

"Open it while I'm here," George said. "That way I can attest to its being broken in transit."

My father drew his handy pocket knife across the box tape and opened the flaps. Out rolled the burnt rolls. A complete dozen.

"Well I'll be!' said George."What in the hell are they?"

Dad broke out laughing, "They're justice," he said. "I never should have started eating burnt rolls."

Ever since, Mae has never burnt the rolls.

ADEQUATE PUNISHMENT

Our neighborhood was really quiet and a wonderful place to raise children. But children will be children no matter where you are. I remember one afternoon I allowed Stephen, Michael and Susan to play in the backyard with several of our neighbor's children. They were all about the same age, from two to seven. The babies, like Susan, who wasn't one yet, usually sat and pulled the grass out of the lawn. You would have to move them every once in a while so the lawn didn't become too bare in any one area. Anyway, this one beautiful afternoon I was observing the children at play. It's amazing that even at the tender age of two and three, children start to acquire attachments and ideas about right and wrong.

I was observing Stephen and Michael playing with our neighbor's three and four year olds. Stephen was three, Michael was two, and Susan was one. Susan was just learning to walk and was toddling along when the neighbor's three years old ran up to her and pushed her down. Not enough to hurt her, but enough to knock her off her feet. Well, Michael and Stephen both witnessed the push, and were standing still trying to decide what to do. Obviously, the three year old girl had done wrong and should be punished. In retaliation, Michael started to run after the girl who pushed Susan. He chased her a short distance and decided that was enough when he found an interesting bug in the grass. He was satisfied justice had prevailed, but Stephen wasn't. Stephen took up the chase. The little girl immediately knew Stephen's intentions were for more justice. He chased her for a minute or two until the little girl got tired. She stopped. Stephen was several feet behind her. When she stopped, he stopped. The little girl turned around, put her hands on her hips, and gave

Stephen a nasty stair. The little girl probably thought, 'what am I running from him for? He's kind of cute. I'll chase him.' She looked Stephen in the eye and her intentions became obvious. She started to chase him. He ran for his life. When she started to chase Stephen he decided to run the other way rather than fight. After all, she was a girl. They kept up the cat and mouse game for about another two minutes until both found something more interesting to do. Then they lost interest in the cat and mouse game. I couldn't help myself but started to laugh. They were acting just like adults.

THE TRAVELLER

While living on the base it was easy for the children to amble from door to door. But seldom did they get lost, until one day when Mae found Michael's overalls in the backyard. Michael was at that age when he preferred to be nude rather than wear scratchy overalls. But nude? Where could he be? One thing about being on an Air Force Base was you could be pretty sure the kids were safe and couldn't get off the base. On this particular afternoon, out of a clear blue sky a light blue sedan came driving past the house and from the passenger's side I could see the top of a very blond head. As his eyes met mine I could see him jump with joy and indicate to the driver that this was where he belonged. His face lit up and the car stopped. Once the car stopped, the door opened and Michael came racing towards me. The driver, an officer from the base came around from his side of the car with a big broad grin on his face and opened the conversation with,

"Does this little feller belong to you?"

"He sure does," I replied as I grabbed him in my arms and gave him a big kiss, although I had mixed emotions. I was mad at him for wandering away, but I was delighted to get him back.

"I'm sorry about the lack of pants," I said to my new acquaintance, "but he just hates to wear clothes during the summer."

"I understand," he remarked, "I've got three of my own. I found him walking around the BX. He's a long way from home."

"Thanks so much for taking care of him. Michael is our little adventurer. He still has to be taught the dangers of walking off by himself. I hope it will come in time."

This was only one of several incidents that occurred to us while we lived in Officers Country on the Air Base. Another incident happened shortly after we arrived and were just getting adjusted to the house and the base. To give you some background, I was one of two Lieutenants assigned to the base. I couldn't find the other one, but I imagined that my life would consist of emptying ash trays and getting coffee for the higher ranking officers. To begin with, in our little office there was myself, three Captains, two Majors and one Lieutenant-Colonel. Lieutenant-Colonel Vanderhoven was in charge and a very competent commanding officer. The rumor that circulated around the office was that Lieutenant-Colonel Vanderhoven was wounded shortly after the surrender of Germany during World War II. He was assigned the task of dropping by parachute behind the Russian lines in Eastern Berlin, getting as many German scientists as possible aboard a train and then running that train through the Russian lines and into the American held portion of Berlin. During this evacuation, a hand grenade was thrown into the caboose where he was hiding and the explosion caused him to lose hearing in his right ear. You could never convince me he lost his hearing because no matter how hard you tried to slip something past him, he heard it just fine. He heard everything. He was tough, but he was fair and it was a pleasure to work for him.

One of the Captains in our little group was Captain Larry. He lived directly across from us and on many occasion I could grab a ride to the operations side of the air field. His wife had just delivered their first baby and they were typical first time parents. It used to get me upset when Mae would ask me to take something across the street because Mrs. Larry had asked for it. She, being a social southern butterfly, and an avant-garde woman, enjoyed breast feeding their child, and for some reason she enjoyed it most when there was an audience of young officers in attendance. The first time it happened to me I nearly lost it when she came to the door with a big boob hanging out of her dress with Junior attached. Junior was having a great time but I almost swallowed my tongue when she opened the door and asked me to come in. I couldn't get home fast enough. It reminded me of the time Mae was baking and for some reason was missing an important ingredient.

"Oh! That's all right," she said, "I'll go next door to Nancy Gray's house. She's always baking and I'll bet she has some."

MAJOR GRAY

Major Gray was a member of the Army's top notch team of rangers who are trained to survive in the wilderness. Yesterday he started on a seven day journey living in the swamps of Florida. Right along with the alligators, snakes and other wild beasts. Not my cup of tea, but we knew after every journey he went on we could count on his hanging out to dry the skins of snakes. Again, not my cup of tea, but what could I do, I was a Lieutenant, and he was a Major. Big difference.

At any rate Mae went next door and, as was her way, she opened the screen door and walked in. She was in the middle of the living room when she discovered the happy couple, both totally nude, in a loving embrace. To make matters even worse . . . he wasn't Major Gray. Talk about embarrassing.

She gradually got herself together, turned around, ran for the screen door, went through it and flew across the lawn to our house.

When she entered our living room she was out of breath, red in the face and couldn't wait to tell me what she had just experienced. She was in tears when she told me about the male being other than Major Gray.

"Quick," I said, "Give me something I can take over to their house."

It took a moment for Mae to get the implication, and then she said, "Just like a man," as if, what else could you expect?

Mae couldn't get over the fact that they were both naked and going at it like there was no tomorrow. Maybe there wasn't. I'm sure, had the interruption been by Major Gray, we would have heard some shots and there would be no tomorrow for someone. After calming Mae down, I explained that things like this happen occasionally in every organization. I explained to her that we were going to forget what she saw and make the cake without the required ingredient. As for the naked bodies, it was a rather hot day. And then I added,

"And don't forget to ring the bell before you go barging into someone's house. Give them time to run for cover."

CHARLIE'S TDY

Every once in a while officers and enlisted men alike had to go on temporary duty away from their home. This meant leaving spouse and children while you made your way to another place for training. No one likes it, but it is necessary to keep the people qualified and up to date on the latest in weapons and aircraft. Here is a sample of one of Charlie's TDY trips.

29 September 1959

I would like to digress two months in time to give you a taste of what traveling was like in 1959. This takes me back to July and my preparation to leave for a business trip to Los Angeles. In the Air Force occasionally we had to take trips away from the base and the family. This was called a TDY trip. It means a temporary duty away from your parent station. In my case, the parent station was Eglin Air Force Base. Now, on a TDY your family may accompany you if you so desire, but after considerable discussion, and a view of the fact that our youngest child was only 6 months old, we determined Mae and the children would remain in Florida.

At 08:00, on July 20, 1959- we arrived early at the airport knowing that at the last minute, there is always something left undone. Good thing we did because as we entered the main airport lobby we heard the following message coming over the Public Address System. 'Flight 907, Southern Airways' leaving at 09:00 AM for Los Angles, California is now boarding. In one sense it was quite a relief. The morning had been a hectic one commencing with our oversleeping, breakfast with the children, and them all jumping into the car to drive Dad to the airport. Southern Airways was located on the base and although the terminal consisted of only one small wooden building, the size of a phone booth, it served us nicely. We arrived at 08:00 with baggage, and under each arm, a baby. Why is it at a time like this the children always develop a paralysis of the legs? No one wanted to walk. Finally, Mae was able to curtail the wails of the baby, Susan, by carrying her and her doll Poopy. Two boys; Stevie, 3 years old and Michael, 2 years old insisted on clinging to me. They heard I might be leaving.

Though the sun was only two hours high the beads of perspiration were well up on my forehead. Onto the scales went both of my suitcases and camera bag. Too bad I couldn't deposit the boys. Ten minutes later I still had no ticket for baggage. 'What,' I thought, 'could be taking this idiot so long?'

"28 Sir," was the verbal reply to my mental question.

"28 What?" I asked.

"Twenty eight dollars for excess baggage, Sir."

"Excess baggage?"

In my haste to get my TDI orders, I had neglected to request and receive authority to carry excess weight. It was too late now.

"Well, just forget the $28, and hand me back my bags. Here Honey, take the kids out to the car."

I gave no thought to the fact it just took the two of us to bring them in from the car.

"How much time do I have before the plane departs?" I asked the clerk.

"The Los Angles flight has just been delayed two hours, Sir. Your flight will depart at 11:00 rather than 09:00."

"Thank you".

Back to the car.

"I'll be dammed, Honey if I'm going to pay $28 dollars for baggage. I just won't take my uniforms."

"But your underwear is in the bag with your uniforms," Mae replied.

Placing both bags upon the hood of the car, I proceeded to unzip them and empty shirts, shorts, jock straps, gym shoes, razors, and shaving cream along with other necessities into the larger of the two suitcases. It was a tight fit, but with a little persuasion, a lot off cussing and much stomping, we were able to close the bag and get in just under the 40 pound limit.

My photo equipment? Except for what I could put in my pockets, was left behind. Well at last I was checked in and still had an hour before flight time. Well there never is enough time to say goodbye, but at that moment time hung over us with a quietness you only find in cemeteries.

"Gosh! It's hot"

Finally the last goodbyes. Kissed Michael, kissed Stevie, kissed Susan, and last but certainly not least, kissed Mae. There were tears in her eyes and on her cheeks, but as always a smile upon her face. Guess that's one of the reasons I love her so much. She's a better soldier than I am.

"Goodbye, Honey. I'll call you as soon as I get settled. No crying, OK? ---I love you."

And all of a sudden there were tears in my eyes. So I quickly turned and boarded the plane. From the small window I could see them standing by the car waving. How wonderful I thought it would be to be coming home instead of leaving. The engines turned over and before long, Eglin was just a small tan patch on the ground, slowly disappearing behind an evergreen countryside.

The following are just a few of the notes from my diary during my time away:

Hollywood, California 21 July 1959

My dearest Darling,

Only one day since we parted; seems like years ago. If I ever get to the point of taking you for granted please remind me of this one day. It will serve to remind me not only of how much I miss and need you, but especially of how much I love you . . .

Arrived at L.A. at five o'clock and proceeded via limo and bus to the corner of Hollywood and Webster. It's only a two block walk to Ed's place on Cauka Way. Ed, my former college roommate left the key to his bachelor apartment under the doormat, as he promised earlier. Am now entrenched in his living quarters and will fill you in on some of the folks around here when I get back.

Love,
Charlie

That was how a TDY trip was supposed to be. For me it meant waiting for the time required to pass until I could board the plane for home. I wanted only to be reunited with the family. Ed was on leave and home in New Jersey. When he returned,

I had already left to return to Florida. It was nice to meet new people and seek new adventures, but there was more than enough action at home for me.

DECEMBER DAYS

The December following, we decided we would surprise our parents, by driving home for the Christmas holidays. It seems that every Christmas brings out the best in everyone, and I could tell Mae would not be happy if she had to spend this Christmas away from her family. So we decided we would make the trip from Florida to New York. After all, with all the things that happened to us on our previous trips, what else could happen?

Although the day started off with plenty of sunshine, it quickly turned gray and ominous. Mae and I spelled each other at the wheel so as not to tire early in the day, but found rest nearly impossible. We found ourselves having to entertain our three children, all awhile keeping peace among them. Little by little we made our way north.

We left South Carolina, went through North Carolina, and were practically across Virginia when the sun set on us once again. In Virginia we encountered snow. The roads were clear, but snow had whitened the landscape. About five-thirty that evening, after all day, I said to Mae: "I'm going to have to stop, Honey. I'm so tired I can't go another mile."

Mae agreed. She too needed a good night's sleep.

"There's a Howard Johnson's half mile up ahead," she said, "We'll stop, rest up, eat, and get an early start in the morning."

I registered at the motel office, and, after settling Mae and the children in the room attached to the motel, walked to the restaurant for take-out hamburgers, french-fries and shakes. It was turning into a typical December evening. My breath came out in fog like puffs and quickly disappeared. I breathed in the exhilarating fresh air and stared up at the magnificent sky as snowflakes were starting again. What a wonderful evening. It was wonderful to be alive and with my family. The motel room was small but nice and clean. The large picture window on the left, next to the door, covered by drapes afforded privacy. The twin beds were to the left as you entered the room, and the shower and bathroom were directly across from the beds. An end table was between the beds, and a television on the dresser to the right.

We feasted on the hamburgers, cheeseburgers, french-fries and shakes, and, after bathing the children, we all collapsed in bed for a well deserved sleep. I slept with the two boys in the far bed directly across from the bathroom. Mae, with Susan in the bed closest to the window. It was seven o'clock when we turned out the lights. I set the alarm on my wrist-watch for six o'clock the following morning. With a good night's rest we were sure to make New York by late the following day.

Mae's final goodnight fell on deaf ears as I was asleep before my head touched the pillow. My body relaxed and I was soon in what can best be described as, 'a dead sleep'.

There are some things though, that rouse even the near dead. My state of unconsciousness evaporated with six spine chilling words from Mae, half whispered, half pleading:

"Charlie, there's someone in the room."

It was like a bolt of electricity went up my spine, from my big toe to the roots of my hair. I was immediately awake, tensed for any sound. My breathing stopped. I silently reached under the bed and retrieved my hunting knife which I had placed there before going to sleep. My mind raced through every possibility. Is it robbery, rape, murder, or a crackpot? I settled on robbery. The floor near the bathroom creaked. I leaped from the bed, and in one bounce, leaped across the bed containing Mae and the baby, blocking the exit and protecting Mae and the kids. As I landed with my knife extended, my empty hand hit the light switch at the door entrance. Nothing happened. No lights. I hit the switch again....still, no lights. My thoughts raced wildly. 'This intruder must be a pro. He's cut the wires to the room'.

My eyes widened, trying to see any unfamiliar figure in the darkness. Although my side was throbbing from my recent appendectomy, any movement would bring on my charge. Fear eliminated pain. I crouched, legs apart, arms out in a wrestler's position. Every nerve and muscle tensed. Whoever it was.... would have to go through me to get out. But it was so dark. No movement of any kind. I had to have light. I had to see. The drapes over the window held out the moonlight. With a quick lunge I was at the window and, in a single motion, yanked the drapes off the wall. Down came the drapes, rods and all, hitting me on the head. I disengaged myself from the drapes and whirled around to face the villain. The room flooded with moonlight. Now I could see. Mae huddled over Susan and the boys were asleep in the other bed. No stranger was visible. I quickly realized the bathroom was the only concealed spot in the room. It was directly across from the bed where the boys slept soundly. I moved quickly between the bed and the entrance to the bathroom. Whoever was in there would have to come out and I would be ready.

My eyes widened as I peered into the darkness of the bathroom. A crouched figure sneered back. I let out a roar and pounced on what turned out to be my reflection in the bathroom mirror. Hitting my head on the sink as I lunged into the darkness, I scrambled to my feet, arms flailing. I was still not convinced that I was alone. I pulled back the shower curtain and found nothing. I looked behind the bathroom door. Again, nothing. If there was anyone in that bathroom he would have had to been small enough to hide in the drain.

I staggered out of the bathroom into the bedroom. I looked at Mae, confused and puzzled. Mae raised her head from under the covers and asked:

"Is there anyone in there?"

"No!" I answered. "No one!"

Mae looked like a little girl as she curled up under the covers and said apologetically:

"I thought I heard someone. And then I saw the ladder against the window."

"What ladder?" I asked.

Mae pointed to what appeared, upon closer inspection, to be the shadow of an exterior trellis, cast across our bedroom window by the reflection of the moon. Cast upon the drapes, it did appear to be a ladder. But now there was no drapes, no rods, no nothing to hold up anything. The ladder was gone.

Suddenly, there was a rap at the door, and a voice called out: "We've had a bad snow storm and the power failed folks. Can we get you some candles?"

I was at the window. I looked out at the motel owner and responded: "No, we thought there was an intruder."

The motel owner continued, "The sound you heard was probably my repairman on the top of the building trying to fix the power line. I'm sorry. Goodnight!"

Mae helped me hang the drapes back over the window, as best we could, and together we crawled back into our beds. During the entire time, with all the commotion, the children had not stirred. Despite the presence of the two boys, and the pain that was throbbing in my wounded side, I quickly drifted off to sleep again.

Mae was restless, however, and sleep was difficult for her. She tossed and turned. She was anxious to be on the road, heading for the safety of home. After twisting and turning for what seemed like an eternity, she leaned out of bed and, dark as it was, examine the watch on my wrist. She strained to see the hands on the watch. A sliver of moonlight drifted in from a space she and I had been unable to cover when we put the drapes back over the window. The hands were straight up and down.

"It's six o'clock," Mae whispered.

I awoke and slowly eased out of bed. I turned off the alarm button on my watch, and went into the bathroom. A shower and shave renewed me. Mae was changing the baby and dressing the boys in their snow suites. The children were still sound asleep. Six o'clock was early for them. They usually slept until eight.

"I feel great," I whispered to Mae as I left the bathroom and kissed her on the neck. "It's marvelous how much a good night's sleep and a shower can do for you." I continued in a mocking way, "Am I correct in remembering we had a prowler last night? You see, I've got this bump on my head."

The two of us chuckled over the thought of last night's activities. We continued to talk in whispers as the children showed no signs of waking.

"What would you have done," asked Mae, "if someone was in the room?"

"I don't know," I replied, "but I'll be dammed if I'd let anyone hurt you or the children, or take off with our money."

We chuckled softly and continued to dress. It was still dark when I went to the car to adjust the blankets and pillows. I packed the suitcases into the car and returned to the room. Mae finished bundling the children into their snow suites.

"I've started the car, and have the heater running," I said. "When it's warm enough, I'll take the kids out and get them settled in the back seat."

While Mae showered, I walked over to the motel office and paid the bill. I noticed the owner had a puzzled expression on his face, but thought nothing of it. I was grateful the manager didn't ask me about the drapes. Upon returning to the room, I made a last minute check of the car to be sure it was warm. One by one, I carried the children out and settled them into the back seat.

"Honey! Look, the kids are still sound asleep," I said, "How about having breakfast. Just the two of us. That way, we can drive until the children wake up. I could use some coffee, and we'll fill our thermos."

Mae agreed and I moved the car in front of the restaurant so we could watch the children from a table. A waitress brought water and gave each of us a menu.

❧

Fresh Roasted Young Turkey $3.75

Hawaiian Pineapple Steak $3.75

Sirloin Steak $4.50

Filet Minion $6.00

❧

"The waitress is still asleep," I whispered to Mae. "She gave me a dinner menu."

Mae looked puzzled, "Me too!" she replied.

We signaled the waitress who returned with pencil poised.

"You gave us the wrong menus," I quietly said to the waitress, handing them back to her, pointing with one finger to the words, Dinner Menu. "We want breakfast."

"Breakfast starts at five," said the waitress.

"Five!" I stuttered. "It's after six!"

"Oh! No Sir," the waitress replied. "It's only a little after one."

I looked at my watch for the first time since I left the comfort of the bed. I looked at the watch, looked at Mae, looked at the watch and back at Mae again, obviously expecting an explanation.

"It's just after one!" I finally said pointing to the hands on my watch.

"When I looked at your watch, the hands were up and down," Mae said. It looked like six o'clock. I guess," she hesitantly continued, "maybe, it was twelve-thirty?"

"What day is today?" I asked the waitress, who was still waiting to take the order.

"Monday," the waitress replied.

"Oh!" I said, turning my attention again to Mae. "I thought maybe I was lucky and slept till Tuesday. Now I feel terrible," I continued. "It's no wonder the kids didn't wake up. They just went to sleep."

It was too late to check back into the motel. The waitress shifted from one leg to the other and asked: "Well folks, what will it be?"

We ordered bacon, eggs and coffee....lots of coffee and pastries. As the hot plates arrived, I looked at Mae and remembering a trip north a year ago, dejectedly said:

"I don't care who comes into this restaurant, I'm going to eat my eggs."

Our breakfast complete, we filled our thermos to the brim, and were back on the road. Once inside the car, Mae said:

"I'm sorry. I really thought it was six o'clock."

"Forget it," I replied from behind the wheel. "It's an easy enough mistake to make. We'll be home earlier this way."

"You know," I said with a smile creeping over my face, "I wondered why the motel owner looked at me in a strange way when I checked out. Can you imagine what he must have thought? What a wild couple. No wonder they have so many kids. They checked in, bounced off the walls, tore down my drapes and checked out, all in under eight hours."

We were both laughing now.

"I should be so lucky to have a sex drive like that," I continued, "No one would believe us if we told them what happened."

We laughed until tears came to our eyes. The journey was ending. It was more than eventful, and an adventure we were not likely to forget.

CHAPTER 12

RETURN TO NEW YORK CITY 1960-2000

The time I was obliged to give the Service in exchange for my education was coming to a close. Mae and I had to make a decision, and soon. My mother's health was failing, we had three children, and who, other than God, knew how big our family would grow? My next duty station was scheduled to be away from Mae and the children. Thus, all these factors indicated it was time for us to take a different direction in our lives. This is when I decided to resign my commission and return home to New York. I submitted the papers requesting my discharge due to medical reasons. Mom was not well and there was considerable concern for her life. We thought if we could get Mom involved with Stephen, Michael, and Susan, we could help her get out of her depression. Unfortunately, while we were waiting for the papers to be approved, Mom died. She was only fifty-five. It was my first major loss in this life and one I felt could have been avoided if I had acted sooner. Nevertheless, Mom was gone and my separation papers were on their way.

I was discharged and we returned home to Dad. I must say Dad and my brother Walter were delighted to see us when we first arrived, but as our son-in-law Kevin is fond of saying, "Guests are like fish, after three days they stink."

My Uncle Larry had arranged a meeting for me with Mr. Bill Robertson of Grumman to explore job opportunities. Robertson was head of the purchasing department of Grumman. If I decided to leave the Service, there would be an opening for me at Grumman. Starting salary was $7,500 plus a turkey at Christmas.

FROM MILITARY LIFE TO CIVILIAN LIFE 1960-2000

WELCOME HOME RONALD

We had just begun to get used to each other; that is, Dad and Walter were adjusting to sharing their space with me, Mae and the three children when my brother Ronald arrived at our front stoop with his new wife from Sweden. Just what we needed, newlyweds.

Not only were they newlyweds, they brought to the States some old-fashioned ideas about how husbands and wives were to treat each other. For example, Siv was to minister to Ron's every need. At the table on the first evening when we all ate dinner together, Ron noticed that the salt and pepper shakers were from the kitchen and not the good china. As he held up the salt shaker, he remarked, "Siveon! These are the kitchen shakers, where are the proper shakers for the dinner table?"

Upon Ron's not-so-nice request, Siv immediately jumped out of her seat and ran for the dining room china cabinet. She retrieved the proper salt and pepper shakers and brought them around for Ron's inspection. He approved and she returned to her seat.

The rest of us were in a state of shock. Who was this master of the house who gave such orders? Before we had recovered, Ron was examining the plates at the place settings. Another round was about to ensue as Ron again addressed Siv, "Siveon! This is not my mother's best china."

Once again Siv was out of her chair and acquiescing to her husband's request. With the new china in place, Siv went back to her seat.

Ron raised his water glass and examined it for finger prints. Sure enough, he found them.

"Siveon! The water glass!"

Siv again rose from her seat, but Mae had heard enough. Mae was on her feet and said quite pointedly to Siv, "Sit! Don't move!"

Looking at Ronald she continued, "Who died and left you boss? Who do you think you are? What makes you think you can order this poor child around like she is your slave. It might be all right in Sweden, but not here. If you want something get up and get it yourself."

Mae's tone was not to be misinterpreted. She literally glared at Ron, and he knew better than to pursue the argument. We all went quietly back to dinner.

While Mae was giving Ron a tongue lashing Siv crept back to her seat and silently sat down. Mae looked at Siv, who was trying to hide behind her napkin and continued, "If he gives you one more order, you stay right where you are and I will fill his request."

We all knew what that meant. I thought to myself, by God I'm proud of her for setting Ron straight, but she sure is screwing up a beautiful system Ron had going for himself. Everyone returned to dinner as planned and there were no more requests made by Ron. He did, however, lean over in my direction and ask, "Does she really mean it?"

"Oh! Yes! She means every word. Be careful of what you ask for."

Dinner went quietly for the next forty–five minutes when Ron asked in a very polite way directed at Mae, "May I ask my wife to get me a cup of coffee?"

Mae's response was, "Are your legs broken?"

After a long discussion with my father, it was decided these were not the most ideal living arrangements since everyone involved had to make some adjustments. For example, my father had to get used to the idea that his refrigerator could no longer be used to keep his beer cold. It had to be used to keep the babies diapers moist until we could get them dried or ironed. And he could no longer keep his Liederkranz cheese in the bottom drawer of the refrigerator because it stunk up the diapers something awful. Walter had to give up his bed or sleep with the two boys. Since they still wet the bed, he decided to take the couch. Mae was happy to do the family cooking, until Ron and his new wife arrived. Although Mae didn't mind doing her share of the cooking, she was not happy about having to do all the cooking. Siv, Ron's wife, was going to have to learn to pitch in and do some of the housework and cooking.

Another problem that arose after we arrived was the placement of keys. My father and Walter were accustomed to leaving their money and keys on their dressers adjacent to their beds. Since the assignments were changed, when my father awoke the following morning he could not find his car or house keys. Neither could Walter. The culprits? The boys. They got up even earlier than Dad or Walter. They thought hiding the keys and cash was great fun as my father and Walter ran from one place in the house to another, trying to find the missing items. Well, the keys were in their shoes, but the cash was still missing. Where did it go?

The boys repented that night and gave up the cash. Dad said this was not going to work.

74 TUSCARORA DIVE

Although Mae and I had been taking every weekend to travel out to Long Island to look for a house, it now became urgent that we spend not only the weekends but time during the week as well. Space was at a premium and my poor father had not only given up space in his refrigerator to cool his beer, his bedroom for the two newly arrived lovers, space on his dresser for his car and house keys but also any space where he felt the children would not pilfer his cash. The children thought it was a great game to play with Papa, to hide his money and watch his face get red while he, Mae, Uncle Walter and I pleaded with them to tell us where they hid his money. My father really wanted us to move. He even offered to put a thousand dollars towards our new digs.

SIGN THE PAPERS

Of course we were told the only place to buy a house was on the north shore of Long Island. Only problem? Money. We could afford the south shore, but we were still trying to find that ideal place on the north shore.

Mae and I tripled our efforts to find a house. We went out early on Saturday mornings, often skipping breakfast to be first in the real estate office. We scoured the North Shore of Long Island. There seemed to be only two choices. One was to move into a million dollar homes community like my Uncle John or Uncle Larry, or find a start up home in a Levittown environment. Now here was something I could afford, but Mae was really concerned about the safety of the children. I was getting desperate. We had covered most of the North Shore within an hour's drive of Grumman; we covered most of the central part of the Island and we were now starting on the South Shore. Mae's big concern was the closeness to water. Many of the homes were either too close to the beach or a canal connecting the mainland to the water. Those that were further inland had pools, in-ground or above ground. The children did not yet swim.

It was about twelve thirty on a Saturday morning and we were exhausted from four hours of hunting when the realtor, who was showing us homes for the fifth time in three weeks said as he was headed for his office,

"I'm really sorry folks, but I've shown you everything I have and most of what the other realtors have. There is just nothing left on the Island that will fit your requirements. I wish there was more to show you, but I'm out of inventory."

I told the realtor we understood and sat dejectedly in the rear of his car as we sped back to his office. After a few minutes of silence he received a call on his car phone from his office. He had just received a new listing in a little town east of Huntington. It was a fixer-upper, but considerably less than we were willing to pay for a house. It was close enough to my job and worth taking a look at. He apologized for the call and explained the listing had not even been posted. It was a real fixer-upper and probably not at all what we had in mind, but he asked if we wanted to take a look at it.

It was only five minutes out of our way and knowing how my father was feeling about the current living conditions, we agreed. Joe, our realtor, changed course and for the next ten minutes was apologizing for the condition of this house.

"Please excuse the condition of this house. It hasn't been lived in for the past four months and is a real fixer-upper. I wouldn't show you this house, but I know how desperate you are."

"At this rate," I began, "We're ready to buy a plot of land and a pup tent. I'm afraid when we get home tonight we'll find our clothes on the sidewalk with the kids on top of them."

We traveled to a small hamlet just east of Huntington to a village called Centerport. Huntington was a relatively large town so Centerport was considered small. And it was. It consisted of a post office at the bottom of Mill Dam Road and sitting on Centerport pond. At the top of Mill Dam Road were a series of eight stores; a pharmacy, a butcher shop, a hardware store, a delicatessen, a general store (candy, news papers, cigars, soda etc), a laundry shop, a barber shop and a card shop. They all existed at the intersection of Mill Dam

Road, Huntington Bay Road, Centerport Beach Road and Ridgefield Drive.

The school bus stopped at the intersection, and the neighborhood elementary school was a few blocks around the corner. Add to the convenience of the stores, the school, and the beach; it was ideal. We couldn't ask for a better location. This house located on Tuscarora Drive, was two blocks off Mill Dam Road and two blocks off Ridgefield Drive. We drove pass it three times before we stopped at what was 74 Tuscarora Drive. The house was small. It was built in the old-fashioned salt box style. The roof on the front left corner appeared to need some repair work, as did many other parts of the house. A gigantic tree grew between the house and what appeared to be a two car garage. A long dirt driveway wound around three magnificent oak trees located directly in front of the house. Directly across the street was a beautiful new house that appeared to have been finished last month. Next to the trees was a boulder that even Paul Bunion couldn't lift. A split rail fence wound around the front of the house and the property tapered off to the left and down the hill that was called Hillside Drive. From the street, the property appeared to be shaped like a large piece of pie. It measured almost three quarters of an acre. The yard was mostly wooded, although the backyard was open. Trees lined the backyard and a small fence went around the entire property. In the rear back left corner was a large grouping of French Lilacs. When they bloomed they scented the entire neighborhood. In the right hand corner of the property were several varieties of blackberries and blueberries. The birds got most of them. Anyway, we were shown the house and property and then were told the asking price was $13,500.00.

We arrived back at Dad's house looking dejected and down on our luck. Poor Dad. He took one look at us and said, "No luck again, hugh?"

"No Dad," I said, "We had to put a down payment on an outhouse and a tent, but you'll be rid of us pretty soon."

His expression brightened up immediately as he asked if I was kidding or if we really found something. We spent the rest of the day and evening discussing the house, where it was located and what it was going to cost us. When I told my father how much they were asking he couldn't believe you could buy anything that cheap on the Island. He immediately became skeptical and said he wanted to go out and see this house.

Some weeks later, as we were leaving my father's house to make the final drive out to our new home, I could see my father waving goodbye with both hands and a big grin upon his face. It wasn't that he was happy to see us leave but I'm sure he was thinking about getting back his refrigerator and bedroom. Who wouldn't?

When we went to the closing and to take possession of 74 Tuscarora Drive in Centerport, Mae took one last look at it and said, "This is it, Charlie. Sign the papers."

MEET THE NEIGHBORS

It seems the location, the size of the property, and the fact that we could walk to the stores was all that Mae required. There were plenty of woods surrounding the property and we were on a seldom used road. Mae felt she could turn the children loose in the backyard and they could play all day and never get lost. On the other hand, she could go to the stores around the corner, or to the beach just down the hill. Perfect for the summer, and it was a plus that when the kids got old enough, the elementary school was within walking distance from the house.

Once the house was purchased and we moved in, things started to fall into place. The first thing we attended to was finding out who our neighbors were and what they were like.

Upon our arrival, a day that was overcast and threatening rain, we pulled into our new driveway, and, like the Keystone cops, the children piled out of the car and started to explore their new surroundings. Little did I know it but our neighbors directly across from us, the Liotta's, were gathered around their living room blinds observing the commotion.

"I heard he was a Captain in the Navy," Sal said.

"He's a big shot in the Air Force," replied his son Joseph.

"You're both wrong," said Sal's wife Rita. "He is a Captain or something like that in the Air Force."

"It looks like he's trying to give the kids some orders," said Sal, "but each one of them is going their own way. Maybe if the kids don't pay any attention to him he won't be too bad."

It was near lunchtime so Rita suggested they invite the new neighbors over for lunch. While they were thinking this over, Charlie and Mae had ambled up to their new home, opened the door and called the children in to examine their new quarters. Upon entering the house there was a small receiving room. To the left was a living room about 15 by 20 feet. Behind the living room was a dining room with a fire-place. Behind the dining room and to the left was the kitchen and adjacent stairs that led up to the bedrooms. At the top of the staircase were two bedrooms one on each side and a bathroom in between. To the right of the receiving room was a small bedroom or den, and directly behind that was another bathroom.

As they were exploring their new quarters, Rita Liotta came over, knocked on the door, welcomed them with a bas-ket of fruit and invited us over for lunch. This sounded great since none of us had eaten since seven o'clock that morning.

While Mae started to unpack a few things, Stephen and Michael decided they would explore the neighborhood. They had seen a little boy about Stephen's age come over with his mother to welcome them. His name was Joseph. He was Stephen's height but much thinner than Stephen. And he was considerably more self-conscious. He was constantly hiding behind his mother's skirt.

Stephen and Michael were dressed in their fall outfits; long sleeved woolen shirts, overalls, heavy red jackets, cowboy boots and hunter's red peaked hats. Together they ambled down the driveway dragging sticks behind them. They were the image of city tough-guys.

Since they lived in the back of the woods, there was lit-tle automobile traffic. Dragging their sticks, they crossed the street and were now on the Liottas' property saunter-ing down the front path to the front door. Sal, always a kid-der, decided he would have some fun with the boys. He hid behind the curtain that shielded the front door and waited until the boys were about two feet from the front. Then he quickly opened the front door and yelled,

"What do you two want?"

The boys were so shocked at the sudden surprise their mouths dropped open ...they dropped their sticks, turned on their heels and ran for the safety of their new home. It was hilarious to see the two of them running across the front lawn making a beeline for our front door.

"There's a real monster over in that house," they kept telling me.

It took all I could manage to convince them it was only Mr. Liotta having some fun with them. On the way over for lunch it was their turn to remain hidden behind Mom's skirt. For the next few months things went as one would hope they would go. With children, you never know what to expect, but you should be ready to expect almost anything. And so it was... I was getting comfortable in my new job and Mae was starting to understand all that was entailed with being good neighborhood mother and the children, well . . . they were being children. Shortly after we moved in, we received some wonderful news about a new addition; Mae was pregnant.

Along with the purchase of 74 Tuscarora Drive came a number of repairs that had to be made. When we bought the house we paid $11,500. I can't begin to guesstimate the amount of money we put into minor repairs.

FINISH THE HOUSE

I've already mentioned when we bought the house it was in terrible shape and needed extensive work throughout. A major repair that had to be attended to immediately was the roof. My father came out one Saturday with two gigantic fans that he proceeded to make an integral part of the roof. They would circulate the air in the attic thus giving the roof and the attic air to breathe. I didn't know they had to breathe. My father showed me sections of the old attic where he could put his hand into and take out a handful of two-by-six. Leaks in the roof had caused the timbers to rot. They had to be replaced. When it finally came down to where the entire roof had to be replaced, the fans went with the old roof. You see, eventually, we had to add a new second floor. This was due to the expansion of four more girls to the family. We had to add onto the house as the children were taking over the place. Mae and I spent many a nights sleeping on the floor, but I loved it. I feel sorry for the father who does not have a daughter. They give meaning to a father's life.

When it came to adding a new upstairs, the first thing that had to be attended to was a gigantic oak tree that was situated directly in between the house and the garage. The tree was about forty feet tall and had a diameter of at least thirty six inches. We decided we would take the tree down one weekend and dig out the root the following weekend. Boy, were we optimists.

When we decided to take down the tree we were fortunate to have the help of Ken Swan, one of our neighbors who had some experience in removing trees. Along with Ken we had Sal, my neighbor and from the family, Pops, Jeff, Tom

Flanagan, Gus and myself. First project was to lower the main bottom branch that crossed the left corner of our house. We had to be careful because if it fell straight down, it would fall onto the corner of the house and collapse that corner of the house. We thought we could pass a rope over a branch about eight feet above the branch to be removed and six feet away from the corner of the house. That way, when the branch we were trying to remove was cut free, it would swing out and away from the house, providing the rope was anchored on the ground. Jeff volunteered to be in charge of the grounding of the rope. I volunteered to climb the tree and cut the branch free after tying the rope securely to the branch and the ground. Pops and Ken would help to lower the big branch to the ground once it was cut free.

In my haste to cut the branch free and get it to drop and swing away from the house, I neglected to check on Jeff. He, in the meantime, was winding the rope around his waist so he could bring added pressure to the branch when it was cut free. As the branch broke free it went straight down, landed on the corner of the roof of the house, toppled to the left and fell the rest of the way to the ground. I looked for Jeff, but he was nowhere to be found. I was going to scold him for not exerting enough pressure to make the branch swing out rather than go straight down. As I looked about I saw Jeff sprawled on the ground covered by leaves at the end of the branch that had just been cut free.

"What are you doing, Jeff?" I yelled "Why didn't you pull on the rope?"

"How do you like them apples," was all Jeff could say.

He was not only out of breath, but had a big lump on the front of his head. What we failed to take into consideration was the weight of the branch we were cutting free. It weighed much more than Jeff and lifted him off the ground and at least eight feet into the air. It seems that when Jeff wrapped the rope around his waist, he didn't have time to remove it before the force of the falling branch overtook him, hauling him eight feet into the air. Poor Jeff landed on his head and then was reprimanded for not pulling on the rope. He mentioned more than once that he probably should be dead were it not for the fact that his family has extremely hard heads. Jeff was dirty from head to toe, but his pride was what was damaged the most.

Not a very pleasant sight. We decided we had better spend more time preparing our plans before we put them into action. The balance of felling the tree went through without incident. Once the tree was down, we started on the job of cutting up the tree and digging out the root. We had dug quite a hole around the root and had a sizable hill of dirt in front of the house. In the hole, still digging, were Ken, myself, Gus and Tom Flanagan. As we looked up, there on top of the hill of dirt was Jeff, with a cup of tea in his hand overseeing the work in progress.

"What are you doing up there Jeff? Aren't you supposed to be down here with the rest of us digging?" Tom Flanagan asked.

Jeff replied in his fine Irish brogue, "Well I would Tom, only the pace at which I dug was so furious the tip of me shovel got so hot I had to put it down. When it cools I'll join you again!"

We all examined our shovels to see if we couldn't use the same excuse. It took us all winter to dig out the root to where we could haul it out with the help of our English Ford. With the root finally out, we were ready to add some rooms to the house.

LORD'S PRAYER

It was a weekend between Thanksgiving and Christmas and with the new roof and a new second floor I wanted to complete the hanging of the gutters. The last part was in the front of the house.

I started the project just before the holiday but was delayed in completing it due to the inclement weather. Rain, rain, rain, and more rain. Finally a weekend that promised no rain. Unfortunately, as I was preparing to hang the last of the gutters across the front of the house, who drove up for a visit but my father and Aunt Edith. Naturally, the project had to be shelved again until time permitted. My father felt bad that they had interrupted my project. He knew how frustrating it was to be in the middle of something and have it delayed due to unexpected company. He told me to go ahead with my plans and he would entertain the girls, Mae and Edith, in the living room.

This was a break and I intended to take full advantage of it. Winter was setting in and I had these last minute repairs to make before my tools were put away for the winter.

I got my extension ladder up and placed against the facer of the roof. Luckily there was just enough room for the ladder and the gutter so I could place the gutter in a slightly declining way so as to bring the water down to the downspout. I gingerly climbed up the ladder, tool belt hanging off my hips, gutter and hammer in hand, and no distractions from the children. Susan was next door playing with her new friend Chucky and the boys were off hunting bugs in the woods.

All was peaceful. Almost like God had willed it. I found the gutter was more of a problem than I anticipated, in that I could get it parallel to the ground but didn't have the room to be able to incline it downward. I struggled to move the top of the ladder just a quarter of an inch lower than it was, not realizing that all the rain the previous few days had softened the earth so that the ladder sunk further and faster in the sandy earth. As a result, before I could make any further adjustments, the ladder fell off the facer and out from under me. I quickly realized I was falling and that unless I did something drastic I would fall into the ladder and probably break both knees, when and if I was lucky enough to survive the fall. I could not afford to be laid up for any length of time. So back I jumped. It's amazing what can go through your head in a moment like this. Here I was falling two floors, with a ladder between me and the earth, and this is what went through my head. First I thought it was bad luck for my church to have rescheduled the Men's Mission from last week to this week. If they had held it as originally planned I would have attended the sessions, gone to confession and be in the state of grace. I would be right with God. But because they made the change, my mission was going to start tonight. Tough break. Then I thought, by golly, I had better forget about the missions and say a few prayers. I started on the Our Father when I hit the ground. Fortunately for me when I jumped I was able to propel myself slightly backwards, enough to give me some momentum in that direction. I hit the soft earth and rolled backwards. I was stunned, but nothing was broken. As I lay in the grass trying to catch my breath, my daughter, Susan, came running up with her playmate. They were both laughing and Susan said,

"Oh! Daddy! Good! Good! Do it again, Chucky didn't see it."

Well I picked myself up after I had time to catch my breath, dusted myself off and decided I would go in and tell Mae, my dad and Aunt Edith what had just happened. Upon entering the house I found the group laughing over some story my father had just told them. I had still not completely recovered but was able to get their attention. I shouted,

"Fine thing…here you three are laughing and having a great time over your tea and crumpets and I could be lying out on the front lawn dead. Little do you care."

Of course they immediately got up and came over to me to make sure there was nothing broken. As they were firing questions at me Mae asked how it happened. I told her exactly how the fall came about and how I hardly had time to complete my prayer before I landed. Mae asked me what prayer I was saying.

"The Lord's Prayer," I replied.

"Oh! Dopey you! You had to pick a long prayer. Don't you know you should have a short prayer prepared for just such occasion?"

"That's gratitude for you," was all I could reply.

With the winter approaching I knew work could only be done on the inside the house, not on the outside. Fortunately, I was able to finish putting up the gutters.

SECOND FLOOR

After a few years it became evident that we needed more room. The number of girls in the family was growing and space was becoming a premium. I learned very quickly, with girls privacy was essential. More rooms were required. The obvious plan was to replace the roof and entire second floor. We would convert the saltbox to a full Colonial.

The weather man had predicted beautiful weather for the weekend. Good. Dad Hackeling, Pops Corry, Tom Duddy, Gus and Jeff had promised to come out this weekend and help us replace the roof. Pops came out early that Friday which allowed him and me to cut open a quarter section of the roof. We covered that with plastic sheeting before quitting for the night. Just in case.

Well, that night a summer thunderstorm erupted and poured ton's of water on our half opened roof. The rain came down in buckets full. Unfortunately, the plastic covering I had stapled to the opened portion of the roof didn't hold and the water poured into the ceiling above the top two bed rooms. The sheetrock on the ceilings started to bow from the weight of the water. Sooner or later they were bound to burst and the upstairs would be drowned. In addition, the water would flow over the upstairs floors and down into the sheetrock onto the downstairs ceilings. Nothing but disaster.

Fortunately, Pop came up with a brilliant plan. We put buckets on the floor directly under the center of the sheetrock ceiling, and then punched a hole in the center allowing the water to run into the buckets. As they filled, we replaced them with new buckets and dumped the water from the full buckets out the window. We did this until the rain abated and we could figure out a better plan of action. At the very least we prevented the rain water from invading the ground floor. It worked beautifully and once we got into the rhythm we felt good.

All this started about two o'clock in the morning. Our neighbor, Sal was awakened by the thunder and looking out his front living room window saw the buckets of water being thrown out of the upstairs windows. Naturally, he hustled into his clothes and scrambled over to find out what was happening. One look told the entire story. The next thing you knew Sal was part of the bucket brigade. At four o'clock that morning the rain stopped and we went about assessing the damage.

We had confined the damage to the upstairs bedrooms. But it was obvious the house was unlivable until the roof could be repaired. Sal and Rita were great and offered their house for us to bunk with them until the following day.

On that Saturday the city crew arrived about eight o'clock in the morning and after reviewing what had transpired the night before, got to work removing the rest of the roof and installing the walls and roof of the new upstairs. Once enclosed, we assigned different jobs to each of my helpers so as to get maximum return on their muscle.

Jeff and Sal were in charge of covering the roof with the underlayment. A hole had been cut for the chimney and my Dad was in charge of raising the chimney so as to bring it through the hole cut in the new roof. Others had jobs closing in the sides of the outside walls of the new second floor.

As I was helping Sal and Gus with the underlayment Sal was rolling out the black tarpaper. He covered half of the chimney hole going one way and the rest of the hole going the other way with tarpaper. I warned Sal as he was approaching the hole about the fact that with the hole completely covered, someone could fall through. Sal straightened up, looked at me and smiling said, Charlie! Don't you think I know what I'm doing?"

Of course I had no intention of offending Sal, so I backed off and said, "Sorry Sal, I just don't want anyone getting hurt."

"I know," said Sal. "Believe me; I've seen this done a hundred times. First you roll it one way then the other, then you cut an x from corner to corner of the chimney hole and fold them back."

"OK!" I was convinced.

But I was cautious and watched as Sal completed the next row of roof covering. Back he came...bent over with sweat running down his face. Completely absorbed in what he was doing. As he got close to where the covered opening was, I said,

"Sal! Remember the hole?"

Sal stopped, straightened up, adjusted his glasses, smiled at me and said, "Gee! Charlie, I almost forgot."

With that Sal turned towards me and took one mighty step in the direction of the hole. Bam! Sal went through the hole like a shot of ammunition. In an instant he disappeared. All that was left of him was his two arms which were clinging to the sides of the chimney hole and his eyeglasses, which he had just adjusted, were now gradually hopping down the roof towards the edge from which they did a swan dive down two stories to the grass below. Slowly, Sal's head came up in the middle of the chimney hole and with shock written all over his face he looked at me and all I could think of was the WW2 slogan, "Kilroy was here."

I immediately reached down for Sal, made sure he was not hurt and looked into the hole to see what had happened. Fortunately, Sal fell through the hole and landed on the chimney top of the old house and was able to stand up. I couldn't help myself and I started to laugh.

"Sal," I said, "I just told you about the hole. Why did you step into it?"

"I don't know Charlie; I thought it was further along."

I pleaded with Sal to take another job, one less dangerous. I helped him down to ground level and told him that although I could afford to provide for my family, I was not sure I could provide for his as well. Please, take a less dangerous job. Sal went over to mixing concrete. Wouldn't you know it, as he was mixing the concrete his glasses which he had just retrieved, fell into the mix. Before he could retrieve them they were gone. What a day.

The following weekend, my Dad came back out to the Island to finish the job of bringing the chimney through the roof.

"Are you sure you're up to this?" I asked him.

"No problem. I've done this all my life."

"OK! Dad," I said and provided all the concrete Dad would need to complete the project.

That evening, as we were all eating dinner Mae called me aside and asked me to accompany her to the backyard where we could get a good view of the completed chimney.

"Do you notice anything peculiar about the chimney?" she asked me.

I looked hard and sure enough the chimney swayed first to one side then to the other. "Holy crap," I said. "I better get Dad back out and quick."

When I brought Dad out to inspect his afternoon handiwork he took a good look and said, "Yeah, what's the problem?"

"What's the problem?" I said, "The chimney waves from side to side instead of going straight up."

'Oh! Yeah!" he said upon further inspection, "Well just tell everyone Snow White and the Seven Dwarfs live here."

"OK!" Back we went to our stew, coffee and dessert.

TOM'S APPARTMENT

Our first house was an old house, but at the time, it was all we could afford. But with four children and a fifth on the way, it was heaven.

It was on a rainy August morning when the roof started to leak. It was then that I decided to send Mae and the children to her mother's in the Bronx for two days. Nana lived in an apartment on Hillside Avenue. That would give me time to make the necessary repairs unencumbered by the family. By six o'clock, Mae and the children were packed and on their way. As it turned out, when Mae arrived at her mother's, she was told her cousin, Tom, an Irish bachelor, was away and his three room apartment was empty. He lived in the same building as Nana. Nana was on the first floor, and Tom was on the fifth.

"It's just been freshly painted," said Nana, "and Tom wouldn't object to your staying there until the roof is fixed."

Years had passed since Mae lived in an apartment. The adventure seemed to thrill her, in an unusual sort of way. She had been away for over six years. Now she would have a chance to renew her experiences with her mother, father and sister. After dinner that evening, Mae and the children walked up to Tom's. Nana and Pops accompanied them.

"You'll be comfortable here," Pops said. "Just make sure you close and lock the front door before going to bed."

The two boys occupied the couch in the living room. Susan, the oldest girl, slept in one of two twin beds. The baby was made comfortable in a make shift crib. Mae would sleep in the other twin bed. Mae relaxed. She was exhausted. She wondered how Charlie was doing with the roof, but was just too exhausted to call him. Maybe after she had a nice hot bath, she would make the call.

With the children asleep, she drew a hot bath. Nothing relaxed Mae like a bath. She could close her eyes, with water up to her chin and drift off to some faraway place where all was peaceful. And she did. When she awoke, the water was still comfortably warm. She relished her bath, but remembered that she had promised herself to call Charlie. After that, she could crawl under the warm blankets on the bed and sleep. Her bath completed, Mae slipped into her nightshirt and grabbed the handle to the bathroom door. A light tug did nothing to dislodge the door. A second and third try, each with increasing pressure still failed to open it. She grabbed the knob with both hands and jerked with all her might. Still nothing. 'Oh my God!' she thought. 'The door was freshly painted, and now it's stuck.' Mae knocked gently on the door at first, trying to awaken the boys. They were the oldest and the lightest sleepers. Nothing. She knocked louder. Nothing. She pounded on the door and screamed, "Stevie! Michael! Wake up! Help me!"

Nothing. After a full day of traveling and visiting their grandparents, they slept the sleep of the innocence. 'What am I going to do?' she thought. 'I can't get out, and I forgot to lock the door before I took the bath.' Mae tugged, jerked, pushed and ground her teeth. She even cursed, although in silence. Nothing seemed to work. The thought of the unlocked front door offered both hope and despair. Suppose some unwelcome visitor decided to enter? Her children were unprotected. She remembered the conversation with her mother and sister that evening about the burglaries and rapes that were becoming a part of city life. 'Oh! My God!' she thought. 'I must get help! Please God, help me!' If she could only get someone to push on the other side while she pulled, she knew she could dislodge the door. The only way to get help was from outside.

She opened the bathroom window and leaned out, head and shoulders. From the fifth floor she had an unobstructed view of the street from the apartment to the church a block away. To her amazement three women were walking down the street in her direction. 'Oh, thank God!' Mae thought. 'You've answered my prayers!'

As the three ladies approached, Mae called, "Hello! Hello! Up here! Hello!"

The startled women stopped short. They stared, unsure from where the voice originated.

"Up here," Mae called.

The three women quickly put their heads together, mumbled, and then hurried off at a gait three times their normal speed.

"Oh, please don't leave!" Mae called after them. "Please. I need your help!"

Panic was beginning to get its icy grip around Mae. In desperation she looked back toward the church. A man was now coming in her direction, walking rapidly. Mae pulled back instinctively so as not to be noticed. She realized a man would be more likely to respond, but fear was now present. There was no way she could protect her children if the wrong person responded to her plight. The man passed and walked on. Mae looked out again. She was in luck. Evidently there was a service at the church this evening, and a second group of ladies were coming within shouting range. Mae was desperate. With tears in her eyes she screamed, "Oh! Please help me! My bathroom door was painted and I'm stuck inside. I can't get out. Please help!"

The startled women looked up, saw Mae, and asked, "What apartment are you in dearie?"

"Apartment 5D," Mae responded. "Please hurry. My children are asleep in the other room and I can't get out of the bathroom."

The women entered the building, climbed the five flights of stairs, an accomplishment in itself, and knocked on the door of 5D. Mae rushed to the bathroom door and placed her ear against it, awaiting the sound of her saviors. Mae heard a faint knock on the door. 'They're probably not sure it's the right apartment,' thought Mae. She reared back and started to yell, "Open the door. It's not locked. I'm in here. Come in. Please help me!"

Now these two women were from as fine Irish stock as can be found in the City of New York. And fearless, well, almost fearless Mrs. Murphy turned to Mrs. O'Shea and asked, "Should we open it?"

Mrs. Murphy put her ear to the door and heard Mae's muffled cries. "Oh, the poor dear" returned Mrs. O'Shea, and courageously turned the knob of the door. The door opened easily. The kitchen light was on and the women could see directly down the hallway. Mae's voice was pleading from the end of the hall,

"Oh! Please help me!"

There on the couch in the living room were two small boys sound asleep. There is nothing like the sweet form of innocent children to melt even the most frightened hearts. Now, confident and self-assurance, Mrs. Murphy headed directly down the hall toward the bathroom.

"Are you in there dearie?" she asked.

"Yes! Yes!" Mae shouted. "Oh! Thank God! Please, I'm stuck. I can't open the door. Could you push on it while I pull?"

"Yes! Yes! Of course," said Mrs. Murphy. "Come on now Mrs. O'Shea, help me get this poor child out."

Together they applied the shoulder to the door. With the two women pushing and Mae pulling, the door finally gave up its tenacious grip. It came unstuck on the third try.

"Oh! Thank you!" said Mae as she grabbed and hugged Mrs. Murphy.

Mae was in tears, but trying to control herself in order to thank her two fine benefactors. The motherly instinct arose in Mrs. Murphy. She put her arm around Mae and said, "Now, now dear, it's all right! It's all right!" Turning to Mrs. O'Shea she added, "See Margaret, Father was right tonight when he said you mustn't be afraid to go to the aid of your neighbor. For when you go with good in your heart, God goes with you."

That night Mae slept an exhausted sleep, but not before she thanked God for Mrs. Murphy, Mrs. O'Shea and the kindly priest, who that night chose to, talk to his flock about the Good Samaritan.

As for Charlie....I was still fixing the roof.

CHAPTER 13

ADJUSTING TO CIVILAN LIFE

We were now completely separated from the Service and life as we had known it was gone forever. From here, we would have to sink or swim on our own. After getting to know some of our neighbors we started to pick out those we really wanted to get to know better. The Liottas were to become our best friends. Sal was associated with the construction industry, so I relied on his advice for many of the things we had to do to make this house livable. In addition, we had to get to know our external environment. Who lived around us and where were the resources we would need in case of emergencies? It was time to examine our neighborhood.

DOUBLE MEETBALLS

Our in-laws, Nana and Pops, lived only an hour away. Today, they drove out to see the new house. They agreed to babysit the children while Mae and I went to dinner. This was our first dinner out for Mom and me since we had moved to Tuscarora Drive.

"Let's go Italian," I said as we drove into the nearby town.

Salvatore's sat on top of the hill overlooking the village. When we entered we were the only couple there. We settled into our seats and ordered a bottle of red wine. We sipped the wine and let the magic of the grapes intoxicate our thoughts. With five children, it had been a long time since we were out together, alone.

I examined the menu. I knew what Mae would order. She loved 'Chicken Parmigiana'. The wine was making me hungry. I wanted something substantial. The menu read Spaghetti and Meatballs, $3.50.

"Can't beat that," I said. "I think I'll have a double order of meatballs."

The waitress, a young girl of fifteen or sixteen, had dark hair piled high on her head. She was short, but the hair added another foot to her height. She ambled over to the table, stuck out one hip, pulled an order pad from her apron, and, while chewing gum asked, "What'll yuh have?"

I gave the order, "My wife will have the Chicken Parmigiana, and I'll have the Spaghetti and Meatballs, with a double order of meatballs."

I smiled at the young waitress and handed her the menus, stressing as I did that I wanted a double order of meatballs.

"No Problem!" said the girl. She turned and swaggered toward the kitchen. The way she wiggled, I thought she might dislocate a hip.

Mae and I sipped the wine and talked softly about our new home and our new life here in Centerport. Without the children, we were like new lovers. It was wonderful to find each other again.

The food arrived. Mae's Chicken Parmigiana' was steaming hot and looked delicious. The cheese was a golden yellow, browned around the edges. The tomato sauce seeped along the edges and promised a delight under the cheese. My spaghetti dish was huge. The spaghetti leaned over the sides of the dish looking like they were trying to escape their final resting place. The red sauce, which covered the spaghetti, was in turn covered with the shredded Parmigiana. On top of the cheese sat two meatballs.

"Excuse me!" I said to the waitress, "I ordered a double order of meatballs!"

"Yeah!" said the waitress, chewing her gum and looking at me as if to say, "So! What's your problem?"

"Well!" I continued, "There are only two meatballs here!"

"So!" said the waitress, looking puzzled, and putting her hand on her hip.

"Well!" I said, "A double order should be four meatballs, not two!"

"No!" the waitress replied, "With Spaghetti you get one meatball. A double order is two. That's what you got!"

"Wait a minute," I said, trying to be patient. "The menu say's 'Spaghetti and Meatballs'. Meatballs is plural. That means more than one!"

"Are you kidding?" the waitress replied, looking incredulously at me. "What's plural got to do with meatballs?"

I was baffled. I couldn't believe the girl didn't understand me.

"Meatballs," I continued, "means more than one. If meatballs are two, then it stands to reason that a double order would be at least four."

The waitress, now annoyed at me, said, "I don't know what your problem is, but a double order of meatballs is two."

I didn't want to ruin the mood that the wine inspired, but I also didn't want to appear a fool. I looked at the waitress and said, "If you only get one meatball with spaghetti, your menu should say, 'Spaghetti and Meatball', not 'Spaghetti and Meatballs.'"

"Sure! Mister! Sure!" the waitress said as she retreated to the kitchen.

I looked at Mae and asked, "Am I crazy, or is it possible she really doesn't get it?"

Mae, deep into her Chicken Parmigiana said, "You're right! I wonder what college she's going to attend."

A PUPPY FOR MICHAEL

The telephone rang as Mae, the children, and I had just finished dinner. I answered, "Hello!"

It was Mae's best friend, and Michael's godmother, Joan. She lived in New York City about an hour away.

"Ready for your dog?" she asked.

"What dog?" I said.

"I want to buy my Godson a dog for his birthday," she returned.

I, who on past occasions has had my differences with Joan, handed the phone to Mae. "It's your kooky friend, Joan," I whispered.

Mae, delighted to hear from Joan, spent the next half hour talking and laughing. "Oh! Joan! A dog! He'll love it!"

From the tone of the conversation, I realized the gift of a dog was a *fete e comple'*. I asked for the phone when Mae was through talking.

"Joan?" I roared into the phone. "Here are the ground rules. It must be a puppy. A German Shepherd, a male, and loveable. Good disposition! Got it?"

"Sure," Joan replied. "I'll bring it out tomorrow." The following morning, I went to work. About eleven o'clock I called home to see if Joan had arrived with the dog.

"Mae, did Joan arrive?"

"Yes!" was Mae's reply. "The puppy is big."

"It is a puppy, isn't it?" I asked.

"Yes!" replied Mae.

"Well, how big can it be?"I thought. "Three months, six months, a year? It's a puppy."

I went back to work in the comfort of knowing Michael finally had his puppy. When I arrived home, I found on the front lawn, frolicking with Michael and the other children, a puppy, the size of a small bear. I got out of the car and started to scream,

"It's too big. I told her a puppy. Where is she? She can take it home. It's a monster. It'll eat us out of house and home. Where is she?"

Very calmly, Mae said in as normal a tone as possible, so as not to upset the children, "She's gone. She had to get home early."

"Gone! Gone!" I repeated, "I told her the rules! A puppy! A puppy! This is a monster. She's a coward! She ran off before I could get home. She did this to irritate me."

I was furious. But as mad as I was getting, so much closer were the children getting to the puppy they had dubbed, Lady.

That evening, after my blood pressure declined to normal, Mae broached the subject of Joan's visit. She told me how good it was to see Joan again. How Joan's car had stalled on the hill approaching their house. How Joan wasn't sure whether it was the hill or whether the car was beginning to give her trouble. She decided to leave before the daylight disappeared. As for Lady, Joan said she was only six months old.

"I think she was just afraid to confront me," I insisted. "She knew I wanted a small puppy. This is a big overgrown bundle of hair and muscle. She's big enough to saddle. She's huge!"

"But the children love the dog," Mae said in Lady's defense, "and it's apparent the dog loves the children."

"She's no pedigree, that's for sure. What is she, a cross between a bull-moose and an Alaskan Bear?" I asked sarcastically.

"She is beautiful." Mae replied.

"She's not even a male!" I lamented. "And she's not a German Shepherd!"

Michael came into the room. He was six years old, with a round head and face, and straight blonde hair. As he entered the room he went up to Lady and gave her a big hug. The dog in turn licked his face as if to say, 'Thank you!'

Then Michael looked me in the eye and said, "We gonna keep her, huh Dad?"

With a sigh of resignation I asked Mae, "Does she have her shots?"

"Oh! Yes!" Mae quickly added. "Joan saw to that."

"She did! Huh!" I muttered under my breath. Then I took Michael into my arms, hugged him, looked at Lady and said, "Welcome to the family, Lady."

And I thought, 'Joan, I owe you one!'

SAINT PATRICK'S DAY PARADE

As life goes on we start to realize that unless we take hold of all the things that go into making our life, it will slip past us before we know it. And we will regret all the time that was wasted when we could have made a significant difference in the lives of all those around us. We now lived in a small house, in need of many repairs, but what we most required was the will and determination to make this small house a home full of many loving wonders. We were determined to make life at 74 Tuscarora Drive one of the happiest homes in all of Long Island. It began on our very first Saint Patrick's Day after the closing.

Mae was feeling down. There was very little Irish music on the radio and there didn't seem to be any spirit in the community. Mae was determined to fix that. She rounded up all the children in the neighborhood, made shamrocks out of poster board and told the children these were badges that made them official St. Patrick Day police. She went through our entire case of music discs until she found one of Irish music. This one she put on our little hand held recorder and with an American and Irish flag flying, marched the children, single file around the neighborhood. Over to the stores the children paraded, singing Irish party song at the top of their lungs. Around the beach club community they went, down Tuscarora Drive and up Ridgefield Drive until they arrived back at 74 Tuscarora Drive. Believe me they were tired, sweaty, and hungry. Mae had a bunch of cookies and Kool Aide ready for her team of Irish fighters, even though the only true Irish person in the parade was Mae. But it brought the community, which up to now was almost invisible, to life. Parents came by to say their child had the best time in Mrs. Hackeling's parade. We were starting to be recognized. Thanksgiving and Christmas were fast approaching.

THE POWER OF SUGGESTION

In our house, Christmas Eve was always hectic. Not only is it the eve of Christ's birth and arrival of Saint Nick's visit, it's also Susan's birthday.

On one Christmas Eve, I remember Mae saying to me:

"Tonight should be special. Make sure you get Susan a Barbie Doll. Susan's been asking for one all year and tonight we should give her one."

I grunted and headed for the door. I knew this evening would be a long one. I bought the Christmas gifts for the children; plenty for everyone. But Mae insisted on a Barbie Doll for Susan's birthday. As yet, I had not found one. The air outside was cold, raw, and I was reluctant to leave the warm house but the thought of the Barbie Doll haunted me. 'Oh well! Another trip won't kill me,' I thought as I headed for the car.

The stores, a short distant from home, were brightly lit, this night before Christmas. I entered the toy store and said to the clerk, "I need a Barbie Doll. Got any?"

"Sure!" the clerk said, adding, "Have you seen the new Barbie Doll Showcase?"

"No! . . . Where is it?"

"Over here! . . . Isn't it a beauty?"

"Sure is!" I said as I examined the gadgets on the Showcase. "She'll love it. I'll take it!"

"Want some clothes for Barbie?" the clerk asked.

"Sure. Throw in a couple of sets."

Bundling up, I climbed back in my car and headed for home. The party that evening was a smashing success. Mae was right, Susan jumped with joy at the sight of the Barbie Doll.

"Put the showcase together, Dad!" she pleaded. Nothing comes assembled these days.

"Sure Honey!" I said and joined her on the living room floor. Susan played with Barbie while Daddy began the chore of assembling the Showcase, piece by piece.

"This is the best birthday ever!" Susan said as she smiled at me.

I returned the smile, but sensed I was in for a long night, as my finger tips began to ache from bending the little metal tabs that held the Showcase together. What I thought would take a few minutes, passed into an hour. Father and daughter were consumed in their respective tasks. Susan spread Barbie's clothes on the floor. Each set of clothes had to be modeled. I struggled with the Showcase.

"Daddy," Susan said, annoyed at a hat that didn't fit. "I can't get this hat on Barbie! Can you help?"

I leaned over, absently took the doll and the hat, and began to fumble with the doll's head. 'How hard can a hat be?' I thought. Funny hat! The strap isn't long enough to go around the back of the head and it isn't long enough to go under the chin. I'll bet they gave us the wrong hat.

My attention was divided. I was trying to put the hat on Barbie, while my main concern was finishing the Showcase assembly. The instructions were as clear as mud. I was lost in thought as I continued to struggle with the hat and getting it onto the Barbie's head. Finally, in frustration I handed the doll back to Susan and said, "I don't seem to be able to get the hat to fit. Maybe your mother knows. Take it to Mom, in the kitchen."

Susan hurried to the kitchen. I went back to the Showcase. I was in deep thought, when, from the kitchen I heard Mae exclaim, "I know he didn't have a sister, but he had a mother. This isn't a hat, it's a brassiere!"

I was stumped. I thought for a moment, then shouted back in the direction of the kitchen, "I thought there was something familiar about that hat! Must have been the strap! No clips!"

THAT CHILD GOES

Everything doesn't always go exactly as planned. Trying to raise eight children and paying particular attention to each of their needs can take a real toll on a body.

One winters evening I arrived home and hadn't taken my hat and coat off yet when behold, before me was Mae in tears, sobbing and pointing to the bottom flight of stairs. There, perched on the next to last step was Denise. Right thumb in her mouth, left hand twisting her hair in little circles, with eyes that flashed defiance at every turn.

"Either ... that child ... goes ... or I go!" was all Mae was able to shout at me.

Then after a short period of time she continued, "I love her so much but she twists me in circles. She enjoys inflicting pain on me. What am I to do?"

I looked at Denise and then at Mae before I said, "But Mae, she only four years old!"

"I don't care," Mae replied, "I swear she stay's awake at night and plots against me!"

"But Mae," I continued, "She's only four years old!"

"She torments me and is defiant at every turn. Why? I love her so much but she pushes me to the very edge."

"But Mae, she's only four years old."

Mae was beside herself. I knew she loved Denise as much as I did but Denise did seem to enjoy pushing her buttons.

I let my coat fall to the floor along with my hat and walked over to Denise and sat down next to her. Mae retreated to the kitchen in tears, completely defeated. Mae was really stressed out. She was losing control and all I could think of was how much Denise was exactly like her mother.

I called to Mae, "Mae, I know you love her. She does have a streak of defiance in her. It's what gives her determination. But where would I take her. She's only four years old?"

"Please Charlie, what am I to do? She has to go! Either she goes or I go!" . . . was all she could say.

I moved over to Denise still sitting,

"Denise," I said as I tried to put my arm around her, for she was struggling to free herself, "you know Mommy and Daddy love you very much. Why do you torment Mommy?"

What a silly question to ask a child of four. I knew the answer was, "Because!"

I knew my next move was out the front door if I didn't bring this to a satisfactory conclusion so I released Denise, kissed her on the top of the head and said, "You know Mommy and Daddy love you very much. More than we love ourselves. Now go play with the other children."

I then went into the kitchen, took Mae in my arms, swore I would be personally responsible for Denise and kissed her on top of the head. . .twice. After all, she was only four years old.

NANA, ONLY TWO RULES

Now there was the time when it became our turn to care for Nana. Disregard the fact that there were already ten people living in the house. Could one more make a difference? It could if that person was Nana.

Kate and Jeff were just leaving, having dropped Nana off at our house. For the foreseeable future, Nana would live with us. As they waved good-bye from the driveway, I looked kindly at my grand-old, ailing, Irish mother-in-law and said,

"Nana, please come in. I want to talk to you."

Now that Nana was to live with us, I wanted to set down guidelines. I had witnessed the damage to self-esteem that Nana inflicted on my nephew Jeff. Several years of critical Irish humor was cruel and unnecessary. Nana had a way of ridiculing Jeffrey, unmercifully. Jeff's father had deserted the family when Jeff was thirteen. He was old enough to sense the rejection, but not old enough to understand the fault was with his father, not himself. It was a sore and sensitive area with Jeff. The worst thing Nana could do was remind him of his father's desertion. And she did it at every opportunity.

She also played favorites. John, Jeff's younger brother was her favorite. I must admit John was a good boy. Jeff was more the Tom Sawyer type. If there was trouble to get into, Jeff found it. On those occasions, Nana reveled in reminding him, 'Why can't you be more like John?' Years of this Irish torture had taken its toll.

I would have none of this type of berating in my house. My children were too important to have Nana, or anyone else

270

for that matter, tear down their self-esteem by ridicule or unfair comparisons.

I sat Nana down in a comfortable wingback chair in the living room. As I carried a chair over so that I could sit directly in front of her, I said, "Mom, I want you to know that my house is your house and you are as welcome here as anyone else. This is now your home."

"Ah! You're too good to me!" was Nana's reply, as she let the words roll off her tongue with her delightful Irish brogue. She looked at me with the smile of a child on her face, but I could tell, behind that smile lurked the spirit of the Banshees.

"Don't be silly, Mom, I love having you," I continued. "But if we're all going to live together in one house, we have to have rules."

"Ah!" sighed Nana as she reached her hand across the space diving us and patted me on the knee. "You're better than a son to me." She looked me in the eye with the warm affection of a puppy-dog.

"There is only one problem," I continued, knowing Nana wanted to defuse the pending rules. "In this house, we have two rules. If everyone obeys the rules, we'll all get along." I paused, then continued, "The first rule, Mom, is that nobody gets 'round the clock' care. Everybody, who can, must do for themselves. You understand that?"

"Oh, sure I do. You're a fine boy."

"The second rule, Mom, is," and here I paused, as if to accentuate that which was to follow, "if we can't say something nice about someone, we say nothing at all." I stressed and repeated the 'nothing at all' part. "Is that clear, Mom?"

"Ah! You're such a good son-in-law. The best that I have. You'll have no trouble with me," was her response. But I knew that old habits die hard. So I reinforced the rules.

"Remember Mom, there are only two rules . . . .. One, don't expect someone else to do the things you can do yourself, and, two, if you can't say something nice, say nothing at all. I mean that." A shake of her head and the smile on her face assured me that Nana understood everything I had just told her.

Feeling pleased with myself at how deftly I handled Nana, I started to get up when Denise, fourteen, and the third of my six daughters walked into the room. Nana seized the chance to change the subject and, looking at Denise asked, "Denise, did you get a new haircut?"

"Yes! I did. Do you like it?" asked Denise in return as she touched her bobbed hair with her hand, smiled at Nana for noticing, and started to twirl around so Nana could get a full view.

"No!" came Nana's terse reply. "It looks terrible. You look like a boy."

I slumped back into my chair. Our talk wasn't thirty seconds old and already Nana had broken rule # two. I immediately went to Denise's defense and said,

"Denise your hair looks beautiful. I like it." Then turning my gaze on Nana, I said, "Nana! . . . .. Remember the rules? There are only two. How could you forget so quickly?"

Denise left the room in a huff. I sitting rather dejectedly, on the verge of exasperation, looked at Nana and said, "Mom, you just broke rule number two! The rules. . . . . . . .remember the rules?"

Nana smiled impishly at me, and returned, "Oh! Don't be silly, the first time don't count."

I knew Nana's stay was to be a long bumpy ride.

JEFF & JOHN

One last story before we move on- this one concerns Jeff and John. I have one serious flaw in my life that I'm constantly aware of, and that is that I didn't pay enough attention to Jeff and John while they were growing up. I wish they had spent more time living with us.

Mixed in during these years, we had occasional visits from cousins Jeff and John. John, as many may remember, would only eat baloney sandwiches. No matter what else we were eating, John would ask for a baloney sandwich. There were times I wanted to hit him off the head with the damn baloney sandwich. He reminded me of my brother Ron and his peanut-butter sandwiches.

It wasn't until years later I found out I was referred to as 'The Up To Bed' Uncle. This goes back to the summers when Jeff and John would spend time with us. They were younger then. Jeff spent more time with us because he was the same age as Steve and Michael. Jeff also spent time with us immediately after graduation from high school.......well almost graduation. At his graduation party, that his mother was throwing for him, he took me aside and said, "You see Uncle Charlie, I really didn't graduate."

"What do you mean?" I asked. "Your Mom is throwing you a big God damn graduation party!"

"Yeah! I know! You see, Mom doesn't know I didn't graduate. It seems I don't have enough credits or something."

"Or something?" I said, looking him in the eye.

"Oh! I just have to get some gym credits. I can get those standing on my head. But until I do, I can't get a graduation certificate."

"Listen, maybe you had better start standing on your head. In the mean time, I'll ask your mother if you can spend some time with us. Then we'll go over to see a friend of mine, Jim Malone. He's a guidance councilor at Harborfields, H.S. and he can help us sought through your mess. This way we can get you to finish high school and start college. Your mother never needs to know that you really didn't graduate. OK?"

Well as it ended up, Aunt Cathleen was left with the impression Jeff graduated and the party went on as planned. Jeff never said another word about his dilemma, and we all settled on Jeff living with us for a few months while he got established in college. Of course he had to finish high school first, but no one needed to know that. Fortunately, Jim Malone was able to get Jeff the courses he needed to get his high school diploma. Once Jeff had that in his back pocket he was able to sign up to be a full time student at Oneonta College. With a little help from Uncle Tom (Tom, as in Flanagan), he graduated from there four years later. Thank you Jeff . . . . . Thank you Uncle Tom.

THE CAR

I have to tell you of my experience with my once new car.... my AMC Hornet Station Wagon. Oh! It only took three years and it was ready for the junk pile. I just have to get this off my chest.

I'm beginning to wonder whether there is any limit to my patience. My wife on the other hand, wonders if there is any limit to my stupidity. I had just completed the last three miles of my journey from my office in Greenlawn to my home in Centerport. What's unique about that is I completed it on foot. I walked! Not by choice mind you, but by necessity. For the umpteenth time my automobile failed me. Conked out and refused to start. As I walked the three miles, on this hot muggy June afternoon, I had plenty of time to contemplate.

In 1975, four years ago, I purchased new, an AMC Hornet Station Wagon. In justice to the manufactures, I must admit it worked fine for the first year. After that, it was one disaster after another. Something was always going wrong, which required dealer maintenance. The car was in the shop more than on the road. But I had AMC's 24,000 mile or 24 month guarantee. The 24,000 miles came in 14 months. When the 24,000 miles appeared on the odometer, the roof caved in, the suspension system needed replacement, windows leaked, mufflers and tail pipes were replaced, the radio stopped working, the heating system would only work in the middle of summer, the doors sprung loose, and the springs in the seats came apart. At 45,000 miles the engine blew. I was going to say that nothing on the car functioned properly, but that would be an exaggeration. The paint didn't peal. But everything else failed. AMC, keep the paint, don't change that.

It was an experience to be on the Jersey Turnpike one February morning, in a torrential downpour, when I heard what sounded like a blowout. I pulled over to the side of the road with a dead engine, only to find a hole 6 inches round in the side of the engine block. A piston rod had blown. Talk about feeling helplessness. There I was standing in a torrential rainstorm, one hundred miles from home. No one in sight but the cars on the turnpike that raced pass me at seventy miles an hour.

But the points of my comments are not about my patience or the vehicle, but the indication of what they represent. The car was unquestionably, a hunk of junk; a disgrace to American engineering. But it is systematic of the "built in obsolescence" philosophy that seems to permeate the entire American work force. Gone are the days when workers took pride in the quality of their work. The new philosophy is, *do as little as possible, as poorly as possible, and get away with it.* After all, the more things break the more work there is in replacing them.

As I walked in the hot sun I wondered why I was taking this insult so tolerably. Had this occurred in the days of our pioneering forefathers, my great-grand-father, having received a defective horse for example, would have returned the horse to the dealer, received a refund, or blown the dealers head off.

Oh! I know! We're more civilized than that now. And such action would really be uncalled for. But in contemplating my situation, I'm amazed that I am so powerless in the face of what is a massive fraud. The automobile industry, has conditioned us, the public, to accept crap. They have done away with the concept of 'pride in workmanship.' They have conditioned us to want what is new and discard what was yesterday's.

We've so embraced that philosophy that we have reached the point where we will accept, patiently, whatever big brother deems advisable to give us. We have abrogated our right to choose. We failed to recognize all awhile that, industry was molding a new value for us. The value of newness. If what we give you today is junk, forget it, be patient, tomorrow you can buy newer junk. We were lulled to sleep with the concept of newness, while the automobile industry established its new value-profit.

Profit above everything else. Even life. Review the Ford Pinto's history. It is better to let some die than recall vehicles with potentially deadly defects. Why? Because the cost to the company will be less even with the loss of a few law suits. Profit is king.

I wonder as I sit here now at my desk, more relaxed than when I first walked through the door, body temperature back to normal, whether there is any hope for us- the consumer. Will we continue to practice patience? Are we really so helpless in the face of 'big business'? It appears that way.

Look at your car. New? If it is, it's probably because Madison Avenue told you it should be. If it isn't it's probably in need of constant repair. Can you imagine if God designed us the way the automobile companies designed their cars. Hands would fall off; legs would break, to say nothing of our heads and other vital parts.

I think I'll go out and repair my son's 1960 Volkswagen Bug. It still runs. My AMC? It's on the side of the road in the next town. With a little luck, maybe someone will steal it. They'll have to tow it though.

CHAPTER 14

DAD'S TIE

Kathleen was our seventh child and a true pleasure. When she was in the sixth grade she decided she would make a tie for me as her Father's Day gift. Sunday, being the day set aside for fathers, Kathleen presented me with the gift she had labored over for almost three weeks. It would have made a beautiful wall hanging. But it was a tie. It was one inch wide at the tail, four inches wide at the face and six feet long. It was red plaid, and made of a thick, course material better used for tapestries. But the tie had one quality all other ties lacked. It was made by Kathleen.

We were seated at breakfast the Sunday morning she gave me the gift. As I opened the box she sat quietly in her chair, eyes cast down and a shy smile stretching from dimple to dimple. I could see the pride and love she put into that tie reflected in her every move. As I opened the box, Mae said, as if preparing me,

"Kathleen made this at school…with her own two hands!"

I opened the box, withdrew all six feet of tie, held it above my head and exclaimed, "Why Kathleen, I had no idea you were so talented. The tie is.... beautiful. I'll wear it tomorrow when I go to work."

Getting up from my chair I walked around the table to where she was sitting, displaying the tie to the other children as I moved.

"Thank you darling," I said as I bent over and covered her with kisses.

That evening as I was getting ready for bed, I asked Mae, "What did you think of my new tie?"

"Oh! Charlie!" she said, obviously pained, "She worked so hard on that tie. I don't know what to tell you. Will you wear it?"

"I can't wear it to work," I said. "But I'll think of something."

Early Monday morning, I arrived at the breakfast table dressed in my best blue suit and my newly acquired red plaid tie around my neck. It is true the knot at my throat was large. It looked like it was two inches across and big enough to cover two buttons. The tail of the tie, about a foot and a half of it, was tucked into my pants. The face of the tie looked more like a bib. But I wore the tie with grace and class. Kathleen, already at the breakfast table, beamed. Tracy, younger than Kathleen by three years, was already eating her cereal. Tracy never missed a meal. She glanced at me, smiled and said without hesitation,

"I like it!"

"So do I," was my reply, as I puffed out my chest and smiled at Kathleen.

When breakfast ended, Kathleen delayed leaving for school, obviously waiting to see if I was really going to wear the tie to work. I picked up my briefcase, kissed Mae, and then Kathleen. As I was getting into my car, I rolled down the window and called to Kathleen,

"I'll be the best dressed salesman in the office today."

She smiled and ran down the driveway to catch the school bus.

When I arrived at the front door of the office I fished out of my pocket a concealed silk tie. I looked at it, looked at the tie around my neck, and thought, "What the heck. I'll wear Kathleen's. It comes with a lot more love."

When I returned home that evening, Kathleen was the first to greet me. I noticed how carefully she examined the tie around my neck. She said, "Do you really like the tie, Dad?"

"Of course I do," I responded, pretending offense at the very thought I might not.

"Good!" Kathleen continued, "I'll make you another one!"

DENISE & SMOKING

One thing I was always proud of was none of my eight children smoked. At least that was what I thought. Until one day, after dinner, I was in the vestibule of the house when one of the children said,

"Dad, Denise smokes!"

It came like a bomb shell exploding under me. "What do you mean, Denise smokes?" I asked, half in a state of shock.

"Just that… Denise smokes cigarettes," said Maureen.

As it happened, for some reason Denise was upstairs in her bedroom when the news was given to me. Although there are fifteen steps going from the entrance to the house up to the second floor where the bedrooms are, it took me only two steps to go the fifteen, while yelling at the top of my lungs, "Denise! Where are you?"

Of course I found her in her bedroom, quietly sitting on her bed doing her journaling, very unperturbed that her father was standing in front of her about to have a heart attack. I began my tirade about the dangers of smoking and how dangerous it was to life and limb. What could happen, the illnesses she could come down with, etc. When I finished I just looked at Denise, steam coming off my head, my face as red as a beet. I asked her for an explanation as to why she would do such a foolish thing as smoke.

Denise calmly looked at me uttered those infamous words that every teenager thinks will get them off the hook,

"So what! It's my life! I like it!"

That was all I needed. I exploded. "Your life? You think it's your life? Let me tell you something young lady, the last fifteen years have been out of my life...out of my hide. You're only here because of the grace of God and the effort of your mother and I. It's a miracle every time a parent can bring a child along for fifteen years and get her to that point without some catastrophe or another. There's danger around every corner and it takes a little piece of the parent's life every time there is even a drop of a child's blood that's spilled. The parent feels it most of all. It's not your life. It's my life. And your mother's life, so don't you think for a moment that it's your life. It's not! Don't ever let me see you with a cigarette in your mouth or even in your possession, because I'll forget you're fifteen, sixteen, seventeen or any other teen and you'll be treated like a two year old."

I was shaking with controlled rage. With the tirade over I walked out of Denise's room and went down to the kitchen where Mae was finishing up the supper dishes. I leaned up against the kitchen sink, spent, sweating, and at a loss for words. I was a man defeated. I looked at Mae and sadly said,

"I guess I didn't handle that very well, did I?"

MARY, PAUL AND QUASIMODO

One evening, just after dinner, Marianne had the nerve to tell me I wasn't nice to her new boyfriend Paul when he came to pick her up for a date. This was all because I didn't acknowledge his presence in the room. In my defense, I was busy reading the paper. The following story reveals how I had some fun with said boyfriend and, at the same time, had a hand in getting rid of him.

Mary was sixteen, sweet, beautiful, and popular. It seemed she had boys chasing her since she was five. But no boy is ever good enough for a father's daughter, and Mary was no exception. Besides, I didn't like the idea of Mary dating at such an early age. Thirty, in my mind, was a better age.

Mary wanted to go to the Senior High School dance with a new boy, Paul. But Mary was only a sophomore. And besides, I liked to get to know Mary's dates before giving my approval. Mary realized I would have to meet Paul, and that could be a problem. The dance was only one day away. Mary decided to meet the problem head-on.

At dinner that night, she turned to me and said, "Dad! I'm going to the dance tomorrow night with Paul."

"Who's Paul?" I asked.

"That's what I want to talk to you about," Mary continued. "He's very nice, and I want you to be nice to him when he comes to pick me up."

"Oh!" I replied, as I paused and gently placed my knife and fork on the table. My eyes lifted from the dinner plate and looked directly at Mary, who was avoiding my gaze.

"Why?" I asked, "What's wrong with Paul?"

"Well!" continued Mary, "There are a few things I think you ought to know about Paul before you meet him."

"Like what?" I asked, my eyes narrowing my suspicions aroused.

"Well!" said Mary, "For one thing, he drives a truck."

"Strike one!" I shouted and stuck one finger into the air above my head.

"For another," Mary continued, ignoring my remark, "He wears a leather jacket."

"Strike two!" I shouted emphatically, shoving two fingers into the air.

Mary continued, ignoring my behavior. "And the third thing is," she paused, "he's going to get a tattoo!"

"Strike three!" I shouted and jumped out of my seat giving the umpire's signal, "He's out!"

I looked at Mary, smiled a devilish grin, and followed up with, "Got anyone else in mind?"

With strike three still ringing in her ears, Mary turned to her mother on the verge of tears and cried, "Maaaa!!!"

Mae looked at me as I was now resettling with great satisfaction and said, "Charlie, he's really not that bad."

I looked at Mae, then Mary, again at Mae and said, as innocently as possible, "I gave him three strikes!"

Mae said to Mary in a quiet tone meant only for Mary to hear, "We'll see Mary. Don't get upset. I'll talk to Dad."

And so she did.

The following evening, when Paul arrived to pick up Marianne, I insisted on meeting him. Paul was wearing a tuxedo. The collar was tight, and beads of perspiration dotted his forehead. He carried a bouquet of flowers for Mary and a single rose for Mae. I wondered where my rose was. Paul's dark hair was slicked back. His face, freshly scrubbed, was red with embarrassment. Mae welcomed him and took Paul into the living room to meet me. I, at six feet and two hundred thirty pounds towered over Paul who was five six and maybe one thirty. I looked at Paul as only a father can look at a competitor for his daughter and said,

"Paul! Do you know who Quasimodo is?"

Paul looked puzzled. Mary entered the room and Paul seemed to seek refuge behind her.

I continued, "I thought not! Well do you know who the Hunchback of Notre Dame is?"

With this said, I put my hands on my hips and stared at Paul, waiting for a response.

"Oh! Yeah!" Paul said smiling, proud of himself for knowing the answer.

"Well," I continued, "Quasimodo is the Hunchback! You know how crippled he is. Well, if Mary isn't home by the strike of midnight, you're going to look like Quasimodo before you leave here. Get my drift?"

"Huh! . . . Oh! Yes, er . . . Yes . . . Sir!" Paul shuddered at the thought, and his puzzled look turned to one of fear and confusion.

Mary grabbed Paul's arm, swung him around and headed for the door. As she was leaving she turned to look at me and said, with some embarrassment,

"Thanks Dad! That's all he needed!"

At the stroke of midnight, Mary was home.

KATHLEEN

Kathleen introduced Mom and me to the marching band. Of course I had to drop her off at band practice every day, and although she protested, I knew she loved it when I would send her a kiss by blowing it across the parking lot. Of course I had to get out of the car, stand on the front seat so I could elevate my voice and shout at the top of my lungs,

"Kathleen, I love you!"

To this day I do not know what children find offensive about the words 'I love you'. Her friends use to like it! Now admit it Kathleen, you did love those kisses, didn't you?

Kathleen played the flute and was getting very good at it. When Mae's father died, Kathleen played Danny Boy at the end of the funeral ceremony. It brought tears to every eye.

Kathleen was very tall for her age and when she was involved in gymnastics she would injure her shin bones by hitting the lower bar with her long legs. Every time she hit the bars I use to cringe. Anyway, Kathleen found another sport she excelled at, dance. I was unaware of it but she had been taking lessons.

One weekend Sal Liotta, his family, Mae and I and our entire family were invited to a dance recital featuring Kathleen. I believe it was at Washington Drive Auditorium. Well! I couldn't believe my eyes.

Kathleen was the star of the show and she danced like a Hollywood star. What a show. As we were leaving the theatre, Sal, our neighbor and Kathleen's Godfather, who rarely says nice things about school plays, leaned over two rows of seats and said to me,

"Charlie, that was better than a Broadway show. Kathleen was outstanding."

Of course she was… she's his Godchild.

TRACY

When it came to children, our eighth and last child was Theresa. Tracy was her nickname. You older children say we spoiled her, but if you ask her she will tell you that is not true. She will tell you she earned everything she got. And you know something? She is right! She did!

I spent a lot of time watching soccer games and helping her through some tough losses. But it was worth it...every minute of it. Tracy's biggest problem became display space for her trophies. When last seen there was a trunk load of trophies stored someplace in Stephen's house.

From the time she was a little shaver Tracy knew she wanted to go to the best college she could get into. Mae and I never had to remind her to do her homework or turn in a report on time. If a lesson had to be in by Wednesday, Tracy made sure it was in by Tuesday.

She was the most determined child; she expected nothing but A's of herself. As a matter of fact, I never remember her bringing in anything but A's.

And when it came to soccer, which was her sport, she excelled. Coaches were clamoring at our door from the time Tracy entered high school. Harvard followed, offering a scholarship...thus they won out, and Tracy spent her next four years there, graduating with honors and receiving the Scholar-Athlete Award her final year. She is some kid. She knew what she wanted, knew what she had to do to get it, and never wavered in her determination. No matter how hard the task, Tracy was up to it.

Way to go!

CHAPTER 15

74 TUSCARORA DRIVE

No history is ever complete without the influence of those immediately surrounding the principal actors. To say I am one of the principal actors would be an exaggeration. All I really am is a Masters of Ceremony, directing the lives and adventures of this family of ten. These ten people have made my life not only meaningful, but also most enjoyable. Then there were times like these:

MAUREEN AND THE BACKYARD FENCE

I was at work. I left on the 5:35 out of Greenlawn for New York City. Mae had just arrived back at the house. The children were ready to head off to school. In order to catch the bus the children went out the back of the house, over the chain link fence, across Defleson's backyard, down 50 feet of road to the corner of Mill Dam Drive and Washington Drive. They could actually walk the short distance to the Washington Drive School, but they liked to take the bus because they could meet their friends that way.

Today started as a cold gray morning with small snow showers here and there. Mae was about to sit down to a peaceful cup of coffee after getting the children off to school, when she thought she heard a whimpering sound coming from the backyard. Sure enough, when she looked out the kitchen window she saw what looked like one of the children's coat hung up on the chain link fence. She couldn't imagine any of the children would go off to school without their coat, so she went out to investigate. When she got to the fence, there was the coat with Maureen in it. What in God's name are you doing here? She wanted to know. Upon inspection Mae found that Maureen had gotten caught on the top portion of the fence. Somehow, the crossed portion of the chain link had penetrated Maureen's behind. There she hung, attached to the fence by the top two thongs of the fence. She was unable to extricate herself and each time she moved the chain link seemed to go in deeper. How both pieces had gotten into her bottom, I'll never know, but there they were and there poor Maureen hung, whimpering and starting to get very cold. Mae couldn't get her free. She was stuck, permanently. Mae immediately took off her overcoat and put it around Maureen to keep her from freezing. She instructed her to keep hanging on to the top of the fence while she went for help. She then ran back into the house and called Sal, our neighbor who lived directly across the street.

SALLY PAJAMAS

Sal had his own estimating business, worked mostly at night, and went to bed when most people were just going off to work. In a frantic state Mae called Sal. Rita, Sal's wife, answered the phone. Mae explained the situation to Rita, who immediately hung up, ran into the bedroom, and pulled Sal out of bed while explaining what Mae had just told her. She started to dress Sal. Sal wanted to see for himself, so he threw his overcoat over his pajamas, put on his slippers and crossed the street, came down my driveway and into the backyard. Sure enough, there was Maureen, tethered to the fence. Once he saw the condition poor Maureen was in he ran back to his house, jumped into his car and drove around the corner to Stanley the hardware man. He jumped out of his car, ran into Stanley's hardware store, went right to the heavy equipment section and got the largest pair of fence cutters Stanley carried.

"Can I help you?" Stanley called to Sal.

"No!" came Sal's response, "I'll explain when I come back," and out ran Sal, overcoat flying open, shears in both hands and back into the car.

Sal was a Scout leader and had been one for many years, so he was used to emergencies. He went into the backyard and with Mae, together they cut the fence so that only about a foot of fence remained attached to Maureen. When she was released from the fence, Mae got into Sal's car, took Maureen face down on her lap while Sal got into the car and headed for the emergency room of the nearest hospital about ten minutes away. Remember now, Sal was still in his pajamas. When they got to the emergency room the doctors were waiting and immediately took Maureen into the operating room where they removed the remaining fence from Maureen's backside. While this was going on Mae realized it was time to pick up Denise at Kindergarten. The school was in between the hospital and our house.

"Sal would you mind going to Washington Drive School and picking up Denise?" Mae asked.

"Are you kidding," Sal said, "What school is going to release a little girl to a man dressed in an overcoat and pajamas?"

"Oh! Yea!" Mae said, "You've got a good point there. Suppose you take Marianne and Kathy, two of Maureen's younger sisters with you, and they'll testify that you are an uncle or something."

The trip was made and the school released Denise after they got the local Suffolk County Police to come to the school and vouch for Sal. With a police escort, Sal went back to the hospital to pick up Mae and Maureen. Sal then went back to Stanley at the hardware store and explained why he wasn't going to buy the shears, but only needed them for this one emergency. Stanley said it was OK, only because he had never before seen a man running around town all morning in his pajamas with a pair of shears in his hands. With a snow storm starting and a little girl in so much pain, Stanley relented and called out to Sal as he left his store,

"Go home Sally Pajamas," and the name stuck.

FIRST FISHING TRIP

While Sal was getting comfortable with his new name, the Hackeling's and Liotta's were getting used to each other and becoming fast friends. I liked Sal and we found there were many things we enjoyed doing together. For example, there was our first fishing trip with the boys; now ages 10, 11, and 12. Sal's son Joseph was 12; Stephen, our oldest was 11, and Michael was 10.

Sal had an outdoor fishing boat that was big enough to hold Sal, myself and the three boys very comfortably. I got home from work (in those days I worked for Grumman Aircraft) and found Sal and the three boys sitting on the fence in front of my house with fishing poles in their hands and smiles on their faces.

"I take it you guys are ready to do some fishing!" I said as I pulled into the driveway.

"You bet!" the smiling faces answered.

We all embarked on Sal's boat and headed out to Sand City, where the fishing was supposed to be good this time of the year. By the time we got to Sand City, set up our tents and got our fire going to heat the dinner Rita had prepared for us, it was starting to get dark. The sun was fading behind some clouds that hung low in the sky and the higher clouds were taking on shades of purple and red. The scene was to die for.

Sal unpacked dinner. Rita packed lobster tails stuffed with crab meat and melted butter. Corn on the cob was our vegetable along with a baked potato with sour cream and, once more, butter. We had chocolate milk for our drink. The dinner was better than you could get at a 5th Avenue res-taurant. We sank our teeth into the lobster and corn and thought we were in heaven.

For desert Rita had prepared strawberry shortcake with whipped cream and berries of all design. After dinner we sat back and enjoyed the campfire and the closing of the sun. Heaven could not be much better than what we had just digested. Michael slid over to me and said he had to go to the bathroom…number two. I explained that was not a problem and he should follow me. I picked up a small shovel and we headed down the beach a short distance but out of sight and sound of the rest of our crew.

Michael stood next to me as I dug a rather deep but nar-row hole. After my part of the job was over I told Mike I'd wait for him a few yards further up the beach.

As I was starting up the beach, Michael called after me and asked me what the hole was for. When I explained to him how people of years ago took care of their hygiene problems he dropped his shovel and told me he no longer had to go. It's amazing how so many problems seem to solve themselves if you let them sit awhile.

VERISANOS BRIDGE

There was one more story that I recall about our visiting Grandpa and Uncle Walter in Florida. We were coming home from Florida after a two week vacation to see my Dad, Uncle Walter, Aunt Helen, and the rest of the Hackelings.

It was a typical February day with the dusk and the sun hidden behind the overcast clouds. We were still driving a station wagon, with the spare tire and several large bags strapped to the car rack on the top. It was a homemade rack and could handle the spare tire and several suitcases. I had the window partially open, the children were in rare form and those who weren't fighting were either asleep or grouchy. My patience was wearing thin and all I could think was, 'Thank God' we only have a few more miles to go before we pull into Tuscarora Drive. What a foolish thought. With the children, even five minutes could wind up being a lifetime.

Then it happened. It sounded like a freight train going over the roof of the car. I don't know how you duck your head in a station wagon, but we pulled in our heads so as to be even with our shoulders while we wondered where the horrific sound was coming from. From on top of us the entire rack, spare tire, suit cases, bags and everything else was sliding from the front of the car to the rear and off the back. Clash, clang, bang. Everything was flying off our car and into the oncoming traffic behind us. Cars were swerving left and right trying to avoid the tire, the suitcases, and . . . each other. Not an easy trick. There was a considerable amount of traffic but I managed to swing the car into the right hand lane and finally up onto the divide. Everyone was screaming except the boys.

"Good driving Dad!" was all they could manage to say. And they meant it.

Good driving indeed. It took the skill of a Mario Andretti to get off this highway and onto the green side space.

I looked at Mae and between breaths said, "Thank God you at least had the presence of mind to put our last two hundred dollars in your pocket before we got in to the car."

As soon as the words left my mouth I knew they were the wrong words. To make matters worse, I continued, "You did put the two hundred dollars in your coat pocket, didn't you?"

Mae's glance from my eyes to her lap told me all I needed to know.

"Where did you put the money?" was all I could get out in short whispers.

"In the suitcase up on the roof."

At this point, I realized there was nothing to gain by exploding all over the car and its occupants, although that was what I wanted to do. I slowly got out of the car and closed the door behind me.

I leaned into the open window on the driver's side of the car and said quite calmly,

"Listen to me very carefully; I'm only going to say this once. I am going to try to dodge the cars on the highway and retrieve as much of our belongings as possible. Hopefully, I may even find all the money we have to our name. In the meantime I want all of you to stay in the car. I do not, and I repeat, do not want any of you to help me. If you do, that is probably the way I will get killed, or you will get killed. Do I make myself clear?" ...

Silence. Nine sets of eyes were concentrating on me very carefully.

"Nobody helps me. Is that clear?"

"Yes Dad," The children said in unison.

"OK! I'm off to get our clothes."

"Don't forget my new underwear," came a timid voice from my own Marianne.

Mae had said nothing.

I started waiting for a break in the traffic. When there would be enough space between cars to allow me time to dash out from the grassy divider, pick up whatever was available on the road and rush back to safety.

First I had to find the clothes, or the tire, or if I should be so lucky, the money. In the darkness of night I had to rely on the car headlights to identify our objects dispersed over the highway. I had to plan how I was going to make my dash. Which item would I get first, which next, etc. Most important was avoiding the cars. Three tries gave me the confidence I needed to make longer and longer excursions. I had piled up two of the suitcases and most of their belongings, parts of the rack that held to the car, and finally I located the tire. It was right in the middle of the highway. I could make it on the next break. When the last car passed me I ran as fast as I could over to the tire and yanked it up under my arm. Gosh! I had forgotten how heavy these tires were. But I cleared the tire and raced back toward the divider. As I ran I spotted what appeared to be Mary's new underwear about seven feet forward of where the tire had been and on the edge of the grass of the center divider. Next trip, I thought.

Sure enough on the next trip across the highway I headed for the spot where I thought I saw the underwear. But when I got there they weren't there. Maybe I overshot the spot. I looked up and down the center divider and was beginning to think I was hallucinating when all of a sudden a car roared past me and the wind from its speed blew over a piece of paper that was hiding the undergarments. Thank God, I've saved at least some of Mary's underwear. As I picked up her undies, directly under them was a roll of dollar bills. Two hundred dollars worth. God works in mysterious ways.

With the clothing retrieved and the money stuffed safely in my pocket, I now had to wait for an opportunity to fly across to the other side. When I did land safely on the right side of the parkway, I collapsed on top of the gear I was carrying and thought it a good idea to just take a moment to catch my breath. As I was drawing in a rather deep breath, I thought I heard a sound that was out of place for this situation. Sure enough, as I raised my head and looked in the direction of my car, here it came barreling down on top of me at full speed. It was all I could do to get out of the way and let out a blood curdling scream. I was ready to kill whoever it was who didn't understand my instructions. The car was not to move.

When the car came to a stop I got up from my kneeling position, blessed myself and walked slowly towards the car. Mae was behind the wheel. I asked in the most controlled manner, "What did I tell you about moving the car?"

No one answered. All sat stone faced looking straight ahead. Oh Well! All's well that ends well I thought.

"Open the trunk and the back door, and we'll get most of what I retrieved back into the car."

"Don't forget my underwear," screamed Marianne.

A glance up at the Heavens and a silent prayer was on my lips as I slowly returned Mary's panties, minus the two hundred dollars. The rest of the trip was driven in silence and believe it or not, nothing else happened, until we reached the front door.

"Who has the key to the front door?" I asked.

Once again, silence. Fortunately, I had a spare key in my wallet and my wallet in my pocket. As I said, "All's well that ends well."

CHICAGO PIZZA

Friday nights were always good nights for going out to dinner with the family.

"How would you all like to go out for dinner tonight? It will be Pizza night and Dad will treat?"

"Yeahhh!!!"

A general round of approval. It was the Pizza that sold the idea. A new Pizza place, called Chicago Pizza, had opened on Jericho Turnpike and was receiving rave reviews. What Chicago Pizza was I had no idea but I was willing to take the chance.

We arrived just ahead of the crowd. We were seated, all ten of us, right next to a party of eight. They were the first in and their order had already been taken. The arrangement of the large room in which we were seated was partitioned by a break in the floor. This portion was an accommodation typically used for the band or whatever other entertainment they had in mind. On this night however, all ten of us were seated in a raised up portion of the floor, right next to the other party of eight. At any rate, we ordered three large pizzas, one pepperoni, one sausage and one cheese. The entire family was in a good mood, it being Friday and a pizza night to boot. As we were awaiting the arrival of our pizzas, someone, not me, decided to play the record machine. *Great Balls of Fire* was their first selection. Little did I realize how appropriate that selection was. As the record was winding up, out came the waitress with the other party's pizzas. They too had ordered three pizzas. It was a very delicate operation to carry three Chicago style pizzas any place, no less over a divided floor. All eyes were watching this young girl moving swiftly towards the table directly opposite us. Just as she reached the table she tripped on the incline in the floor and projected herself and the three pizzas directly at the oldest member of the party. He, realizing what was about to transpire, was trying to dislodge himself from his chair. His girth made that somewhat difficult and he was the recipient of all three pies directly into his lap with the waitress on top. Once the hot pizzas hit, it was amazing how fast the old gentleman could react. He jumped up and spun around so as to dislodge himself from the very hot pizzas. Of course the waitress was full of apologies and was trying to wipe off the cheese and tomato sauce to keep the burn to a minimum. The old man howled, the waitress screamed and my kids went into a bedlam of laughter.

Now, now, I cautioned them. It was not nice to make fun of someone else's discomfort, although I had to confess it was rather comical. In very short order the three pizzas were picked up and deposited in the dumpster. Apologies were coming from all directions and the waitress insured the party they would get the very next pizzas out of the oven. There go our pizzas I thought to myself. Might as well settle down for a longer than expected dinner hour.

While the next three pizzas were being prepared for delivery the waitress decided she would bring the four jugs of root beer that had been ordered. Naturally as she walked across the floor towards their table, all eyes, including mine were glued to her progress. Closer and closer she came to the bump in the floor. Oh! No! She couldn't make the same mistake and trip a second time.

Well, she did. And as she did she pitched the four gallons of root beer right in the direction of the older gentlemen. He couldn't believe it. Neither could anyone else. But there they went, four gallons of root beer hurdled directly at the gentleman trying to cool off his pants from the hot cheese. Not to worry. They would be cool enough soon enough.

When the four jugs of root beer landed, the waitress screamed before she split out the front door and was last seen running for the nearest bus stop. The entire audience was in hysterics. All but the gentleman covered with root beer from head to toe.

Now the manager came out, towels in hand and full of apologies.

"Oh Please! I'm a so sorry. The waitress is new. The dinner is on me."

"No! No!" shouted the old gentlemen, "the dinner is on me."

When our pizza's arrived they were served by the manager himself. Believe me; he was cautious when it came to the step up in the floor.

We left shortly after the laughter subsided and we were able to get ourselves under control. As for the waitress, it seems that was her first day … and it would be my guess … her last.

CHINEESE RESTAURANT MANNERS

There comes a time when you observe the children and their manners, or lack thereof. This happened one evening when Mae had served a meal of chicken over rice. It was one of the children's favorite meals. To observe them you would have thought they were a team of hungry athletes instead of children. I was appalled at their manners and said to Mae:

"Honey, have you been observing the children and their manners? I think it's time we started to give them instructions in manners. Tomorrow night let's take them out to a restaurant and see what we can accomplish."

The following night Mae, the eight children and I started out for the restaurant. We decided to go to the Chinese restaurant for several reasons. One, they had a table big enough to accommodate us all. Second, if we went early enough they wouldn't object to so many children. And lastly, if they ate like pigs we wouldn't have to worry about our friends observing us.

Once seated, I ordered for the entire family. Wanton soup was to be the first course. Second course was to be Sweet and Sour Pork and Chicken with cashew nuts. Dessert was fortune cookies and jello with cream.

With the serving of the wanton soup Mae and I showed the children how soup was to be eaten when out with company. Everything was going along fine. Each child used their big spoon and, while the slow children were finishing their soup the waiter brought around finger bowels for everyone. All hell broke loose when Michael mistook the finger bowl for a drink. When I spied the finger bowl going towards Michael's lips, I quickly tried to correct him and tell him this was a finger bowl, not a drink, but as I leaned over a noodle got lodged in my throat. I couldn't talk and what was worse, I jumped up overturning the table and started spitting over most of the children in my attempt to dislodge the noodle. For a few seconds there was bedlam. Mae was trying to do the Heimlich maneuver on me while I was struggling to get free. The water glasses and ice tea went everywhere but where they were supposed to.

Once everyone was calmed down and realized I was not going to choke to death it was time for the waiters to bring out the main courses. Mae had sense enough to advise everyone that the training session for manners was over and they could go about eating dinner as they pleased. She turned to me and said, "That was a great session. What was it called?"

In my embarrassment I said she could name it anything she liked. For me, it would be,

'What not to do at the dinner table.'

CHAPTER 16

I told you at the beginning that we considered certain friends family. The Duddys, the Flanagans, the Mittens, Les Wooley, the Liottas, and several more. These are people we love and we hope they love us back. Here are some stories that involve them.

BRIDGE WITH THE MC PEEKS

Bill McPeek was a West Point Cadet and met Dad in Tucson. His wife, Barbara, was a hoot! This is how a bridge game with the McPeek's went down at our Tuscarora Drive house.

The game pits Mae and me against Bill and Barbara. Bill dealt and was the first to declare.

"HUMM..." Bill McPeek scratched his head, pulled on his chin, eyes together, neck arched, looking to heaven for an inspiration, "Two clubs!" he said.

I passed.

Bill's wife Barbara responded, "Well finally. Two spades, you louse!"

Mae passed.

Bill replied, "Now, God dam it dear, don't call me a louse!"

"I'll call you anything I want." A pause.

"What did you bid?" asked Bill.

Responding in an exasperated tone, Barbara replied, "I said two spades." She jerked to an erect position.

"I'm sorry, I didn't hear you," sighed Bill.

"Well, you'd better listen."

I offered Bill some peanuts. "Here, have some peanuts Bill. They're making me sick."

"I shouldn't really," Bill replied, "They're not good for the gut, but I think I'll take some anyway."

"You know they'll make you sick," Barbara said rather disgustedly.

"I'll take them anyway," Bill replied.

Taking a hand full of nuts, Bill promptly popped them into his mouth, slid them over to his cheek and then commenced to chew them one by one.

Mae passed and it was up to Bill again. Chomp, chomp, chomp, one by one. Like a volcano about to erupt, Barbara started to smolder. Her neck and face got red.

"I told you I hate that," she spouted at Bill.

Bill, half in a stupor concentrating on the bids, drawn from his state of meditation raised his eyes, puckered up his lips and responded, "What, ... what's the matter with you? Three spades."

"Don't put those peanuts in the side of your mouth!"

"I like 'em that way."

"It's disgusting. Four spades."

"Oh! For god's sake," Bill responded, "I pass."

"About time," Barbara said, and the rest of the table passed.

"You've got it Barb…for 4 spades."

"Humm … I wonder if we shouldn't be in a different suit, Barb," Bill reasoned.

"No, we'll make it."

"I hope so!"

"Don't count on it …" I said.

"If you've got just one trick Mae we'll have it made," I said.

"Humm… could be," said Mae.

Bill put down his hand and Barbara was shocked when she saw he had only one spade trick.

"Drop dead," said Barbara in disgust.

The night wore on much in the same manner. Bill tried harder and harder to win and Barbara grew angrier and angrier by the minute.

"You louse." One of Barb's favorite descriptions of Bill, and in return, Bill's "shut up!" The only thing I got from this sort of bridge was an ulcer, but to keep peace I passed a bottle of Budweiser to Bill, filled Barb's glass with coke and brought out the sour cream and onion dip and the potato chips. Next we settled back to some serious playing. We reorganized. Boys against the girls.

"You better not win," is all Barbara said to Bill as the cards were shuffled and dealt. Both Bill and I got the point. We lost.

BRIDGE AT THE HACKELINGS

Have you ever forgotten to tell your wife that you're expecting company? And what's worse, forgotten it yourself? One lovely Sunday afternoon in late September, Sal, my neighbor, invited my two sons and I to go fishing on his boat with Joseph, his son, and himself.

We returned from the trip about six-thirty to find my wife Mae had already returned the favor by insisting that Sal, Rita and their two children Joseph and Victoria join us for supper. This in itself was not uncommon since we were very close friends, and lived right next door to each other. And having four more for supper was hardly any extra bother since with six children of our own and the seventh only six weeks away, the Liottas were easily lost in the crowd.

With supper over, the children retired to the TV room while Mae and Rita sat back, sipped their tea, and eagerly awaited the stories Sal and I were about to relate to them concerning our trip that day. We were in the early stages of inebriation, having finished three bottles of wine during supper. Two Chianti and one Boudreaux. I slid back in my captain's chair, stretched out my legs and puffed like a connoisseur on the cigar Sal had just given me. Sal, on the opposite side of the table, learned forward, propped both elbows on the table, squinted through his salt stained glasses at the tip of his brightly glowing cigar and giggled to himself. His wind-blown hair and gray stubble beard caused me to remark that he reminded me of Hemingway's old man from the book *The Old Man and the Sea*. He of course retaliated, and justly so, since my condition was no better than his. The most obvious and pungent trait that characterized us both of course was the smell of fish. But to add to the flavor of course was the dry windblown hair, rosy cheeks and eyes half shut. Our turtle neck sweaters, khaki trousers and sneakers added to the picture.

The conversation was just beginning to warm when the phone rang. I reached over from where I was sitting to answer it.

"Hi," said a voice from the opposite end of the phone, "I'm at Link's Log Cabin. Can you direct me to your house from here?"

Obviously confused, I replied, "What's this in relation to?" There was a pause and then a somewhat dumfounded voice replied, "We're the Peterson's. We're supposed to play bridge with you tonight. Eight o'clock, right?"

If a bolt of lightning had hit me, I couldn't have reacted any differently. In one motion I was propelled upward into an erect position. The chair went flying over backwards and with my cigar quivering between my teeth, I responded,

"Oh yes!" Covering the mouth piece, my eyes popped open. I whispered to Mae, who was standing in the doorway to the kitchen,

"Are we supposed to play bridge tonight?"

All of a sudden the same bolt of lightning hit Mae. Her face registered panic as she recalled she had made arrangements last Wednesday to the long overdue bridge game which was required by the school bridge marathon. She let out a scream and went headlong into the kitchen.

That's going to help, I thought. She quickly explained to Rita the situation and both girls cleaned off the dining room table like the Keystone cops. I returned to the phone and gave the Peterson's directions to get from Link's to our house- the long way.

Normally, I would blow my top at Mae for something like this, but tonight I didn't have time. After hanging up the phone I ran to the front door to open it for Sal, who by now had realized what was happening, picked up Victoria, said out loud, "Oh, my goodness" and was running toward the front door.

Sal couldn't stand emergencies. I yelled to the kids in the TV room to turn off the TV, run upstairs and jump into their pajamas. Rita and Mae finished cleaning the dining room. I yelled back over my shoulder,

"They'll be here in about ten minutes. I sent them the long way."

Sal ran across the front lawn like a penguin, his cigar shaking on one side of his mouth and Victoria shaking on his other side. Sal was holding Victoria at arm's length because she had dirtied her diaper and Sal couldn't stand the smell. He never would have picked her up except for the emergency. And even then, he would have left without her had he realized she'd had a load in her pants.

I bounded upstairs, flew out of my old clothes and right into a new pair of slacks and a sport shirt. The children, also sensing the emergency, came bounding upstairs. The oldest ones were dressing themselves while Mae hurriedly threw a new diaper on Marianne and put her into bed. Denise, Maureen and Susan were already in their PJ's. Mae told them they could read in their rooms but don't dare come downstairs. As she left the girl's room, she collided with me in the hall.

"We ate the dessert," she said, "hurry around the corner and buy a cake."

I went out of the house like a shot, over the fence in the backyard, around the corner, and directly into the Deli. I brought a cake and returned the same way hoping I wouldn't run into the Petersons.

The company had arrived. The Peterson's were there. When I entered, the company was already seated in the living room. I introduced myself and hoped they didn't smell the fish on me. As everyone relaxed, I laughed and tried to explain my comment, 'What's this in relation to?'

"You see, Friday Mae and I went to the World's Fair and I spent most of the day signing up for free encyclopedias, World Knowledge, etc. When you called I thought you were one of the agencies calling about an appointment."

"OH!" they said, but did they believe me?

Throughout the course of the evening, over a few drinks and sixteen hands of bridge, we discovered that Bill Peterson and I had graduated from the same school and Bill was working for the firm where I had just interviewed for a position. The evening wore on and the last hand of bridge ended at about eleven thirty. After the Petersons left, Mae and I both settled for a nightcap in the living room.

"We're a fine pair," I said. "You with your wig on backwards and me smelling of fish. We're the social smash of the season."

"I wonder when Bobby and Ethel are going to invite us for tea?" asked Mae.

We enjoyed a good laugh, but I never heard from Bill Peterson's firm. I wonder why?

FREE FOR ALL CAMPING TRIP
(Told by Susan)

It was just early morning, for me at least, when I was awaken by my sisters. They're all younger than I am. I'm fifteen!

"Wake up Sue! Come on! Get dressed and bring your stuff downstairs. Dad's loading everything now."

"Okay! Okay!" I struggled with my clothes and hurried downstairs to meet the rest of the family. Everyone else was dressed and had already eaten breakfast. Now this was your typical family of ten getting ready for a weekend of camping in the Adirondacks. Mother and father were outside loading sleeping bags, air mattresses, duffel bags and everything else onto the roof of a 1964 station wagon which looked and sounded a hundred years old. Steve and Mike, my older brothers, were sitting in the kitchen complaining as usual.

"Oh! Gee! I can tell this will be fun," Mike joked.

Then there was "Mother Maureen," as we called her. She was an eleven years old, going on forty, who knew and applied all the tricks of the trade of motherhood to three-year-old Tracy.

At the end of the driveway, was Denise, ten years old, with a pack of neighborhood boys. She was considered the "cute tomboy" of the family. "Yeh! Well I gotta go you guys, so I'll see you when we get back," she said. As she ran up to Marianne, the next youngest to her, she slapped her on the backside and said, "Hi Skinny Bones!"

"Don't touch my dress with your dirty hands!" Marianne yelled.

There was something about dresses Marianne liked. Even when she played football she wore them. Then there was Kathleen, two years younger than Marianne, three years older than Tracy, and definitely the feminine type. We were all fooling around in the front yard when Dad asked, "Is everything ready? I hope so! Well, let's get going."

"Everyone into the car," Mom said anxiously.

After everyone was settled comfortably, Dad said to us,

"You've all gone to the bathroom, I hope. There are no stops."

Just then five of the girls crawled back out and headed for the house. We waited a few minutes and then, one by one, the girls returned and crawled back into the car.

"Well which route do we take first?" Dad asked, starting the car.

"I don't know, I thought you took the directions," Mom answered.

Dad just sat there, looked at Mom, then turned off the engine.

"Oh no! Well what do we do now?" Mom asked him.

Both of them decided to go back into the house at the same time to look for the map.

"We'll be right back," Mom said to us.

Dad didn't say anything, and we were all glad he didn't because he looked like he might explode. It seemed like we sat there for an hour. The morning had turned into a roasting hot afternoon. With all of us cramped into the car, we started getting impatient.

"Move over, I'm hot."

"Where's Mom?"

Then out walked Mom.

"Okay! We're ready to go. But since it's almost noon, why don't we have lunch and make a fresh start after lunch?"

"Yeah! It's about time," I said.

The boys, as I call my brothers, were totally indifferent to the idea but I was so tired by then all I could think of was that I could have had four more hours to sleep. But looking at Dad's face, I decided not to say that. After lunch we were on our way. Pee breaks were over.....no more breaks until we reached our destination. The ride was unbearably hot but the worst part was that after the first hour and a half, it was boring. We played a guessing game that Dad had taught us. After that, we read some comic books and then played some cards. Stops were occasionally made for sodas and the bathrooms. Dad relented; some of us just couldn't hold it any longer. Of course there were some slight mix ups here and there, taking the wrong turnoffs, or having to take detours which threw the directions off. We managed eventually to arrive at the town of Summit about seven PM and found the camping grounds. The old woman in charge explained where our camp site located.

"You're the Hackelings aren't you? Well, your site is just up that tiny hill there and to the right. In case you need anything just let me know, I've got a little store back here. You can go in through the side door."

She didn't tell us there was a supermarket a couple of miles away. She just happens to own a little store behind the office which had ridiculously high prices. Driving up that tiny hill, our car had a nervous breakdown. While we were bouncing around inside we could hear the bottom of the car scrapping the gravel. It was about a mile to our site which was the size of a postcard. When we arrived Mike said,

"You're kidding! We have to fit three tents on this?"

The total area was about 175 to 200 feet.

"Well who's going to bunk with me?" I asked.

I guess no one was particularly amused at this point. Mom suggested we use the adjacent site as well as our own since no one seemed to have claimed it. When the tents were pitched, Dad suggested we go for a swim. There were mosquitoes and gnats galore! No one had noticed it until we returned from swimming. While we were changing, I kept hearing from the others,

"Those damn gnats bit me on the butt!" Denise said.

While everyone else was getting dressed, Dad helped Mom get supper.

"What shall we have tonight?" she asked.

"Whatever will cook fast. How about your specialty Mom?"

"Okay! Hamburgers it is!" she said.

It was getting dark and slightly chilly by the time dinner was ready. The boys were sent to get some logs and the girls to get some twigs for later. After twenty minutes, I decided to look for some wood myself. Right down the hill was a pile of logs that could keep the fire going for weeks. The boys finally returned with empty arms.

"Where did ya get the wood?" they asked.

"Well, if you opened our eyes and closed your mouth and stopped complaining we might get organized around here," I said.

I told them I didn't want to pursue the argument with them because I could see Mom's specialty was sticking in Dad's chest. When he dropped his hamburger and sighed, I took the clue. Wood was now the one item we didn't have to worry about. But we still hadn't decided who was going to bunk with whom. Right after Dad gave out the sleeping assignments there were objections from everyone.

"Susan, Maureen, Denise, Mary and ..." Dad started, but then was interrupted by Kathleen, "Hold on! We can't all sleep there, and what's worse, something moved back there. I'm not going in that tent."

Maureen then chimed in, "Wait a minute, we can't all sleep together. Mary snores!"

"Oh no I don't!" Mary responded.

Not to be left out of the discussion, Tracy piped in, "Hold on! What's that behind us, up there in that tree?"

Kathleen screamed, "I just saw something fly up in that tree."

Stephen boldly (ha ha) stepped over the line holding up the tent and shook the tree. A bat flew out over our heads and all the girls started screaming.

"It's a vampire!" screamed Denise.

"Sh-h-h! No it's not a vampire, it's just a little bat," Dad claimed as he was trying to get some control over the situation.

"How do you know?" Denise asked him. Dad was reaching the limit of his patience.

"What do you mean, how do I know? I know because I said it! OK? Now that's the end of the discussion and the end of the bat. I'm sure the bat flew away more confused than anyone here."

As the evening wore on everyone found themselves a spot in one of the tents. The girls decided they were most comfortable when they all slept in one tent. Crowed, but comfortable. Marianne started to give lessons on how to fold clothes so they didn't wrinkle.

"You fold them inside out then fold them up and roll them before you put them back in your duffle bag. They make a great pillow and don't wrinkle."

"How can they not wrinkle?" Susan asked.

"I don't know," Marianne answered, "They just don't."

This went on until everyone was so tired they dropped off to sleep. I was still wide awake, just staring out the screen door surveying the land. The only good thing about this camping trip so far was the scenery.

Things began to change the next morning. I woke up early and found myself cramped to the underside of the tent wall. After getting untangled, without waking the entire camp ground, I dressed and started to make bag lunches for later. The plan for today was to visit the Catskill Game Farm and then the Howe Caverns. A friend had given Dad directions on how to get there from our camp site.

"He said it was only a half hour trip," Dad told Mom after we had been driving for a good hour. "Stick to the plan!" and we did. All of a sudden we came upon the Game Farm. "A miracle!" Dad shouted, and we all applauded.

I had the feeling everyone liked the Game Farm except Mom. It all started when Mom went into the llama cage with a hand full of cookies. The attendant said he never saw anyone attacked by these gentle creatures except Mom. As the llamas started for Mom she started running away yelling,

"Help! Get away from me you things."

Just before mom toppled over a bench, the llamas swerved away from Mom and headed for another woman who had a big sandwich in her hands. You should have seen the expression on the other woman's face when the llamas turned in her direction. Pure panic. While the rest of us were laughing hysterically, Dad was over by the bench helping Mom get back up on her feet and brush her off. The other woman had turned away from the herd of llamas, threw her sandwich up in the air and was running for her life. We couldn't have asked for a funnier show. Mom didn't think so. That ended it for Mom.

"Too dangerous!" she said.

FATHER KNOWS BEST: STEVE, CAREER

It isn't every day you get a chance to be a wise father. You rarely recognize the opportunity when faced with it. You hope that when the time does come, you're prepared.

I had such a chance some years ago. My oldest son was home during summer break, having completed his sophomore year at college. It was unlike him to be mopping around the house. He seemed downcast. Very unlike himself. I sensed an opportunity to have a father-son talk.

"Steve! You seem a little up-tight today. Anything I can help you with?" I asked.

"Yeah! Dad! Thanks! There is something that's been bothering me!" he murmured.

What an opportunity, I thought. Father and son talking.... passing on wisdom from one generation to another. We walked into the kitchen and sat in chairs opposite each other.

"What is it Steve?" I asked, concerned, as we leaned toward each other, on the front of our chairs.

"Well! You see, Dad," Steve began, "Here I am, half-way through college, and I don't know what I want to be!"

It was almost more of a question than a statement. But I sensed he was troubled. I sat there staring into his clear blue eyes. I thought, 'Doesn't he have any simple questions? Ones with Yes or No answers?' After what seemed like an eternity, I realized he was waiting for my response. He was asking me to help him make a decision that could alter the rest of his life. Fathers are supposed to have answers. As I looked into his eyes I saw tears and I realized how important my answer was going to be to him. 'God,' I silently prayed, 'give me the wisdom of Solomon.' Moments passed before I finally said,

"Steve, I have the solution for you."

"You do?" he said, bolting upright in his chair.

"Yes, I do!" I said, as I reached my hand across the space between us to grasp his. "When I know what I want to be, I'll tell you exactly what you should be."

For a moment his face went blank. My heart stopped. Did I blow it? Then a broad grin spread across his face and he said,

"I get it, Dad! You're telling me to keep my options open, to put myself in a position to do many things."

"That's right, Steve!" I returned. "As you go through life, there may be several careers you would like to experience. Don't lock yourself out of any, if you can avoid it. An educated man can do many things. Your role now is to acquire knowledge. Wisdom and direction will come with experience."

Stephen stood up, said, "Thanks Dad!" and walked away a different person.

I could see his demeanor change. His step was less fatigued, more lighthearted. After thanking God for the proper words, I thought, 'Boy! This job of being a father isn't easy.'

MIDDLE FINGER

Tracy, age four and our youngest child, was on the back porch, playing with her older, more mature friend, Kathy Cavanaugh. Kathy was five. Ever since Kathy started Kindergarten all I heard from Tracy was,

"Kathy said this, Kathy said that; Kathy did this, Kathy did that."

Kathy, having achieved the advanced station of Kindergartner, knew everything. Tracy awaited her return from school each day so she could hear the important things Kathy learned that day. I, on the other hand, was only her father. As such, I knew nothing. I'm also the family repairman. But I still knew nothing. With eight rambunctious children in the house, there was never a day when I could honestly say I got the edge in the game of "Break the House. Fix the House." It seemed it was always me against them. Not only was I always behind, but I fell further behind every day.

One day I was working on a plumbing problem in the kitchen. Nothing is more frustrating than a plumbing problem. It looks so simple before you start. Only after you have everything disconnected do you find the problem is of gigantic proportion. In addition, the parts you took apart no longer go back together. Don't ask me why! Take my word for it. It's demonic.

I was under the sink trying to fix a leaky pipe. When I started, it was a small leak. Now, several hours into the repair, it was a major leak. Tracy and her friend, Kathy, were in the living room playing. Well, not exactly playing. More like fighting; only not fighting. It just sounded like fighting. It's something God gives little children to punish their parents for having them. The repair was not going well, and my nerves were as tight as violin strings. I was working myself into a state of heated anxiety, and it was easy to blame the noise in the next room as the source of my anxiety. I crawled out from under the sink, on edge and ready to scream. I stumbled into the next room as Tracy and Kathy reached a feverish pitch.

"Stop!" I shouted at the top of my voice. "Be quiet, for God's sake! Be quiet!"

I then went into a tirade of why children should be seen and not heard. I was sweating more than I needed to be. By now, my face was the color of a radish, my hair was standing straight up and my pants were entirely too tight. I explained, in a heated frame of mind, that they were driving me crazy with all the noise. How was it possible that two little girls can make so much noise? As I look back on it now, I realize it was not the best way to handle the situation. But I excused myself on the basis of 'Do It Yourself' nerves.

Having exhausted myself yelling, I turned around and started to leave the room. My head was sunk between my shoulders and I thought of what a fool I just made of myself. All of a sudden I realized there was more I wanted to say. Maybe even apologize. I quickly turned on my heels to read-dress God's gift to fathers: there was Tracy, seated next to and looking at Kathy, with a smile upon her face, the middle finger of her left hand extended in my direction. Kathy was the first to realize that I had turned around. Her smile disappeared and she turned an ashen white. The expression on her face gave warning to Tracy, 'All was not well.' Tracy's eyes quickly darted in my direction. First to my face, then to her hand and the extended finger, then back again to my face. She was caught. I was dumbfounded. Can this be? My daughter, giving me the finger? Tracy knew I would not stand for this kind of disrespect. She had a dilemma. As I tried to think of an appropriate response, she smiled at me, nodded in the direction of the finger and said demurely,

"That's half a peace sign, Daddy."

"Half a peace sign ..." I stammered. "Oh! Of course. That's what you had in mind, is it?" Of course I had completely forgotten what I wanted to say so I turned again and left the room. This time I refused to turn back.

I found Mae, my better half, in the upstairs bathroom and told her what had happened. Mae said, "Ever since Kathy has started school Tracy has been picking up things that amaze me. Most of them bad."

With much indignation I said I was shocked that a child of mine would do such a thing, then added, "But you've got to admit, she's a quick thinker."

That was the last time Tracy gave me the finger. At least I think it was. Of course, as I age, I'm getting slower, and she's getting faster. Anyway, I've learned to take these little surprises for what they are, a part of life. And by the way, I gave up plumbing.

MICHAEL CARLSON

Michael Carlson was my cousin via Aunt Rosalie. He was Aunt Rosalie's brother, therefore my relative. Michael worked for the Budweiser Beer Company. He lived with Aunt Evelyn on Staten Island. But all this is beside the point. The reason for my even bringing Michael up is because of his involvement with Stephen's sixth grade teacher, Ms. Hanratty. The story goes as follows:

It was ten-thirty on a Saturday morning and I was ready to get back to fixing the house when the phone rang.

"Hello!"

"Hi! This is Michael. I'm at Link's Log Cabin. How do I get to your house from here?"

"Michael who?" I asked.

"Carlson!" he replied, "Who else would be calling you at 10:30 on a Saturday morning?"

Not having heard from Michael in the last twenty years, it was reasonable to expect that I was not exactly up to speed. But I'm a quick learner and so I replied.

"Hi! Mike! It's great to hear from you. I'll tell you what. Stay exactly where you are and I'll come down and get you. Be there in five minutes.

I quickly told Mae that Michael Carlson was at Links, and I would go down to get him and asked her to put on another pot of coffee.

When I entered Links, there was Mike sitting at the bar sipping a beer with the owner, Frank Gerts. We exchanged greetings and I led Michael back up the hill and around the block to our home on Tuscarora Drive. When I asked Mike if he would like a fresh cup of coffee, he smiled and asked me if I had any Budweiser on hand. Of course I did and while he continued to drink his form of morning awakening brew, I had a large cup of coffee with Mae.

Naturally we were delighted to see Michael and asked him to fill us in on all the activity from Staten Island. We in turn told him about the children and although he said he was delighted to make their acquaintance, he was obviously ill at ease when they crawled all over him. But he was used to it having lived in close proximity to the Hackeling's and Keeling's all of the last fifty years.

Earlier in the week, Mae had made arrangements to have a surprise party for Sal and Rita. It was to take place at our house that evening about seven. Our neighbors, plus Sal and Rita's best friends, were all invited, including Stephen's sixth grade teacher who was married to a Keeling. As a slight deception we invited Sal and Rita to join us for dinner at the local Chinese restaurant that evening. It got to be about four o'clock that afternoon when Mae asked me quietly when Michael was going to leave. I had to confess I had no idea. We'll play it by ear.

As the day progressed, Michael consumed all of my Budweiser and then graduated to my last bottle of Scotch. When it became time to leave for the restaurant I told Michael of our plans. He was delighted and said he hadn't had Chinese for a long time and relished the opportunity to join us. Well, that settled when Michael was going to leave.

We all adjoined to the restaurant and Sal, who is very particular about his menu, was about to order when Michael interrupted him and declared he would do the ordering. I looked at Sal and Sal looked at me as if to say, Gee! This is nice of Michael to take responsibility for the entire meal. Guess he must be used to doing things like this being a rep of Budweiser. So we let Michael proceed. Michael made the mistake of asking little Stevie, who was sitting next to him, if he liked Chinese food. Steve, of course, shook his head yes.

"Swell," said Michel, "and what would you like?"

Steve gave Michael a big grin and responded, "a hot dog." That settled the request for dinner suggestions.

"We'll start with Bird Nest Soup," Michael ordered the little Chinese waiter. "Then we'll have some ribs and ----- for appetizers. We'll top all that off with roast duck for everyone."

Well it obviously was Michael's treat so we all settled back to enjoy dinner and listen to the wonderful stories Michael was telling us. Michael was a master story teller and he kept us in stitches throughout the evening.

Mae was not concerned about our guests who were already arriving at our house. She had informed them where the drinks and appetizers were and instructed them to start the party without us. We would join them shortly.

As our meal was coming to a close the waiter arrived with the check. A review of the table revealed Michael had already headed for the bathroom. It quickly became obvious that Michel's only contribution to the meal was the ordering. He would not be expected back in time to pick up the bill.

It should be pointed out that all during the meal Michael indulged in his favorite drink, Budweiser. He was starting to totter. But not so much that he couldn't find the bathroom when the check was presented. Cleaver villain. My cousin, my bill.

We arrived home and insisted Sal and Rita join us for a night cap. Michael didn't need one but he wholeheartedly agreed it was a wonderful suggestion. As we entered the house, pandemonium erupted and Sal and Rita were truly surprised. All of their friends were there and as the evening wore on Michael consumed more liquor than any one person was entitled too. I was amassed at how much he could drink without falling over. As the evening wore on and the hour was approaching midnight, Mae asked me if she should suggest to Michael that perhaps he would like to retire to the guest room. I told her I didn't think that was a very good idea because Michael might start thinking she was inviting him to an after party tryst. As it was, Michael was sitting on a large window box next to Stephen's teacher, Ms. Hanratty. He wasn't exactly sitting next to her as he was sliding off the front of the window box and in front of Ms. Hanratty. Out of a clear blue sky Michael bent all the way over in front of Ms. Hanratty, looked up her skirt and shouted for all to hear,

"Not a bad pair of gams Ms. Hanratty."

Mae, Pat Fallon, and I immediately rushed over to Michael just as he collapsed in our arms. Michael had finally had enough.

I asked Mae what sort of grade Stevie should expect after Michael's pronouncement?

CHAPTER 17

SILVER! SILVER! SILVER!

Stephen and Michael were preparing to return to college. Stephen for his final year. Michael for his junior year. Together they had about one thousand dollars more than would be needed to cover their expenses for the year. What to do with this gigantic surplus? Naturally, they turned to me, their father, for advice.

"Do you have any investment ideas, Dad, about how we could double or triple this before graduation?"

Earlier that morning, Art Gregory, my banker, suggested I might consider putting some money in silver. "It's going through the ceiling!" he told me. "Better get in early, before it's too late."

I looked at Steve and Mike and told them what Art had said.

"Do you think it could double by the end of the year?" they asked.

"Art tells me it could triple or quadruple," I answered.

Greed oozed out of their eyes. Ebenezer Scrooge grins spread over their faces.

"Great!" they exclaimed. "Will you invest the thousand dollars in silver for us Dad?"

"Sure!" I said. "I'll call Art today."

About two weeks after the boys' biggest investment, the Hunt brothers were accused of trying to corner the silver market and the bottom fell out. The boys' investment plummeted. Their thousand dollar investment rapidly became a six hundred dollar investment. Much concerned, they came to me, dejected and forlorn, and said with the saddest eyes you could imagine,

"Gee Dad! What did you do to us?"

You can imagine how I felt. I thought to myself, 'Well, I could always replace their losses out of my own pocket. But what would that teach them?' Then it dawned on me. This is one of those special moments between parent and child where wisdom is required, and if dispensed properly, can lead to better things later on. Besides, I wasn't crazy about giving away four hundred of my own dollars.

I turned to the boys, put my hands on their shoulders, looked them directly in the eyes and said, "Steve! Mike! You have just learned a very valuable lesson. When it comes to money, don't trust anyone. Not even your father."

It wasn't much consolation, but years later, after both boys became financially successful, they said to me,

"We never forgot what you said about our silver investment Dad! By the way, how much did you lose?"

I looked at them, smiled, and replied, "Nothing, I don't believe in speculating."

To this day I feel guilty and feel I owe both boys a debt to be cleared some day in Heaven. The moral being that when it comes to money, don't ever give advice.

VACATION AT SHIRLEY'S

Mae, the children, and I were headed for the mountains of Pennsylvania for the long awaited vacation. Mae had doted on the kids and I for years, and she finally put her foot down. We're going for a week's vacation, whether you like it or not, she told me.

"I need it! And twenty years of waiting on you is enough. We're going!"

By the tone of her voice it was evident to me that this was not a battle I should take on. We were to join several nursing friends of Mae's, and their families for a week of sun and fun. Getting reacquainted would be an added benefit. The ride took four hours. Even in our newly acquired station wagon (in the 1960's, Vans were for business, not for families) it was crowded with ten people, and the paraphernalia that accompanies young children and babies. When they arrived and checked in, I instructed Mae to get the kids settled in.

I would unload the car, set up the crib and playpen for the baby, and bring the suitcases into the rooms. Everything went smoothly until I started to unload the suitcases. One for the new baby. Check! One for the two boys. Check! Two suitcases for the five other girls. Check! One suitcase for Mae. Check! Now this is where the problem developed. I had run out of suitcases. Where was mine, I wondered.

The children were excited about the fun that awaited them at the lake. The other family members had arrived earlier and were already at the lake front. Mae and the children were in their bathing suites and ready to depart for the lake. As Mae marshaled the troops for the short trek to the water's edge, I called her aside and said,

"Mae! There's a problem. I've unloaded a suitcase for everyone but myself. Where's mine?"

Mae, exhausted after the journey, replied, "Didn't you pack one?"

"Didn't I pack one!" I responded. "Didn't I pack one? That's your job!"

"My job?" Mae returned. "You're a big boy. If you didn't pack a bag, I guess you don't have one." And off she went with the eight little children in tow.

I sat down dumbfounded. As I pondered my situation I gave thanks for remembering to stick an extra set of underwear in my back pocket. But I wondered who, amongst the new friends I would make today, would loan me a razor?

DINNER WITH LES WOOLEY

Remember I mentioned there were some friends who were so close we counted them as members of the family. Les Wooley was one of them. Dinner parties were always painful for me. I hated dressing up. Felt it was pretentious. A sweat shirt, loose fitting shorts or baggy pants, and shoes that still had bottoms, were my idea of dress-up.

Mae, on the other hand, enjoyed dress-up affairs, especially dinner parties. Tonight was special. We were to dine with Mae's employer and several honored guests.

"You're going to look nice tonight if it kills you," she said, leaving no doubt about her intention. "We're going to dinner at the Steere's," she continued, "and I want you to be on your best behavior!"

"Why?" I whined, "Is the Pope going to be there?"

"No!" Mae said between clenched teeth, "But Les Wooley will. He's the artist I told you about, only you weren't listening!"

"So! I should be impressed because he's an ar-tist?" I said in a sarcastic drawl.

"No!' came Mae's quick response, "But, Les is a little different. And I know you! You'll put your big foot in your mouth before the entree is served." Mae continued, in no mood for a debate tonight, "Les has Muscular Dystrophy. He can't use his hands."

"I thought you said he was an artist," I interrupted, "How in the world does he paint?"

Mae dropped her hands to her sides, let out a long sigh, looked me directly in the eye and said,

"For God's sake! He does! It's a long story, and I don't have the time to go into it now. Get dressed, and remember, be nice!"

'She wants me to look like Lord Fauntleroy,' I thought. 'Be nice! I'll be nice all right!' But I knew better than to pursue the discussion. Certain subjects, sensitive subjects, where I delighted in playing Devil's advocate, were off limits. Not wanting to be embarrassed, Mae launched into the 'Do's and Don'ts' for the evening.

"All right! All right!" I said disgustedly, "I'll keep my mouth shut!"

The drive to the Steer's was less than fifteen minutes, but it seemed a lot longer in total silence. The less said, the better I thought. When we arrived at Howard's, Les, the guest of honor hadn't arrived yet. 'Just as well' I thought, 'I'll need a drink if I'm to survive this evening.'

As the drinks arrived, so did Les. He was in his late sixties, thin, about one-hundred and fifty pounds, and six feet tall. He had gray hair and a wild beard that made him look like a pirate. He wore a large black hat, reminiscent of the Three Musketeers, with a large gray feather sweeping from the front to the rear of the broad brim. He had a black velvet cape from his shoulders to his knees, black shirt trimmed with silver, black pants and black shoes. Over his left eye was a black patch. A large bump stood out on the lid of his good eye. To my horror, two earrings dangled from his left ear. Les didn't just arrive, he swept in. A cane supported him on one side and a girlfriend, Louise, supported him on the other. He entered with a big "Hello!" His hat, removed by his companion, was gracefully swept in front of him as he bowed to the ladies.

'Who is this character?' I thought. 'He acts like the King of England. Looks more like Bluebeard if you ask me!' I had to admit though, anyone who would make such an entry might not have brains, but he had to have guts. Mae's caution returned to torment me, 'I want you to be on your best behavior.' I grit my teeth and thought, 'I'll be good all right, at least for awhile.'

With Les's arrival, dinner was served. Guests had to be seated to adjust for Les's handicap. His companion on his right to help him with his drinks; a friend of sorts on his left to help him with his food. The rest? It was the luck of the draw. I drew the seat directly across from Les. 'Just what I need,' I thought, 'I have to look at, and converse with the ar-tist.'

I was curious about how Les would handle dinner. Who would feed him? To my amazement, Les's companion cut his food into bite size, and put the plate directly in front of him. With effort, Les swung his right arm onto the table. Louise lodged a fork in his hand, and Les, shoveled the food from the plate to his mouth. His drinks contained a straw, placed, so Les could lean over and sip from it. I noted Les rarely let people do for him what he could do for himself. I admired such independence.

Another surprise came with the dinner conversation. Les jumped in with both feet. He talked about philosophy, current affairs, and politics. What's more, he made sense. My opinion of Les was changing. The conversation ultimately got around to,

"What do you do Les?" I asked.

Les said he volunteers lecturing at the local schools where his art was on display. He felt children had a vast potential of untapped talent, but were afraid to express it. By showing them how he could paint, despite his handicaps, he hoped to inspire them. To impress the children with the extent of his disabilities, he made a grand entrance from the back of the auditoriums, to the music of 'Vincent.' It was a struggle to make the long walk alone, but necessary to teach them perseverance. Then he demonstrated his art. Without the use of hands he developed the 'free throw, flow and blow' method. Les used a makeshift table and on this table were cans of different sizes. Tomato cans, green beans, tomato paste and fruit juice cans. A variety of sizes, on top of which was a canvas, lying at a jaunty angle. With jerking motions of arms and shoulders, he threw paint on the canvas and watched it flow. He redirected flow, direction, density and effect by blowing on the paint with his mouth, or knocking over a can to shift position of the canvas. I was impressed. As Les joked and poked fun at his shortcomings, I realized he was a person of unique quality.

As dessert was served, I, thinking about how good I had been all night, thought I'd have a little fun and test the whit of Les Wooley. A grin spread over my face as I thought about the two earrings hanging from Les's left ear. Leaning over the table, I inquired,

"Les, why do you have two earrings in one ear?"

Les leaned back in his chair, startled and replied, "Why Charlie! They came in a pair!"

Everyone at the table laughed and Les continued, "You know Charlie, with all my disabilities, which I'm sure you've noticed, you know what bothers me the most?"

I shook my head, 'no!'

Les continued, "This damn pimple on my eye!"

I burst out laughing and replied, "You know Les; I think I'm going to like you."

After dinner, as we were saying goodnight and walking toward the car, I pulled off my tie and opened my collar. I looked at Mae and said, "You know Mae, I could have worn a barrel and fit in fine with that guy. I like him!"

IT WON'T BITE

It wasn't very often you got an invitation to Les Wooley's for dinner, so when you did you had better take it. Anyway, Mae and I were invited to Les's for dinner with himself and Louise, his lifetime flame.

We arrived with the usual bottle of wine and curious as to how Les was going to carry this dinner off. After all, he suffered with Muscular Dystrophy, and had sparing use of his hands and feet, along with a myriad of other minor problems. But Louise was a real good sport and handled just about everything from the cooking to the place settings.

"They'll just be the four of us," Les said as we drifted into the living room.

Les's apartment was in a house owned by Louise. It was not only his home but also his studio. You see, Les is an artist. He paints mostly in oils but lately had been dabbling in acrylics as well.

"No problem", I said, "Just more for us to eat".

"Well", Les began, "Charlie, you serve the drinks while the girls get the food ready. There are some rules I ought to tell you about right up front," Les advised us.

"First and foremost, when I'm tired I'll tell you. That means it's time for you to go home. Secondly, come to think of it, there is no second. Just one rule".

"That's OK by me!" I said, "These days I've been going to bed rather early anyway."

"OH! Yes! Now I remember what the second rule is. You," and here Les pointed at me, "You'll have to help me get in my bed when it's time for me to sleep."

Well that didn't sound like such a hard job, I thought, 'a piece of cake.'

"No problem Les, now let's get to those drinks."

I should tell you a little about Les's apartment so you will better understand the dilemma Les has at times. His apartment consisted of two rooms and a bath. The largest room was made up of Les's living room, studio, bedroom and library. In the main part of the great room Les had constructed a large table, four feet by eight feet, and in the form of a box 4 inches deep. On top of the box was chicken wire covering the entire surface. Strung tightly, so a variety of cans and canvases would fit on top without falling off. The table had six sturdy legs, two on each end and two in the middle. This gave a sturdy foundation. On top of the chicken wire he had cans. These were cans of different size. Tomato paste cans, fruit cans, large fruit juice cans and a few other cans of different sizes. The reason for these cans was that when Les managed to get a canvas on top of the table, it would sit at an uneven angle. That way, when Les poured paint on the canvas, it would flow in the downward direction depending on the way the canvas was positioned. Once the paint started to flow, Les could redirect the paint by knocking a can out from under the canvas and off the table. He was able to then blow or smear the paint with his hand or paint brush. Whatever was handy at the time; it was ingenious. Les was able to mix paint on the floor by grasping a stirrer between his wrists and putting his wrist between his knees. Once the paint was mixed, he had built a little dolly system whereby he could lift the paint up to the top of the table. From there he would muscle the can of paint to a point where he would tip the can over and allow the paint to flow. Once the paint started its journey down the canvas, all Les had to do was redirect it. It worked remarkably well. Les became an expert at what he called his *Flow, Blow, Slow Method* of applying paint to a canvas. He was a genius at times.

Anyway, this evening went just as Les had planned. We had a double round of drinks when Les announced,

"Mae, you have to dish out the salads. I have them in the bottom shelf in the refrigerator. Charlie, you have the task of cutting the pork roast and putting at least two pieces on each plate. Louise, you're in charge of heating the gravy, and pouring it on the pork roast after it's on the dishes."

Remember, Les couldn't use his hands, so Louise had to position him in his favorite chair so he could turn his head and reach the straw that was stuck in his drink. Believe me, Les had no trouble downing those drinks once he was secure in his chair.

"Fill that one up, will you Charlie," Les would say while tilting his head towards his straw.

"OK," I giggled, as I poured Les #2. Everyone else had just started on # 1.

When dinner was ready, Louise announced dinner was served and we all moved to the dining room table. Dinner went as planned and before you knew it we were ready for dessert. Only problem was, Les, who had been knocking down the drinks like they were water, was now feeling the effect and was tired. As he was struggling to get himself erect he looked at us and said,

"Sorry folks, dessert will have to wait until tomorrow. I'm tired. Charlie will you help me over to my bed?"

"Sure Les," I said, and immediately went around the table and half carried, half dragged Les to his bed which was in the room directly opposite from the dining area.

I have to admit I was looking forward to dessert, but Les had warned us. When he was ready for bed the party was over. I wasn't quite sure how Les handled getting ready for bed so I thought I would just follow his lead.

"Help me out of these pants and shirt, will you Charlie."

"OK Les," I said not knowing what was to follow.

Once out of his clothes Les pointed to his dresser and said, "In the top drawer of the dresser you'll find my nightshirt. Will you get it for me and help me into it?"

What was I going to say? What I said was, "Of course, Les."

By now I thought my duties as Les's nursemaid were over but I was mistaken. Les had a few too many and had difficulty standing when he was sober. After the drinks Les had consumed this evening, I was surprised he could stand at all. But he did. He then dropped his drawers and asked me to help him get into bed. Fortunately his bed was low to the floor so getting him into bed was no problem. The problem came afterwards. Once Les was settled in his bed I was going to place his blanket over him when he said,

"Oh! Shit! Wouldn't you know it? I've got to take a piss."

"OK!" I thought, "how do we do that?"

Les pulled up his nightshirt until he had it waist high. Naturally, that left everything below the waist exposed.

"You see that jar on top of the bureau, Charlie. Will you get it down and bring it over to this side of my bed. Then I can pee in it easier."

I had no trouble getting the jar for Les, but once I got it on the other side of the bed I was stymied.

"What do I do now?" I asked Les.

"You put my pencil in the jar so I can pee," he said nonchalantly.

"Er! …You want me to put your pecker in the jar?" I asked knowing Les had no use of his hands. "You know Les! I really hadn't given that much thought. And if you weren't such a good friend I'd take a short walk home."

"Just pick it up," Les continued, "It won't bite. The bite left it a long time ago."

"OK! Les, but if that thing moves while I'm getting it into the jar, I'm out of here."

And so ended dinner at Les's.

GOODBYE LES WOOLEY

Les died in his sleep one evening and a celebration for Les was held at the Unitarian Church. It was there that people from all walks of life were able to pay tribute to the man who was there when they needed him. The Cavanaugh boys were there to tell us how Les had taught them to be excellent cooks and get jobs as chefs at local restaurants.

A young girl told how Les hired her to clean his house so he could pay her enough to continue her dance lessons at the local college. Another boy told us how Les had stimulated his interest in horticulture and he was now making this his career. The testimonials went on all morning and it became apparent how many lives Les had touched.

Now that you have had some idea of what Les was like, let me tell you about how he left this world and how he left his imprint for all to admire and love.

Stephen, our oldest son, received a phone call at his law office in Huntington one summer afternoon, and although he had his secretary monitor all his calls, this was one call he decided to take out of respect for Mae and me. He explained to Les that he didn't handle wills and such but as a courtesy he would come over to Les's home and draw up the necessary paperwork. During the last few years Stephen had become one of Les's patrons and had purchased several of Les's large paintings. They adorned the walls of his home and his offices- both his law office and his political office. Les knew that upon his death, members of his family, those who had not attempted to socialize with him for the last many years, would start to come out of the woodwork to lay claim to his many paintings. There were hundreds of them in the basement of his home. Whether they were worth anything or not would only be determined by time. But Les wanted certain paintings to go to specific people. Most he wanted to remain with Louise. He also wanted to be buried in a most unorthodox way. He wanted his ashes to be spread under a beautiful dogwood tree that spread its branches over most of his backyard. His ceremony was to be a bubble blowing contest in the backyard, with prizes for the biggest and most imaginative bubbles. He suspected his relatives would object to this and asked Stephen to help him find a way to overcome their objections.

Stephen drafted Les's will and provided all the quirks and stipulations Les wanted. Still, Les felt there was still room for his relatives to out maneuver his intentions.

"Well," said Stephen, "if Louise were to spread your ashes immediately after the cremation, what could your relatives do?" he asked Les.

After a short period of silence Les's voice came over the phone, soft and grateful,

"Thank you, Stephen."

CHAPTER 18

The children were a continuous joy to both Mae and I. Although there were times when the word 'joy' might not be the best description.

DANCE BALLERINA DANCE

Denise & Maureen

I was very proud of our daughters Denise and Maureen, just as I was proud of all my children. Why shouldn't I be? The girls were natural-born ballerinas, and they looked adorable in their tutus. Denise was three; Maureen was four. They had been taking dance classes for six months and were now ready to perform on stage, for the first time.

The girls were so excited; they twirled and curtsied all afternoon and throughout dinner, performing for us. Tonight they would perform in the school's graduation exercises. Our neighbor, Sal, thought dance lessons were a waste of time and money.

"Dancing comes natural to girls," he argued.

"Nonsense," I said. "Lessons give the girls grace, poise and self confidence. You should send Lisa and Victoria."

Sal wouldn't hear of it.

"A waste of money!" he repeated.

To convince him otherwise, I invited Sal to accompany me to the performance. We had front row seats. The performance started with the older, more experienced dancers who had been taking lessons for two or more years. The performance was delightful and each child received the admiration and applause of the audience.

The younger children performed last. Denise and Maureen were part of this group, it being their first year of dance lessons. In my eyes, however, they were very talented and mature for their age. I kept telling Sal how graceful and accomplished the girls were. When the time arrived for the first year students to perform, the lights dimmed, the audience hushed, and the girls pranced on stage to the music of, *"It's a Small World After-All."*

They entered stage left, tip-toed across the stage, and circled front, in serpentine fashion. From left to right, back to the left, and again to the right. All looked adorable.

"Yes! There's Maureen." I proudly announced.

She led the parade of angels. At the appropriate time the line halted to accept the cheers of the crowd.

"Where's Denise?" Sal quietly asked me.

"I don't know!" I responded, somewhat puzzled at not seeing her in the line of dancers.

Then I saw Denise. She was on the left side of the stage, half hidden by the stage curtain. Slowly, she stepped from behind the curtain. Only the hands of her teacher, Ms. Bock, could be seen pushing her on the stage.

Denise stood perfectly still and stared into the audience. Her left thumb was inserted in her mouth; her right hand twisting the threads of her tutu, which was starting to come apart. The other children, already on stage, were encouraging Denise to, 'come-on!' Maureen glanced at Denise and rolled her eyes. They seemed to say, 'Oh! No! What now?'

Painfully, step by step, Denise advanced, behind the line of dancers, to the center of the line. When she stepped into her assigned position, the audience gave an approving round of applause and the music started again. The little ballerinas, up on their toes, twirled and twirled. Four times around. All except Denise. She stood there, stage front, thumb in mouth, staring into the audience. People chuckled, shifted in their seats and whispered to each other,

"Who is that little one?"

The dancers did a plie', forward and back. All except Denise. She didn't move. Just stood there, staring, sucking her thumb, and unwinding the threats of her tutu. I smiled, clapped my hands and waived at Denise. Perhaps if she saw me, I reasoned, she would join in with the others and dance. She stared at me and screwed-up her face. The audience was starting to laugh over the little imp in the center of the stage. Her tutu dropped from her hips to her thighs. Even I, embarrassed, was prone to smile. Sal kept asking me,

"Isn't she supposed to dance?"

When the dance ended, the dancers bowed and exited stage left. All, except Denise. Alone, in the middle of the empty stage, she was content to take the audience's applause. They applauded so loudly you could hardly hear the music which was playing, 'exit stage left'. She even bowed. Another round of exit music played, while Ms. Bock, her teacher, could be heard from behind the curtain pleading with Denise,

"Denise! Come this way off the stage!"

Denise turned in Ms. Bock's direction and shook her head, 'No!'

The requests to exit, and the 'No!' response, were repeated several times. All the while, the audience laughed hysterically, while Sal kept asking,

"Isn't she supposed to dance?"

The stage curtain opened wider than normal and revealed Ms. Bock, on her knees, pleading with Denise. Once exposed, Ms. Bock got to her feet, smiled, acknowledged the audience's applause, and crossed the stage in Denise's direction. The audience was in convulsions. Denise took this opportunity to take one last bow. Ms. Bock took Denise by the hand, and gradually led the defiant child off the stage. Of course, Denise got a standing ovation. Sal leaned over gently, placed his hand on my shoulder, and whispered in his ear,

"You paid for these lessons?"

MICHAEL & THE CIGAR

It was just after the children left for school that I looked out the kitchen window and saw a whiff of light smoke coming from behind the backyard hedges. My eyes narrowed, my teeth came together, and my jaw set as I stared particularly hard at the shrubbery. There was a dark form huddled behind the bushes. 'Must be a neighbor's kid, 'smoking,' I thought. 'I'll give him the scare of his life.' I slipped silently out of the house and, by cover of some trees and bushes, crept up behind the offender. I thrust my arms through the hedges and parted them to expose the perpetrator.

"Ah, ha!" I shouted as I looked into the face of my seven year old son, Michael, "Gotcha!"

Michael went into shock as I grabbed him by the ear and dragged him from his hiding place. Smoking was a 'no- no,' and I was proud that my children didn't imbibe. At least I thought that was the case. Here was evidence to the contrary.

"What do you think you're doing?" I shouted at Michael, as I dragged him across the back lawn to the patio. I sat Michael down and tried to compose myself as I thought, 'I have to handle this right.'

Michael whined, "Ah! Dad! All the kids smoke!"

"Not mine!" I was quick to reply. "Not if I have anything to say about it!"

Michael looked at me through sorrowful eyes and pleaded, "Come on, Dad! All the kids in school smoke. You're a fag if you don't."

"But Michael," I pleaded as he sat in front of me. "Don't you realize how bad smoking is for you?"

"Who cares?" Michael carried on, "You have to smoke if you want to be cool."

My chest dropped and I let out a sigh of desperation. How could he overcome such peer pressure?

"Listen!" I continued, thinking I might find a way to get Michael sick of smoking, "O.K!" I started slowly, "If you're going to smoke, smoke a man's smoke-no cigarettes. Smoke cigars! Come on! I'll take you around to Al Marlow's for a couple of good cigars."

Al Marlow ran a candy store-diner around the corner from where we lived. We became good friends over the years as I chose to grab a quick breakfast at Marlow's before heading to work each morning. We arrived at Marlow's and I gave Al the eye as I asked in a loud voice so everyone could hear, "Al, Michael's decided to smoke. Will you give me a couple of good cigars for him!"

Al immediately knew where I was headed and played along. Sure Charlie! How about some of these? They're a man's smoke!"

The cigars were dark brown, bordering on black, about six inches long, twisted and bent.

"They look fine, Al," I said, and then whispered, "Better give me two of them."

We arrived home and retreated to the patio picnic table.

"If you're going to smoke Mike," I offered, "you might as well smoke a real smoke."

I lit up the stogie and handed it to Michael, thinking, 'Shouldn't take more than a few puffs on this cigar before he's puking his guts out.' To my surprise, Michael sat quietly, puffing the cigar, and blowing the smoke like a real trooper. 'Hummm!' I thought, as I watched Michael. 'It's taking longer than I thought!' The cigar was drawn to three quarters ash before Michael leaned back and, looking at me said,

"You're right, Dad."

'Success,' I thought, pleased with myself.

Then Michael continued, "These are better than cigarettes."

My face fell, chin almost hitting the concrete pavement of the patio. Then I looked into Michael's eyes and saw the gloss-over and one about to turn itself inside-out.

"See you later, Dad." Michael shouted, as he dropped the stub of his cigar and raced for the bathroom.

My eyes followed Michael from the patio table to the bathroom as a sly, crooked smile crept across my face. 'Success!' I thought, 'and it only took one cigar.' I looked at the second black, twisted, ominous cigar in my hand and mused, 'I'll save this one, should he need a reminder.'

DENISE AND HER FLOAT

It was a hot August afternoon. After spending the last several hours repairing the roof I plunked my tired six foot, 230 pound body into a chase-lounge by the swimming pool. I removed my sweat-soaked shirt, poured myself my last cool beer, and was looking forward to acquiring a tan and maybe some zzz's. I was tired. So tired I couldn't bring myself to bend over and remove my ankle-high work boots. They would have to stay on until I could summon up the strength to unlace them.

In the pool were three of my daughters; Maureen, age 13, Denise, age 12 and Tracy, age 7.

"Let me on the float!" shouted Maureen.

"No!" said Denise.

"Yes! You're hogging it!"

"So! It's my float!"

"So! It's our pool! You have to share!"

"No! I don't. Get your own float!"

"Dad! Denise won't share!"

'Is there no place on earth,' I thought, 'where I can get some peace?' With a great effort, I raised myself on an elbow and glanced at the three bobbing heads in the pool. 'Why can't they behave like human beings?' I thought. I pleaded.

"Stop the fighting! You're sisters. You're supposed to love one another. Learn to play together!"

I sank back in my lounge chair and raised the cool glass of beer to my lips. But the brew never made it from the glass to my lips.

"Denise won't share?" whined Maureen.

"She thinks she owns the pool," Tracy chimed in.

"Shut up you little twit!" Denise shouted back. "It's my float. I paid for it with my money and I'll do what I want with it!"

It was true. Denise did save her money to buy the float. But she also delighted in tormenting her sisters at every turn. She continued to float under the diving board, driving the others crazy.

I lowered the still full glass of beer to the pool deck and pleaded, "Please! Stop the bickering! Play together like nice children, and let me rest."

Oh! How I needed the rest. Some case.

"But she won't share!" Tracy complained.

"She's selfish," Maureen said. "She thinks she can boss everyone around."

Denise was sitting astride the float backpedaling. She was not about to share. As she paddled away from her sisters, she splashed water in their faces. Maureen was slow to anger, but once aroused, she was a shrew. She leaped on the float, upset the balance and sent Denise cascading into the water. With a cry that would put Cochise to shame, Denise came up from under the surface of the water and seized Maureen by the hair. In the flick of a gnat's eye, the two engaged in a brawl. Great gobs of hair were pulled and twisted. Choice names uttered. I chose to ignore them. Water was splashing. Fists were flying. Heads dunked and surfaced and then punches were thrown. Although Tracy was small she joined in the fracas by jumping on Denise's back and wrapped her arms around Denise's eyes so she couldn't see.

Rest was impossible. I knew there would be no peace. I had to intervene. I struggled to get out of the chaise-lounge, and in doing so, inadvertently upset my glass of beer. That made me really mad. My last beer. Now it's one thing to be mad at someone else but when you're mad at yourself you get really pissed. I got to my feet, which seemed especially heavy. With a great effort I lumbered toward the edge of the pool. I summoned up all my energy and shouted, "Stop it! Stop it!"

My face was red with anger. Not so much because the girls were fighting, but because they had caused me to spill my last glass of beer. The girls disengaged, hair soaking wet, water running out of their ears and mouth.

"Well, she started it!" Maureen yelled back.

"Yeah!" Tracy joined in.

"It's my float," Denise repeated. She used the moment to push her float away from her sisters and jumped back upon it.

"Cry baby! Cry baby!" she taunted the others.

"Enough!" I screamed. "Denise! Give me that float!"

"No!" came Denise's reply.

Her emphatic "No!" was not an answer I was accustomed to receiving. I had never been sassed by my children before.

"What?" I screamed at Denise, who by now had floated close to where I was standing.

"No!" she said again, defiantly.

I grabbed the ladder railing, and swung my right hand in Denise's direction. It was my intention to grab her by the hair, pull her even closer and confront her nose to nose. But the long hot day in the sun impaired my ability to judge distance. As I lunged, Denise ducked. My hand passed over her head, grabbing nothing but air. Worse still, the sun had affected my balance for as my hand made a long, circular arch and came circling back toward my chest, my body continued its arch toward the water. I went head first into the pool, followed closely by a heavy pair of Woodstock working boots.

Fortunately for me, and the girls as well, I landed in the shallow end of the pool. As I gathered myself together and came up for air I was surprised to find I was alone in the pool. Water dropped from my head and shoulder and from every part of my body. Three skimpily clad bodies, viewed from the rear, were scurrying for shelter, in three different directions.

As this was taking place, Mae, my wife, came out on the patio to investigate all the shouting and splashing.

"I guess I don't have to ask what made the girls run for cover," she said as she looked at me and began to laugh.

"You know," I said, in a serious tone, "if I had been in the deep end, I'd still be at the bottom. They could at least have waited to see if I drowned."

MAE'S PRIZE

The telephone rang and I quickly raised the receiver to my ear and answered, "Hello!"

"Is Mary Hackeling there, please?"

"This is Mr. Hackeling; she's indisposed," I replied, as I looked across the dinner table at Mae, thinking I could spare her the pitch of the usual evening sales force. "Can I take a message?"

"Yes, this is Michael Drab from the GWF Sweepstake program. Mary Hackeling is the winner of our sweepstake contest. Isn't that wonderful?"

There was a pause for the information to sink in. 'Oh! Yes, I thought. That's wonderful. Now for the punch line.'

"What's it going to cost me?" I returned.

"Nothing! She's our big winner. Isn't that wonderful?" he asked again.

Knowing that there is no such thing as *free lunch*, and having been, at one time or another, the recipient/winner of untold 'free' this or that, I figured that this could wind up costing me more than a trip around the world. Better make it short I thought. Get right to the bottom line.

"Yes," I repeated, "What did she win?"

"Why Mr. Hackeling, she won our first prize. A Bible."

'A Bible' I thought. 'She won a bible!' I leaned across the table and handed the phone to Mae.

"Here, this is for you. And it's on the level." Anyone who could get as excited about winning a Bible as this salesman must be on the level. Mae was delighted. She had won THE BIG PRIZE.

MEET FRITZ BOHL

Commack is a small town just east of my home, and in the center of Long Island. Someone had advertised in the local Pennysaver, FOR SALE - 1963 Volkswagen- $300 Good running condition. (516) 757-0150, Ask for Bohl.

I called, got the address, and was on my way. I arrived at the front door of 73 Vineyard Road, a small, nicely kept, two-story house with a detached garage. I approached the front door and knocked. A big man answered, six foot with a husky build. His head was balding down the middle and towards the back. But the sparse hair that remained was combed neatly over the bald plate.

"Mr. Bohl?" I asked.

"Ya!" he replied in a German accent, as he opened the door. He wore old-fashioned farmer's overalls, with halter straps over a heavy red flannel shirt. He was neat and clean with a nicely trimmed beard and mustache. He appeared to be in his late seventies; his eyes, bright blue, twinkled with merriment, as if denying his age.

"I've come in response to your ad for the VW" I said. "I'm Charlie Hackeling."

"Oh!, Ya!" he repeated, "You are da chentleman who called me, no?"

"Yes," I repeated, "I wonder if I might see the car?"

He reached for a key on the mantle that stood next to his front door. Then he gestured for me to follow him around the front of the house to his garage in the back. I wasn't really expecting much since the car was fifteen years old. But once in the garage, much to my surprise, there stood a bright, shiny and obviously very well kept Volkswagen Bug.

"Van't to try it?" he asked.

I jumped into the front seat, put the key in the ignition, and turned over the engine. It hummed. After inspecting the car and finding no fault with it, we concluded our business. The purchase accomplished; Fritz asked me,

"Vould you like some cherry brandy to seal our arrangement? I make it myself! It's in da basement."

It seems Fritz owned a restaurant many years before the war. The big war, World War II. When war broke out between the United States and Germany, he felt it was better to sell the business than try to operate a German restaurant.

In 1941, Germany was giving anything German a bad name. But he continued to make his own spirits in his basement. My wife, Mae, is a brandy lover, and I thought a bottle of brandy would be a nice present to bring her to celebrate our latest purchase. As we descended several well worn wooden steps and passed through a cobweb-littered basement door, I observed, on the wall directly opposite the entrance, several brandy casks pilled one on top of each other. Alongside them, stacked to the ceiling and lying on their sides, were bottles of wine that gave the basement the pungent odor of grapes. On the wall to my left and slightly behind the stairs was a workbench with an assortment of small knives, drills and hand tools. On a table adjacent to the workbench were two enormous doll houses. They were three stories high and looked exactly like classical Alpine homes advertised in travel brochures.

"Wow!" I exclaimed, as I rushed up to examine them. "These are beautiful. Did you make them?"

"Ya!" he sighed humbly.

"They're beautiful!" I kept repeating. "They're beautiful! I have six daughters at home, and I've been looking for a really nice doll house for Christmas. These are gorgeous. What do you charge for them?"

"Oh!" he chuckled, as he was rinsing out two glasses by a sink next to an old fashion washing machine.

"I don't sell dem".

"Could I buy one?" I asked.

He chuckled again and said, "Oh! You couldn't afford dem."

I was stunned. What an odd thing for this kindly gentleman to say to someone he had just met. He must have seen the shocked expression on my face because he stammered a little as he comes over to the table. His face reddened as he continued,

"Vat I mean, Charles, is dot I von't sell dem. I mean, not for money."

He continued trying for an adequate explanation….."You see," he explained, "I don't mean you can't afford a doll house, I mean dey are ... special."

As he poured a generous helping of cherry brandy into two juice glasses and slid one across the corner of the table towards me, he continued, "During da year, I make vone, two, sometimes tree doll houses like dese. I make dem like I remember dem in Chermany, years ago. Chust after Tanksgiving holiday, I go to Brooklyn, to da poorest neighborhoods, to da poorest schools, and inquire -'Who is da poorest little girl in da school?' Den on Christmas eve, I send a doll house to arrive dat evening. I enclose a card and sign it, 'Santa Clause.' Un later dat evening, as I sit by my fireplace, in my rocking chair, I dream about da expression dat comes over da faces of da little girls ven UPS knocks.

"You see Charles," he continued, "This may be the only gift the child receives and I vant it to be beautiful."

As I watched and listened to him talk, his eyes took on a life of their own. They twinkled and sparkled, a tear welled up in the corner of each eye, and a grin spread over his entire face. He brought tears to my eyes. He was right; money could never buy the thrill of an unexpected gift from Santa. I drove home that evening thinking about these young girls. How, years from now, they will hold their children and grandchildren on their laps on Christmas Eve and tell them, there really is a Santa Clause.

THE BATHING SUIT

When the children have the opportunity to get a bargain, they're Johnny on the spot. Kevin, our first son-in-law, is usually the first to take advantage of a sale. In this case he was slow and not very excited about Tracy's bathing suit. But Susan made him get excited. She insisted he take Tracy shopping.

There is a big age difference between Kevin and Tracy, our youngest daughter. But despite the age difference, they shared one thing in common. Both are extremely competitive.

Kevin was a Captain of Lifeguards at Jones Beach on the south shore of Long Island. Tracy was just old enough to be tested for a lifeguard position.

"No way she's going to pass the test for lifeguard!" he maintained.

According to Kevin, Stephen and Michael, our sons and also lifeguards, you had to be big and strong to be a Jones Beach Lifeguard. Tracy, they maintained, was too small. They forgot that when it comes to competitiveness, Tracy is twelve feet tall.

"Phoff! She'll never make it!'" Kevin sneered and said to Sue, his future wife.

"She will too!" said Susan in defense of Tracy. "But she needs a new bathing suit. Take her to Herman's. They have a sale going on."

"Why should I take her?" Kevin whined.

"Because you always find good deals. And besides, she doesn't have much money," Susan responded.

So together they went to Herman's. Tracy, always one with a keen eye for bargains, saw a suit marked down dramatically. She tried it on but lacked the chest dimensions to fill it out.

"It's a great buy," she said to Kevin, who was looking over the men's wear. "But it doesn't fit me up here," she said pointing to her chest.

"Take it anyway," Kevin replied, "And stuff it with newspaper. Who's going to know?"

"You're right," Tracy said, "Besides, maybe they'll fill in!"

And they did. And Tracy went on to win a spot on the Jones Beach Lifeguard Squad. Goes to show!

YOUTH'S SCREAM
(Told by Maureen)

I ran across this essay when I was cleaning out the basement prior to our move to Florida. It was in Maureen's box of school papers and when I read it I thought it would be a good composition to save because it demonstrates Maureen's keen sense of fairness and rightness.

"Shut up you creeps! You don't know what you're doing to me. You didn't know him. You never cared about him. Do you really give a damn about anyone besides yourselves? I hate you! Shut up! Shut up!"

This kept screeching through my mind as I ran from my English class one early afternoon. I had suddenly been flooded with so much anger I wanted to burst. My body had a cold piercing ache running through it. I was so hurt and upset. It took everything I had to keep from crying in the middle of the hallway. I felt as though my heart had just been dropped on cement and shattered like a plate of glass. The jolt I had received during class had sent me into a spin. I could barely think straight.

As I continued down the empty hall, I tried to piece together what had just happened. Suddenly, my eyes began to blur. I could feel tears streaming down my face. I tried to understand how my classmates could be so inconsiderate and callous, but couldn't. I guess I just never prepared myself for the big question, "Which do you think Eddie would be suited for, 'most likely to succeed, or class corpse?'" I couldn't believe the question, but the worst part was the laughter that followed. It kept ringing in my ears. Fortunately, I was able to get into the privacy of the locker room before my tears turned into overwhelming sobs. For a few minutes things became so out of hand I could hardly breathe. After ten minutes I was able to calm down enough to be able to lie back without gagging on my own mucus. The cold metal bench seemed to cool my burning face. As I rested, I began to think about Eddie and the preceding incident.

I just didn't understand how my classmates could find anything to laugh about in such a tragic death. Eddie was a seventeen-year-old boy whom I had grown up with. He had been shot in the neck, chest, and right shoulder, three weeks earlier. After struggling for his life for fifteen hours, he died.

It had already been so hard for me to accept the fact that I would never watch him run for the school bus. I would never again wince when he lost his temper or drove fast. I'd never see him walk his dog or take the garbage out. I'd never again listen to his bellowing laugh. Didn't my classmates realize how often I'd already been hurt? The realization that he was gone, after glancing through the neighborhood butcher shop window expecting to find his bright smile and friendly "hello", was enough to send a cold chill through me. A surge of rage suddenly ran through me. I almost wanted to hit them. If they only knew how hard it had been for me to kneel beside him and say "Goodbye." I wonder how many would have laughed if they had seen his stitched lips, his neck filled with cork, and his once strong handsome face now bloated and blue.

I still didn't know what possessed them to ask such a question. Maybe this was their way of venting their own insecurities toward death. I didn't know. The only thing I knew for sure was that he was a friend and he shared a piece of my heart. I cared so much. Maybe this was the time for me to really let go.

The bells rang. School had ended. I got up, changed, washed my face, and went to practice. I played ball that day like there was no tomorrow.

I WISH I KNEW HIS NAME

For the past fifteen years we commuted to work every morning. We were friends for the last twenty five years. Walt liked to drive. On winter days, like today, I liked to look at the passing landscape. Even the City looked good when covered by new snow.

"Is that an angel on your collar?" Walt asked.

"Yep!" I replied.

"Do you believe in angles?" Walt asked in a mocking tone.

"Well," I said, "for most of my life I'd have to say no. But as I think back over the years, I've come to realize, someone's been looking out for me."

"You don't believe that!" Walt went on.

I laughed. "Maybe not! You have to remember, I was trained as an engineer. All my life I've looked for the reason things work the way they do. And most of the time I've found the reason. But occasionally, I can't find an answer."

I continued in a musing tone of voice, "I remember once I let the oil level in the basement tank get too low. When the burner drew on the system for oil, all it got was the water that floats on top of the oil. The burner went out. Naturally, it happened at night when the temperature was below freezing. In the morning, I tried to get the furnace to turn over. The furnace refused. Ice was clogging the fuel line. There was nothing to do but thaw out the line. For hours I heated the oil line with a torch. Morning turned to afternoon, then the night approached. I was desperate. I couldn't let the family go through another night without heat. In a silent moment, as I bent over the exposed oil line in the basement, heating it with a torch, I whispered a silent prayer,

"Please dear God, let this work."

Almost immediately, the burner rumbled and kicked over. The blocked line opened. Naturally, I took credit for being so clever.

"So! Where does the angel come in?" Walt pursued.

"On another occasion," I went on, "I was driving from New York to North Carolina for a Christmas family reunion. The oil light came on accompanied by a buzzing sound. A God awful buzzer. Sounded like the car was about to explode. I checked the oil level. It was O.K. Never- the-less, I was nervous. The problem became intermittent. I didn't know what to think.

I remembered my father telling me that when things go wrong in a car they never get better by themselves. They only get worse. The car was full of presents for the children and grandchildren. Each time the light and buzzer came on, I panicked. I was getting desperate. When the light came on, I'd stop the car. The light would go off. Another few miles, the light came on again. The buzzer screamed at me, 'Stop the car!' When I did, off went the light. I was trying to convince myself there was a short circuit somewhere in the system. But every time the light came on and the buzzer sounded, my heart skipped a beat. From New York to Newark, it was touch and go. Drive awhile; no light, no buzzer. Then suddenly, the light and buzzer would go on. Stop. Light and buzzer go off. Drive a little further, same result. Light and buzzer. In desperation, I prayed,

"Dear God, just get me to North Carolina. Then the car can fall apart. But please don't strand me in no-man's land." The light immediately went out. The buzzer stopped. From Newark to Wilmington, I didn't have another bit of trouble.

We arrived at the hotel, met the kids, and for several days, drove around without any trouble. Again I congratulated myself on my cool handling of the situation.

Walt interrupted, "What does all this have to do with the damn angel?"

"Don't get impatient," I said, looking at Walt. "And don't use profanity when you're referring to my angel."

I went on, "On our return trip home, I was no sooner out of the hotel parking lot than the damn oil light came on. The buzzer nearly drove me through the car roof. 'God!' I thought, 'The oil light again!' I had completely forgotten about it. I was about to ask God for an extension to New York, when it dawned on me. 'You have one hell of a nerve Charlie! You asked him to get you to North Carolina! He did! Now you want an extension?' Realizing I'd be stretching my luck, and remembering I had forgotten to thank Him for getting us to the hotel, I resigned myself to calling Triple A. I did and we got home safely. Now I ask you Walt, how do you explain that?"

Walt looked out of the corner of his eye, a slight grin playing over his lips. He moved away from me and a little closer to his door.

"More recently," I continued, "I was driving from Florida to New York. This time the 'Check engine' light came on. Naturally I pulled over, examined the engine, and listened for obvious signs of distress. I couldn't find anything wrong.

Nevertheless, the 'Check Engine' light continued to flash. No mechanic within earshot. No gas station. With a prayer on my lips I proceeded to the next exit. I was in luck. There was a gas station and a mechanic. He examined the engine, listened, just as I had done, then said he didn't think it was anything major. Could I get home? Sure! Again I thought I was pretty cleaver having diagnosed the problem correctly.

"I thanked him and went into the station for orange juice. As I was waiting for change, I noticed a small display on the counter. It was a display of collar angles. One, in particular, seemed to be laughing at me. I'll take that angel, I heard myself saying. As I got into the car I put the angel on my collar. 'Do your stuff!' I said. When I reached Newark, a buzzing sound accompanied the still lit 'Check Engine' light. I got back on the hot line.

"God! Please! Get us home safely." Reaching for my collar, I felt the angel.

"Are you there?" I silently asked. The buzzing sound went off, and so did the light. I smiled to myself. 'If anyone could hear me, they'd think I'm crazy.' I'm not so sure I don't think that myself. When I got home I congratulated myself again on my nerves of steel and cleverness in completing the trip. I didn't think again about my angel until I took off my shirt that night. There he was, still laughing at me."

I sat silently for awhile. Walt just kept driving. No one talked. Finally I turned to Walt, smiled at him and said, "As I get older I realize I'm not such a genius. And I know God is a pretty busy feller. But you see this angel sitting up here upon my shoulder?"

I wasn't pointing to my collar, but to my shoulder. Walt looked uncertainly at me.

"Yeeear!" I finally uttered. "Well! He is a genius. And a damned good mechanic to boot.

He's become a very good friend. I only have one problem, Walt . . . I wish I knew his name.

CHARLIE

As a follow up to my angel story, I have to tell you about Sean Curzan and the angel I told him about.

It happened one evening when Mae and I were baby-sitting so Tracy and Mark could go out for a quiet dinner. After prayers that night Sean asked me about angels. I told him we all have a guardian angel who watches over us. He wanted to know where he was and if he could see him. I told him I had never seen mine, but I knew he was there. He wasn't satisfied with my explanation so I told him his guardian angel probably sat on his left shoulder. Then he asked me what his name was. Again, I was stumped. I told him I didn't know. I thought the story had been put to bed, but no, not yet.

A few days later Mae told me she had a talk with Sean and he told her he had a guardian angel that took care of him.

"Oh!" said Mae. "And what is his name?"

Without a moment's hesitation he told Mae, "His name is Charlie."

I love that boy.

CHAPTER 19

50 YEARS AND COUNTING

On our fiftieth wedding anniversary the children decided they were going to give us a wing-ding of a party at the Farrington Restaurant and Hotel. I thought I might have to give a speech so I jotted some ideas on paper to talk from.

On December 26, 1955, I married your mother. That was over 50 years ago. It doesn't seem possible that it was that long ago. --- 50 years seems like an eternity when you say it, or even think about it. --- 50 years. But I can tell you, they went by in the blink of an eye and, they were not only the fastest years of my life, but also the happiest.

I was thinking about it just the other day. There was the wedding. I know I enjoyed it, but I really don't remember much about it, except, like any new groom, I was anxious for it to end so we could start on our honeymoon. We didn't have a lot of time. It was Christmas at the Naval Academy and we had ten days leave before we had to return. Two days had already gone by. I had eight days left. Time was a wasting. We were married at Saint Philip and James Roman Catholic Church in the Bronx. We spent our honeymoon at Paradise Valley Lodge in the Pocono Mountains in Pennsylvania.

I have such fond memories of our honeymoon. There was snow on the ground and the pond was frozen over but the ice skating was grand. We had a small cottage in the woods. It was called the Oaks. We spent four days and three nights there and then returned to Mae's mother's apartment on Seymour Ave. We spent New Year's Eve with Aunt Cathleen and Uncle Jeff. We went to Meyer's Restaurant for the midnight event. Then back to school.

TIME OFF AND INTO PARENTHOOD

Shortly after returning to the Academy, we were given time off for St. Patrick's Day. It was an unexpected holiday. I jumped on a train and raced to Mae and our small apartment in the Bronx. It was our first time together since the wedding and our honeymoon. The apartment was small so Mae arranged for her roommate to spend the weekend at someone else's apartment. That way, we could have some time alone. Aside from the fact that Mae decided to cook ham steaks in the microwave oven we huddled around the small kitchen table staring into each other's eyes, and waited for the steaks to cook. Each time the bell rang we took out the steaks only to find they had not as yet heated up. Well, we'll tried again, this time giving it more time. We did this three times and I finally said to Mae, "Whatever we're doing isn't working. Let's go out for Chinese!"

Mae was determined to cook these ham steaks. It was then we discovered the electricity for this circuit was off. It must have blown a fuse sometime during our previous attempts. Oh Well! Fortunately the Chinese restaurant was just around the corner. As we were leaving the apartment I noticed a gigantic nail, a foot long, driven through the front door.

"What's the spike for?" I asked

"Oh!" Mae replied, "I had Johnny O'Conner over this afternoon to help me move some furniture and help with some painting. Before I could stop him he had driven the stake through the door.

The following day, Mae was acting a bit strange. We were out for a walk when Mae said she had to go into our local drugstore, but she didn't want me to come with her. That was O.K. with me. I thought girls probably had things they needed that weren't easy to discuss with boys. She came out of the store with a sheepish grin on her face. We walked a short distance before she broke the news.

"Charlie! You're going to be a father."

I was shocked but I couldn't be happier.

"My! My! What have we done?" I said.

You would think we had produced a Messiah. Well, we felt like we had. Stephen was going to be President one day.

We were on our way to dinner at my parent's house, so I immediately bought a bottle of champagne and tried to sneak it into my parent's refrigerator without them noticing. Some chance… it didn't fool my father. He knew something was up. When I announced we were going to be parents, and that my mom and dad were soon to become grandparents, Aunt Edith, who was having dinner with us stole the news by proclaiming that Bob, my cousin, was also due to have a child. Anyway, we were all happy and looking forward to the adventures of parenthood…and were blessed eight times.

CHAPTER 20

CLOSING

Finally there came the time for grandchildren. And boy did you guys give us a boatload. But as someone once said, "If I knew grandchildren were so much fun, I'd have had them first." We love them all, and as parents, you know you can never love one more than another. And you can never love them enough.

Life sure has changed over the past fifty years. I cherish all the memories I have from the past. Times are different and I consider myself lucky to have lived the life I had.

During these fifty years much has happened. Mae and I have grown closer together and we've grown closer to our children and grandchildren. I can't help thinking as I watch them grow and develop how much effort is put into their development. Despite what people say, it doesn't just happen. It takes sweat and blood and an awful lot of love on the part of the parents and grandparents to bring children from their primal state to the state of loving and caring about their fellow human beings.

Things were different for me than they will be for the next few generations. Christmas Stockings were full of wonder and surprise. Cars were made with pride and honor. Gone are the days when workers took pride in the quality of their work. The new philosophy is, do as little as possible, as poorly as possible, and get away with it. Today's younger generation has been conditioned to want what is new and discard what was yesterday's.

Profit above all is not a philosophy to follow. I hope the generations that follow do not embraced the philosophy where they will accept, patiently, whatever big brother deems advisable and abrogate their right to choose. Don't be molded for the new value of newness. Honor, integrity, pride, and honesty! Stick to what is important.

There are your 50 plus years. For me they went by in a flash. There are very few things I would change. I'd only ask for a little more time to love each one of you. As for your mother, she has truly been my soul mate. I look forward to the next 50 years with you, my dear, where ever they are.

Love,
Charlie

Well I've reached the end of this book. It doesn't contain all that I wanted to say to you, but it says a lot. I hope it tells you how much I love you all. I hope it tells you that without each and every one of you my life would have been incomplete. You are all so precious.

I wish you all had the experience of meeting and getting to know all the people in these stories. They were real people; flesh and blood like you and me. The time will come when you will meet them. Hopefully, I will be there to introduce you.

I want to close with the words from a song written by Gregory Norbet. It goes like this,

"All I ask of you is for you to remember me as loving you."

Love,
Dad, Grandpa

Where to Chief?

Good choices.

Made in the USA
Charleston, SC
03 December 2010